Data Rights Law 2.0

- Key Research Project of Key Laboratory of Big Data Strategy
- Key Research Project of Beijing Key Laboratory of Urban Science Research Based on Big Data
- Publishing Fund Project of Think Tank Program of Beijing Cosmopolis Cultural Exchange Foundation

Data Rights Law 2.0

The System Construction

Key Laboratory of Big Data Strategy

Edited by Lian Yuming

社会科学文献出版社
SOCIAL SCIENCES ACADEMIC PRESS(CHINA)

PETER LANG
Oxford • Bern • Berlin • Bruxelles • New York • Wien

Bibliographic information published by Die Deutsche Bibliothek
Die Deutsche Bibliothek lists this publication in the Deutsche Nationalbibliografie; detailed bibliographic data is available on the Internet at http://dnb.ddb.de.

A catalogue record for this book is available at the British Library.

Library of Congress Cataloging-in-Publication Data: A CIP catalog record for this book has been applied for at the Library of Congress.

LCCN Number: 2020905295

Cover design: Brian Melville for Peter Lang

ISBN 978-1-78997-838-4 (print) • ISBN 978-1-78997-839-1 (ePDF)
ISBN 978-1-78997-840-7 (ePub) • ISBN 978-1-78997-841-4 (mobi)

Published by Peter Lang Ltd, International Academic Publishers,
52 St Giles, Oxford, OX1 3LU, United Kingdom
oxford@peterlang.com, www.peterlang.com

Academically supported by
Research Base of Key Laboratory of Big Data Strategy in
China University of Political Science and Law
&
Research Center of Data Rights Law in
China University of Political Science and Law

Institute Introduction

Key Laboratory of Big Data Strategy, established in April 2015, is an interdisciplinary, professional, international and open research platform co-founded by the Guiyang Municipal People's Government and Beijing Municipal Science and Technology Commission. It is a new-type, high-level think tank for the researches on Chinese big data development.

Relying on the Global City Development Corporation Council, Beijing (GDCC) and the Guiyang Innovation-Driven Development Strategy Research Institute (GDI), Key Laboratory of Big Data Strategy established two research centers in Beijing and Guiyang. And it sets up five research bases, respectively, Research Base in the Party School of the CPC Central Committee, Research Base in the China National Committee for Terms in Sciences and Technologies, Research Base in Zhejiang University, Research Base in China University of Political Science and Law, and Research Base in Shanghai Academy of Science & Technology. In Guizhou Province, three research bases were approved and established, they are, the Block Data Theory and Applicable Innovation Research Base, the Big Data Applicable Innovation Research Base for Urban Space Decision, and the Big Data Innovation in Culture Research Base. The "two centers, five research bases, and three research platforms" have created a new research system and a regional collaborative innovation pattern.

The publications of The Key Laboratory of Big Data Strategy include *Block Data: The Signal of the Arrival of Big Data Time*, *Block Data 2.0: Paradigm Revolution in the Era of Big Data*, *Block Data 3.0: Order Internet and Sovereign Blockchain*, *Block Data 4.0: Activation Dataology in the Age of Artificial Intelligence*, *Block Data 5.0: Theories and Methods of Data Sociology*, *Data Rights Law 1.0: The Theoretical Basis* (published in Simplified Chinese, English, French, German and Traditional Chinese), *Sovereignty Blockchain 1.0: Orderly Internet and Community with a Shared Future for Humanity* and *Blue Book of Big Data - Annual Report on Development of Big Data in China (No.1-No.4)*. So far, big data development theories and key innovative fruits in practice have exerted significant influence at home and abroad.

Editor's Profile

Professor Lian Yuming
Doctor of Engineering
Member of the CPPCC National Committee
President of Global City Development Corporation Council, Beijing
Director of the Data Rights Law Research Centre in China University of Political Science and Law

Prof. Lian Yuming is a renowned urban development expert in China. He is Vice Chairman of the Beijing Chaoyang District People's Political Consultative Conference, member of the Experts Consultative Committee for the People's Government of Beijing, Vice Chairman of Beijing Federation of Social Science Circles, chief expert in the Research Base of Beijing-Tianjin-Hebei Coordinated Development, as well as director of Beijing Key Laboratory of Urban Science Research Based on Big Data. His researches mainly focus on urbanology, science of decision making, and sociology. His works include *Rising of Cities, Beijing Strategic Positioning,* and *Rediscovery of World Cities.*

In March 2014, Prof. Lian took a temporary post as Mayor's Assistant of Guiyang municipal people's government, and was appointed as the president of Guiyang Innovation-Driven Development Strategy Research Institute, the director of the Key Laboratory of Big Data Strategy. From then on, he has been devoted to the researches on big data strategy, and published the following books: *Block Data: The Signal of the Arrival of Big Data Time, Block Data 2.0: Paradigm Revolution in the Era of Big Data, Block Data 3.0: Order Internet and Sovereign Blockchain, Block Data 4.0: Activation Dataology in the Age of Artificial Intelligence, Block Data 5.0: Theories and Methods of Data Sociology, Data Rights Law 1.0: The Theoretical Basis* (published in Simplified Chinese, English, French, German and Traditional Chinese), *Sovereignty Blockchain 1.0: Orderly Internet and Community with a Shared Future for Humanity* and *Blue Book of Big Data - Annual Report on Development of Big Data in China (No.1-No.4).*

Editorial Board

Translation Committee

Senior Translators:	Tian Linan, Ma Jing
Translators:	Zhang Chunyang (Preface, Postscript, etc.)
	Hu Jinhua (Chapter1)
	Zhao Hongfang (Chapter2)
	Xu Xinyan (Chapter3)
	Dai Jiajia (Chapter4)
	Fu Yao (Chapter5)
Translation Reviewers:	Yue Ling, Xi Jinting

Contents

List of Tables

Editor's Foreword

Throughout the history of world civilization, mankind has experienced the agricultural revolution, industrial revolution, and information revolution. Every revolution in technology has brought huge and profound impact on human production and lives. Similarly, the ongoing data revolution is reshaping our lives even more radically. Bringing about overwhelming changes, it does not mean extension or expansion of our world, but, to a great extent, a complete replacement of the ways of life and production that we have been following since the industrial revolution. New types of legal relationships continue to emerge as the digital economy develops and as unmanned driving, gene editing, and other new technologies progress. The experience that mankind has accumulated over time and rules that are now in use in society are being disrupted and restructured. As an adage of an old nomadic tribe points out, "your soul wouldn't be able to keep up if you walk too fast." We may as well use this adage to describe the situation we are facing now: as we charge forward in the development and use of big data, risks and disorders are seen frequently; as the world goes digital, gets connected and becomes smart, traditional legal principles have encountered difficult theoretical and practical challenges when people try to understand and maintain good order in this reshaped world. "If laws are adjusted to the time, there is good government."[1] Big data should be taken into consideration when we work to create the new legal system, so that we can establish forward-looking theories and innovative systems from a new perspective for the three-fold space that mankind is about to enter from a new perspective and be prepared for the upcoming era of digital civilization.

1 Quote from *Han Feizi*, an ancient Chinese text attributed to a foundational Chinese political philosopher, Master Han Fei. It comprises a selection of essays in the "Legalist" tradition on theories of state power, synthesizing the methodologies of his predecessors.

Three Preconditions for the Data Man Hypothesis

People is the logical starting point of law, and law is the manifestation of human nature. The jurisprudential basis of the data rights law lies in human nature, so the data rights law system should also rise out of human nature. It is thus necessary that we design our legislations and their application from the perspective of human nature. Openness and development are part of human nature. Only by constantly renewing our image and creating new regulations can us human beings resolve our own contradictions and make ourselves better. "Data man" represents a new manifestation of human nature in the era of big data. As long as we can set the legal person model for the data man and the path, scope, and way of expression for the data rights system, we will be able to lay the foundation for the legitimacy of the data rights law from the perspective of data ethics. We propose the data man hypothesis for the data rights law because, the data man hypothesis represents the new human nature that should be seen in relevant parties as is determined by the sociality, altruism, sharing and other basic characteristics of mankind in the era of big data. Furthermore, this hypothesis can also guide us to make the data rights law in a science-based manner and to effectively implement it by mitigating or overcoming the plight of security in data governance. However, there are preconditions for the existence and development of the data man hypothesis.

Move from dependence on things to dependence on data. Data depicts the entire life of every person, from the cradle to the grave. We are inextricably dependent on data today and this dependence arises at a time when we are not yet free from dependence on others and on things. The image, connotation and denotation of what we call "man" will change profoundly when production, life and the way we live our lives are all tied to data, when human intelligence and artificial intelligence merge, and when a natural man evolves into a data man. There is no end to either the development of technology or the chain of evolution. In the future, human society will be composed of natural men, robots and gene-edited men. It should be pointed out that the status of the data man is a legal issue that we will have to deal with in the future.

Altruism woven into the foundation of our society. The structure of relationships in a digital society determines that such a society is decentralized, flat, and borderless in nature, featuring the basic spirits of openness, sharing, cooperation and mutual benefit. This means that our society will be people-oriented with altruism as the core value. Altruism enhances people's willingness to transfer and share data rights, and further turns such transfer and sharing into behaviors that are positively perceived in society. When data resources and products are abundant and can be allocated according to needs, the idea of equal sharing will gain popularity, data labor will become a path to a happy life, and altruism will grow and spread significantly. By then, the altruism that has hidden in human nature would be unleashed with the data rights system serving somewhat as the midwife.

Maximization of the value of data. A data man regards value maximization as the ultimate goal of the pursuit, creation and realization of data value. As the legal system governing the ownership, rights, use and protection of data and the basic norm of data-related behaviors that maintains order in the data world, the data rights law system, which is based on the data man hypothesis, mainly aims to realize balance and coordination between effective protection of data rights and making the best use of data, safeguard public interests and public security, and promote the free sharing of personal data. To this end, citizens' transfer of data rights, to a certain extent, is crucial. Legislation on data rights is intended to promote the flow and use of data rather than to impose restrictions via a dense net of justice. A sound data rights system indicates that we have gained a better understanding of the relationship between man and data, and that we encourage transfer for the well-being of society.

Three Rights in the Era of Big Data

As we move forward in time, we are constantly required to acknowledge new rights so as to meet the needs of society. Facing the roaring tide of data, we need to build a rights protection system based on data rights to achieve comprehensive protection of data. Data rights, the rights to share, and data sovereignty are the new rights in the era of big data, and these rights can be established by law. In a sense, data rights arise as the development of society gives our legal system an opportunity for improvements.

Data rights. Data is becoming a kind of resource, asset and capital. At the same time, infringements on or criminal acts related to data rights, such as illegal collection, stealing, trading, and abuse of data are more and more frequent. Strengthening legal support for the protection, development and use of data by establishing a sound legal system is a major agenda for legislators in various countries around the world, as well as researchers from home and abroad. Data rights, as a separate category of emerging rights, include personal data rights, corporate data rights, and government data rights. Data rights protection is an overarching concept that covers data rights in the realm of private rights and data power in the realm of public rights. The core of the rule of law is to regulate public rights, protect private rights, safeguard justice, and give guidance to society. Data rights and data power, as the extension of traditional private rights and public rights in the digital space, have more frequent conflicts now. At present, both data rights and data power are growing rapidly, but in the long run, the spread of data rights and the decline of data power will be the inevitable trend.

Rights to share. Sharing is to put data in to more effective use. It is the ultimate manifestation of data ownership. Different from the real rights, data rights are no longer rights of possession, but rights to share that are not exclusive, which means the data tend to have multi-ownership. Once data rights are upgraded from a natural right to a public right and general will, they will inevitably go beyond what is endowed by the form and become a social right. The rights to share is the essence of data rights, and it is realized via the usufructuary rights of data and the usufructuary rights of public data. It thus becomes possible to separate the right to use data from data ownership, and form a basic pattern of sharing where people seek not to own but to use data. There exist natural conflicts of interests between data sharing and privacy protection because of the game between public interests and personal interests and the discrepancies between property interests and personality interests. Therefore, the balance between the rights to share and the right to privacy must be achieved in order to fully explore the value of data resources. By proposing the rights to share, we are initiating a new jurisprudential rule beyond what has been in existence in the real rights system, which will be a hallmark of digital civilization. It is foreseeable that based on sharing, human civilization will move to a higher level and have a new order that is built on the basis of the rights to share.

Data sovereignty. The digital space has become the "fifth territory" following land, sea, air and space. The scales of data that a country holds in its possession, how active the data is, and the capacity of the country to interpret and use the data will become an important part of the country's comprehensive national strength. Sovereignty is no longer a concept that is confined to geography as data sovereignty becomes a new member of the system and a core part of the whole picture of sovereignty. Data sovereignty is an important part of national sovereignty, and a manifestation and natural extension of national sovereignty in the data space. If data power is the main indicator of a country's comprehensive national strength and international competitiveness, then data sovereignty will become the prerequisite and basis for safeguarding a country's core interests. Countries around the world have begun to establish their own data sovereignty systems so as to better manage and control data. For example, the European Union implemented the *General Data Protection Regulation* to claim extraterritorial jurisdiction over data; the United States has issued the *Clarifying Lawful Overseas Use of Data Act*, which gives law enforcement agencies the right to obtain extraterritorial data; Russia has adopted a sovereign Internet law to establish "autonomous and controllable" cyber sovereignty over Russian network. Countries like Australia, Brazil, Canada, India and South Korea also have similar laws. So far, data sovereignty has become a new field for global competition.

Three Implications of the Data Rights Law

The world today is in the middle of radical changes that we have never seen in the past 100 years and mankind is facing both hope and challenges. As Stephen Hawking put it, "we stand on the threshold of a brave new world. It is an exciting, if precarious, place to be ..." The game around the establishment of the global cyberspace governance system is intensifying, as difficulties abound in the governance process and more disagreements arise regarding the governance model. Although countries in the world have different national conditions, are in different stages of Internet development, and face different challenges, we share the desire to promote the development of the digital economy, address cybersecurity challenges, and strengthen cyberspace governance. The data rights law is a new approach to global cyberspace governance proposed by China. It provides the Chinese wisdom and Chinese solutions to the establishment of a community with a shared future in cyberspace.

The data rights law is a symbol that Chinese legislation has stepped onto the world stage. China is currently undergoing the most extensive and profound social changes in human history, and is working on the most ambitious and unique innovations in its practices of the rule of law. A sound legal system is the backbone of the national governance system. As President Xi Jinping pointed out, "China must make good use the rule of law when she interacts with the world and participates in international affairs as a major and responsible country ... The global governance system is at a key stage of adjustments and changes for the global governance system. We should actively take part in rule-making, and be a participant, promoter and champion of the transformation of global governance." The data rights law, as an innovation and breakthrough in the field of law, leads the way and promotes progress towards the globalization of law and jurisprudence. In particular, the publishing of our book series on data rights law in multiple languages presents Chinese ideas to the world, has our voice heard, and proposes Chinese solutions to global cyberspace governance. It heralds the rise of Chinese laws and their move to the center stage of the world. It is a powerful legal tool for China's participation in global governance in the era of digital civilization and a milestone in our efforts to provide public products for global governance.

Data rights law is an important part of the rule of law in the future. If there is another huge social revolution around the corner, it will be a revolution in legislation that pursues better governance for the digital empire. In today's world, with governance in multiple forms, on multiple levels, and across various fields, our governance model has gradually adapted to this era of globalization. However, as the governance system grows more complex, its effectiveness and legitimacy can easily be hampered. In order to avoid conflicts regarding data sovereignty, we should formulate international rules through international cooperation, establish a data rights system, and create an international legal community, which will lead towards a community with a shared future for mankind in cyberspace based on the rule of law. Looking at the development of laws in the world, it is not difficult to see a trend of integration between laws from different places around the world. Standing at the present, we are trying to envisage rule of law in the future, so that we can figure out what are our options today that will help us better embrace the future rule of law. The data rights law offers insights about what laws will be like in the future and kindles our imagination.

Data rights law is an important step stone for mankind's march towards the digital civilization. "For the past, the law was what civilization produced; for the present, the law is a tool with which we keep civilization going; for the future, the law would be a means we use to push civilization forward." As human society progressed from the agricultural civilization to the industrial civilization and then to the digital civilization, the law transformed from the law of man to the law of things, and to the law of data. The digital civilization is the value justification and driving force of the creation of the data rights law, while the data rights law offers basis for the existence of the digital civilization, helping maintain its systems and improving its order. The data rights law is highly meaningful in that it serves as the order paradigm of the digital civilization and lays the foundation for maintaining order in this civilization (Key Laboratory of Big Data Strategy 2018). In this sense, the data rights law is the product of a leap of our civilization and its order, and the legal basis for the building of a community with a shared future for mankind in cyberspace. It, together with the property law, constitutes the legal foundation of the era of digital civilization, and form a synergy that pushes for the leap of the human world from the industrial civilization to the digital civilization.

Lian Yuming
Director of the Key Laboratory of Big Data Strategy
Director of the Research Center for Data Rights Law in
China University of Political Science and Law
Beijing
January 17, 2020

Introduction

Today, mankind is faced with many unprecedented challenges. Global concerns such as nuclear war, cyberwar, financial war, biological war and non-sovereign power are plaguing the world. The key to these global problems is global governance, and the community with a shared future for mankind is China's proposal for a bright future of the world and for human development on the basis of good global governance. The international legal community, which offers legal support for the community with a shared future for mankind, is a system of shared rules that exists in an interdependent international community. It helps expand the common interests of different countries, form a community of shared interests, and enable international players to fulfill their shared responsibilities. The data rights law is an important part of this international legal community and represents our insights into the development trends of the technology, laws and mankind. It is an important symbol showing that Chinese laws are marching towards the center stage of the world, and it also serves as a powerful legal tool for China's participation in global governance in the era of digital civilization.

I

In the opening plenary of the 2017 annual meeting of the World Economic Forum in Davos, Switzerland, President Xi Jinping said, "Today, we also live in a world of contradictions. On the one hand, with growing material wealth and advances in science and technology, human civilization has developed as never before. On the other hand, frequent regional conflicts, global challenges like terrorism and refugees, as well as poverty, unemployment and widening income gap have all added to the uncertainties of the world." Then, on the next day, at the United Nations Office in Geneva, President Xi raised the question of our times: "What has happened to the world and how should we respond?" More than two years later, at the closing ceremony of the Global Governance Forum co-hosted by China and France, he once again gave his insights into the world situation. "We are witnessing major changes unfolding in our world, something unseen in a century. Peace and development remain the theme of the times. Meanwhile, mankind faces a host of common challenges as uncertainties and destabilizing factors continue to mount."

The world is faced with changes as well as challenges that mankind has not seen for 100 years. One of these is the threat of nuclear war. Since the twenty-first century, major countries in the world have launched nuclear strategies one after another and focused on building their power for nuclear deterrence with both defensive and offensive capabilities. This has given rise to vicious nuclear competition and nuclear game worldwide. Vicious nuclear development may further undermine the strategic stability of the world, triggering the Third World War featured by nuclear weapons, and opening the "Pandora's box" for mankind. The second threat comes of cyberwar which is a completely new form of warfare. Cyberspace has become a new battlefield where countries wrestle fiercely for control. As cyberspace is closely linked to the physical space we live in, cyberwar poses an even greater threat to mankind than nuclear war does. As it rises quietly, cyberwar may become a major source of turbulence and disorder in the world. The third threat comes from financial war. Financial security is important for economic development and world peace, and constitutes a major part of global governance. Considering the trend of economic integration, once a country, any country, is hit by a systemic financial crisis, it will inevitably wreak havoc on the entire world economy, leaving hardly any country out of it. The fourth is the threat of biological warfare. Mankind today faces multiple health challenges such as cancer, Ebola, and HIV/AIDS, as well as social risks in multiple dimensions, including the alienation of gene editing technology. The "super-man" created by gene editing will represent a "superior civilization" compared with the world of natural men, and could deal a fatal dimension-reduction blow on us. Once this gets out of control, mankind may find itself in a catastrophe like never before. The fifth is the threat of non-sovereign power. Democracy Network is a non-sovereign power that focuses on using the Internet to democratize other countries. It can easily go beyond national borders to form a global network, affecting or even controlling and restraining sovereign states, and thereby directly or indirectly change the international geopolitical order, winding up as a new type of global hazard. In addition to all these, we are also facing two "gray rhinos", which can be disruptive and leave us no room to resist at all. One is global warming. A recent UN report has once again warned us about climate disasters that may materialize: By the end of this century, the sea level may rise by one meter and disasters like extreme weather, floods, and food shortage are likely to sink one billion people in the world into crises, driving 280 million people away from their homes, and bringing large numbers of refugees. The other is the clash of civilizations. Are the clashes between civilizations unavoidable, or can civilizations coexist in harmony through communication and mutual learning? This famous old question is now once again on our table as the world witnesses an increasingly complex situation featured by confrontations between seclusion and opening up, and between unilateralism and multilateralism. This is actually an ultimate question for us today: Where should mankind head for?

On June 7, 2019, UN Secretary-General António Guterres said at the St. Petersburg International Economic Forum that "global challenges require global solutions. No country, and no organization, can do it alone." He also emphasized that the world must have multilateral institutions and architecture, because international relations follow international law. As the world's largest developing country and a permanent member of the UN Security Council, China always abide by the global governance principle of extensive consultation, joint contribution and shared benefits. China firmly adheres to the path of peaceful development, unswervingly supports multilateralism and upholds the core role of United Nations in global governance, and actively promotes the establishment of new international relations and a community with a shared future for mankind. It should be noted that the Political Bureau of the Central Committee of the Communist Party of China has had a number of collective studies sessions themed on global governance. President Xi Jinping chaired the sessions himself and delivered a series of important speeches on the topic. This fully demonstrates that China attaches great importance to global governance and is willing to play its role as a responsible major country in global governance, participate in the reform and building of the global governance system, and continuously contribute its wisdom and strength.

II

After President Xi Jinping proposed the concept of a community with a shared future for mankind on March 23rd, 2013, the concept soon becomes a buzzword in international relations and global governance. It has not only been repeatedly mentioned and interpreted by Chinese leaders in various speeches that they deliver at home and abroad, but also written in UN resolutions. This means that the community with a shared future for mankind has, to a large extent, become an international consensus. The report to the 19th CPC National Congress called on "the people of all countries to work together to build a community with a shared future for mankind, to build an open, inclusive, clean, and beautiful world that enjoys lasting peace, universal security, and common prosperity." In the Second Plenary Session of the 19th Central Committee of the Chinese Communist Party, it was emphasized once again that "Following the path of peaceful development, pursuing a mutually beneficial strategy of opening up, and promoting the building of a community with a shared future for mankind are of great significance to the cause of peaceful development for humanity." In March 2018, at the first session of the 13th National People's Congress, *Amendments to the Constitution of the People's Republic of China* was adopted, and "promoting the building of a community with a shared future for mankind" was written into the preamble of the *Constitution*, making it a concept up to the constitutional level and part of China's legal system. Thus, this concept became an important part of the Xi Jinping thought on socialism with Chinese characteristics for a new era.

At present, global cyberspace governance is plagued with problems such as incomplete rules, unreasonable order, and unbalanced development, all are problems that have long been in existence. At the same time, there is also the plight of a poor structure, hegemony and the lack of the rule of law. What appear to be spontaneous rules set by the technological communities is in fact the result of hegemony and domination from countries with the most advanced technologies, and this has produced a monopoly of power under the disguise of "decentralization" in cyberspace. The Internet is by no means a place out of the law. The international community needs a fair legal system for the Internet, and this in turn requires guidance and support from the international legal community. The idea of an international legal community reflects China's new understanding of the social foundation of international law. It is of great value to China's participation in the reform of the global governance system, helps China better understand its relationship with the world, amplifies China's voice in the world, enables China to take a better approach when it communicates with the world, and facilitates the legalization of the kind of international relations that China has always advocated. It can be said that working harder to establish an international legal community is the way we must take towards a community with a shared future for mankind.

The international environment sets the foundation for the establishment of an international legal community, while an international legal community provides legal solutions to the problems in the international environment. Major problems that the world is facing include more and more frequent and extreme global problems caused by the threats of nuclear wars, cyber wars, financial wars, biological warfare, and non-sovereign power, the diversity and fragmentation of international laws, and the absence of and disputes over global governance. It has become an urgent need for countries around the world to strengthen cooperation and deepen communication, to jointly grasp the opportunities brought about by digitalization, networking, and smart development, to respond to global challenges in terms of law, security, and government administration, and to join hands for an international legal community. The international legal community meets the needs of both China and the world and it will soon become a reality as sovereign states have common interests due to interdependence and the need to take common actions because of common threats. This is because they need a shared legal system to protect common interests and respond to common threats, and they shoulder common but differentiated responsibilities in order to implement the shared legal system.

III

The data rights law is an important part of the international legal community. Big data makes a smarter world, and everything in this threefold world of humans, machines and things can be expressed with data. Therefore, we propose the data man hypothesis, and on its basis, we set out to deal with a series of statutory rights and legal relationships that traditional laws fail to cover, including data rights, the rights to share, and data sovereignty. To do this, we need new laws that govern the data ownership, data rights, data use, and data protection in the age of digital civilization. This new law is what we call the "data rights law". Kevin Kelly and Yuval Noah Harari are deemed as great data philosophers of the twentieth century. Kevin Kelly's Future Trilogy (*The Inevitable: Understanding the 12 Technological Forces That Will Shape Our Future*; *Out of Control: The New Biology of Machines, Social Systems, and the Economic World*; and *What Technology Wants*) and Yuval Noah Harari's Brief History Trilogy (*Sapiens: A Brief History of Humankind*; *Homo Deus: A Brief History of Tomorrow*; and *21 Lessons for the 21st Century*) overwhelmed the world with their great insights. They have revealed to us how the Internet smashes the old world, but not how the Internet builds a new world. The data rights law is our answer to the latter question from a legal perspective.

The data rights law studies the three trends in the age of digital civilization. The first is the trend of technological development. After the birth of the world's first general-purpose electronic computer, mankind entered the era of information technology 1.0, whose hallmarks include electronic technology, computing technology and software technology. Twenty years after that, technological progress and ecosystem evolution led us into the era of information technology 2.0, with Internet technology as an important symbol. International online platforms like Facebook pools information from around the world, gets us all connected, and makes our world a global village where people feel they are close to one another. Then, technology continued to evolve, giving rise to new-generation technologies such as artificial intelligence, quantum informatics, 5G, the Internet of Things, and blockchain. Thus, we are now in the era of information technology 3.0 symbolized by digital twin. Mankind is in the middle of migration from the physical space to the digital space and in foreseeable future, the two are expected to merge. Digitalization, networking, and intelligence will gradually become new features of human existence, and digital subsistence will become our most important way of life. This is the technological context of our study on the data rights law. The second is the trend of legal development. A conscious society would see the development of laws. Looking back at the history of legal systems in the human world, we can see the development track from laws for ethnic communities to laws for city states, to national laws, and international organization laws; and in the future, laws will proceed from national laws to transnational to supranational laws. The important trends will be the globalization and integration of laws, autonomy of private rights, and the merging of statute law and case law; and the ultimate pattern will be one that combines global laws and national laws. This is the basic assumption on which our study on the data rights law is based. The third is the trend of human development. Up to now, the holders of rights have always been natural man, but perhaps in the near future, human society will see the coexistence of natural men, robots, and gene-edited men. We collectively refer to these three categories of existence as "data man" and based on this, we have constructed the legal framework of data rights, data rights system, and data rights law. This is the theoretical basis for our study on the data rights law.

"If Chinese laws are to go onto the world stage, laws related to the digital economy are the most likely." The biggest change in international politics in the early twenty-first century is China's lasting and peaceful development. For any country, real peace comes from providing the world with a civilization. The data rights law, as a product of the progress of our time, represents a new order as mankind moves towards digital civilization.

It opens up a brand new field of legal research and is highly meaningful for promoting dialogue between Chinese global jurisprudential circles, and for enhancing bilateral and multilateral exchanges in legal culture. The framework of data rights, data rights system, and data rights law provides us with a new perspective to look at and better understand our world. This is a key that we all have long been looking for. It will open the door to the future of digital civilization. It can be said that the data rights law is not only a grand idea about the future of our life, but also a major discovery made in our studies on the digital civilization. The proposal of the data rights law has laid a legal foundation for maintaining national data sovereignty as well as firmly holding in hand our right to formulate data rights rules and have our voice heard on the world stage. It is of special importance to our progress towards law-based global cyberspace governance and the building of a community with a shared future for mankind.

CHAPTER I

Data Man

Rights are closely bound up with human nature. "Human nature serves as the source and basis of rights and rights embody the requirements and nature of human beings. It is the rights based on human nature that are deep-rooted. Thus, the extent to which people understand human nature determines the extent to which people understand rights and are able to protect rights." Law is a system of rules formed on the basis of the demand of human nature and a representation of the human demand for rules. It starts with man and ends with man. Law derives from human nature and the study of law will lose its theoretical premise if it parts ways with human nature. "What we need is to explain the essence of the law while this essence is to be found in human nature." Human nature is the basis for judging the legitimacy of law and structuring the legal system. We are stepping into a new era of civilization featured by the digital economy, digital government and digital society. The establishment of a digital civilization relies on the design of data rights rules, the arrangement of a data rights system and establishment of the data rights law. As such, legislation on data rights becomes an inevitable trend of the development of human society. For the study on the data rights law, the hypothesis of human nature is the logical starting point and the core value. We propose the data man hypothesis for human nature basis of the data rights law and the core of this hypothesis is altruism. Only when altruism is possible can claims for data rights become possible.

The Human Nature Basis of the Law

All doctrines about man are premised on and start with a certain hypothesis of human nature and different definitions of man and different hypotheses of human nature determine the basic inclination of a discipline's theoretical system. As David Hume put it, "all the sciences have a relation, greater or less, to human nature and that however wide any of them may seem to run from it, they still return back by one passage or another" (Hume 1996, p. 6). Any system design has a certain hypothesis of human nature as its premise. "All systems are based on their different hypotheses of human nature, and they organize, lead, control and stimulate people" (Gao Chengjun 2014). As regard to the building of any institutional system, only when the logical starting point is clear, can it avoid abstraction in theory. As Yi-Hwa Yang, a scholar from Taiwan of China, once commented, jurisprudence is a subject of people-centered study of law. The study on jurisprudence must boil down to the study on humanity and the principles of law are, after all, inseparable from humans, human interaction and the social scenarios where humans seek to survive" (Hu Yuhong 2002, p. 7). The "science of law is a science of human and a 'people-centered subject'. It focuses on the actual legal life of human beings and the legal issues that people face in social life. Legal phenomena are nothing but various behavioral phenomena displayed by people in legal scenarios. Too much emphasis on legal phenomena as the object of study on law might cause us to forget who create such phenomena and make it impossible to probe into the inherent tension between man and law arising out of legal issues" (Hu Yuhong 2002, p. 6).

Man and human nature

The presuppositions of all human sciences are centered on man and focused on human nature. As early as in ancient Greece, wise men attempted to solve the riddle of Sphinx, which is clearly man-centered. Then, in the Middle Ages, people's world view centered around theology and Godship was what was used to shape and explain human nature. It was not until the Renaissance that man received attention with the human body, mind, desires and well-being in the spotlight. This is the "discovery of man" in the studies of history. What is man? This has always been a fascinating question for philosophers all over the world since ancient times and debates on it has never ceased over the past millennium.

Many philosophers, Chinese and foreign, ancient and modern, have expressed their views on human nature, leaving numerous writings on this topic. However, there seems to be no sign of any consensus so far. This might be one of the reasons why this topic is always so widely discussed. Here are some of the views: Protagoras said that "of all things the measure is Man; Aristotle said that "man is by nature a political animal"; a medieval motto reads "man is both angel and beast"; La Mettrie said that "man is machine"; Immanuel Kant said that "rational human beings should be treated as an end in themselves"; an utilitarian view has it that "man is a rational maximizer of his ends in life"; Karl Marx believed the "essence of man as the ensemble of social relations"; Ernst Cassirer defined "man as a cultural or symbolic animal"; Friedrich Nietzsche regarded "man as the will-to-power animal"; in Blaise Pascal's view, "man is a thinking reed"; and Mark Twain once said that "man is the only animal that blushes – or needs to". "These theories provide correct answers to human nature from different perspectives, but they are more likely to be just one link on the eternal development chain along which mankind probes into its own mystery" (Chen Zhonglin 2001). None of them gets it all.

Obviously, there is no end to our efforts to define man and new definitions will emerge one after another. Definitions of man need to be deconstructed and reconstructed. The discussion about what man is becomes necessary, because human life is a reality governed by an institutional framework. Karl Marx demonstrated the essence of man from three perspectives. He

> revealed the distinction between man and animal from the perspective of labor, explained the relationship between persons from the perspective of sociality, and specified that the demand of man itself was the essence of man from the perspective of the development of man itself. (Yang Lan 2018)

The complexity of human beings determines that human nature is multi-dimensional. Different from divinity and animality, "human nature is the general term of various attributes of man". There are natural, social, and spiritual dimensions to it, and the three, in dialectical unity, constitute the complete structure of human nature. As constrained by relations

Table 1. Definitions of Man

Definition	Source
Man is created by God.	This mainly comes from early myths and Christian theology. According to the doctrine of creation stated in the Christian *Bible*, God created the heavens and the earth and, on the sixth day of creating the world, created man in his own image and let man have dominion over every living thing that moves upon the earth.
Man is a rational animal.	With the longest history, this idea is the most influential and is still in wide use today. Socrates defines man as "that creature who has a rational answer when he is asked a rational question"; Xunzi said that "that by which humans are human is not because they are special in having two legs and no feathers, but because they have distinctions."
Man is a political animal.	This idea was first proposed by Aristotle. In his view, a social instinct is implanted in all men by nature, and can thus form such advanced (political) alliance. Therefore, "man is by nature a political animal". As stated by Xunzi, he is not as strong as the ox, nor as swift as the horse, and yet he makes the ox and the horse work for him. Why? Because he is able to organize himself in society and they are not.
Man is a linguistic animal.	Aristotle said that "man is the only animal capable of reasoning". Martin Heidegger said that "language is the home of existence." Ernst Cassirer defined "man as a symbolic animal". Although modern observation and study of animals have proved animals to also have their languages and to be capable of exchanging and sharing information with their counterparts, there are contemporary anthropologists who still insist that human is the only creature capable of using linguistic signs to communicate.

(To be continued)

Table 1. Continued

Definition	**Source**
Man is a moral animal.	Mencius said that "That whereby man differs from the lower animals is but small. The mass of people cast it away, while superior men preserve it. Shun clearly understood the multitude of things, and closely observed the relations of humanity. He walked along the path of benevolence and righteousness; he did not need to pursue benevolence and righteousness." Xunzi said that "fire and water possess energy, but are without life. Grass and trees have life but no intelligence. Birds and beasts have intelligence but no sense of duty. Man possesses energy, life, intelligence, and, in addition, a sense of duty. Therefore, he is the noblest being on earth." Zhu Xi said that man was different from beasts in that there was love between a father and son; righteousness between a ruler and minister; separation of functions and jobs between a husband and a wife, as they should each know their place and proper responsibilities; a proper order between old and young; and loyalty between friends.
Man is an animal of tools.	Benjamin Franklin defined man as a "tool-making animal"; Friedrich Engels defined man as the animals making and using tools; anthropologists George Bartholomew Jr. and Joseph Birdsell said that "man is the only mammal which is continuously dependent on tools for survival"; Chinese philosopher Deng Xiaomang said that "man is the animal making, using and carrying tools".
Man is a spiritual animal.	Georg Wilhelm Friedrich Hegel defined man as a self-conscious animal; Ludwig Feuerbach defined man as an animal with ideological feelings; Wilhelm Dilthey regarded spiritual culture as distinguishing man from animals; Max Scheler defined man as the only superior existence with mental tendency; Erich Rothacker was of the opinion that the essence of man lay in its spiritual activity; Michael Landmann said that man was a spiritual creature.

(To be continued)

Table 1. Continued

Definition	Source
Man is a cultural animal.	Ernst Cassirer defined man as an animal of culture; Michael Landmann regarded man as the one creating and using culture; Shi Zhonglian construed culture as covering everything created by man and said that a true and in-depth grasp of the special property of man could be gained only when man was viewed as the creature of culture.
Man is an unspecialized creature.	Arnold Gehlen stated that the biggest difference between man and animals was that man was unspecialized. Because it was unspecialized or unascertained, man could make up for its defects in activities, excel sufficiently equipped animals and be open to the world without being enclosed by surroundings. This was the way that enabled man to resolve all defects in the structure of creature.
Man is a free animal.	Advocates of this definition include Chuang Tsu of ancient China and a large number of more recent thinkers since the Enlightenment age: Jean-Jacques Rousseau, Immanuel Kant, Karl Marx, and Jean-Paul Sartre, among others. Karl Marx is perhaps the most representative. His definition of human being could, by inference, be that man was a free and conscious animal. This definition by no means precluded him from affirming Benjamin Franklin's definition of man in his old age because making tools is exactly a kind of free and conscious activity.

Source: Han Dongping. 2016. "Solving the Mystery of Man: Deconstruction and Reconstruction of the Definition of Man." *Wuhan University Journal (Humanity Sciences)*, 6th issue.

of production, politics and ethics, among other things, human nature changes constantly in the process of social development.

The natural dimension of man nature covers an ensemble of characteristics of man who, as a natural being, is subject to the nature. Like any other form of life, man develops according to natural law and makes physical and chemical movements. Thus, man has the characteristics of things. As a kind of animal, man performs activities as living things and has the characteristics possessed by animals in general. The natural aspect of man and the desires of man arising therefrom form the material base for the existence of man and serve as the preconditions for all human activities and other dimensions of human nature. As Friedrich Engels put it:

> It is, however, inherent in the descent of man from the animal world that he can never entirely rid himself of the beast, so that it can always be only a question of more or less, of a difference in the degree of bestiality or of humanity.
>
> Man is directly a natural being. As a natural being and as a living natural being he is on the one hand endowed with natural powers, vital powers – he is an active natural being. These forces exist in him as tendencies and abilities – as instincts. (Central Compilation and Translation Bureau 2009, p. 209)
>
> Man (is the) being (of) human nature. (Central Compilation and Translation Bureau 2009, p. 208)

Man is firstly a natural being and then a social being, rational being, cultural being, and ethical being.

The social dimension of human nature is the ensemble of all characteristics of man as a social being. Different from other animals in manner for activities, man lives in social groups, and this is why man is social in nature. According to Ludwig Feuerbach, only social man is man (Ludwig Feuerbach 1984, p. 571). Karl Marx was of the opinion that man was of both naturalness and sociality and that man became human only in social relations. He defined the essence of man as

> No abstraction inherent in each single individual; in its reality it is the ensemble of the social relations, the further back we trace the course of history, the more does the individual, and accordingly also the producing individual, appear to be dependent and to belong to a larger whole: at first, the individual in a still quite natural manner is part of the family and of the tribe which evolves from the family; later he is part of a community, of one of the different forms of the community which arise from the conflict and the merging of tribes. It is not until the eighteenth century that in bourgeois society the various forms of the social texture confront the individual as merely means towards his private ends, as external necessity. But the epoch which produces this standpoint, namely, that of the isolated individual, is precisely the epoch of the (as yet) most highly developed social (according to this standpoint, general) relations. Man is a zoon politikon in the most literal sense, not only a social animal, but an animal that can be individualized only

> within society. Production by an isolated individual outside society ... is a rare event. (Karl Marx 1979, p. 22)

The natural and social dimensions of human nature are only the start, and by no means the whole, of human nature. What is more important is the moral dimension, which is reflected by the tendency of people to take action based on specific codes of conduct when dealing with other people or with society. This is the unique part of human nature that distinguishes man from other animals and makes man superior. In terms of morality and ethics, the moral nature of man distinguishes man from animals not only in content but also in form. In the chapter on the regulations of a king, Xunzi said that:

> Fire and water possess energy, but are without life. Grass and trees have life but no intelligence. Birds and beasts have intelligence but no sense of duty. Man possesses energy, life, intelligence, and, in addition, a sense of duty. Therefore, he is the noblest being on earth.

That is to say, man is superior to beasts and animals in general because man knows about good and evil and has a sense of what is moral. "It reflects the main characteristics of altruism. That is, people show respect and solicitude toward other people living in the same group, pay attention to the group and even the whole mankind and nature, and cause their actions to be in harmony with the surroundings and to benefit others and the development of the group" (Yan Cunsheng 2007). Moral nature is a superior nature that is based on rationality, sensibility and sociality and brings about the organic combination of the three. It is in essence altruism and civilization.

Several hypotheses of human nature

Hypotheses of human nature are assumptions of the essential nature of man. Human nature is where we can find answers to questions concerning relations between man and nature, man and society, as well as man and himself. Moreover, hypotheses of human nature are always the logical starting point of our studies of issues concerning, among other things, management activities, institutional design, innovation in rules, and legislation in reality, because all these represent the hypotheses of human nature in one way or another. There have been countless theories regarding hypotheses of human nature in history, but it is the hypotheses of human nature in some specific disciplines that are truly influential and in wide use in reality (see Table 2).

Table 2. Classical Hypotheses of Human Nature

Hypothesis	**Description**
Economic man hypothesis	This was first put forward by Adam Smith in *The Wealth of Nations*. The core of the idea is that the purpose of human activities is to maximize the benefits of man. This hypothesis has had profound influence on the industrial society and is the basis for the structuring of society and institutional arrangements in the West. Meanwhile, People have also found an invisible hand unconsciously but effectively increase social and public interests as individuals pursue the maximization of their own interests. This hypothesis and relevant thoughts have contributed to the establishment of the scientific management theory.
Political man hypothesis	In *Politics*, Aristotle presented the idea that "man is by nature a political animal". According to this hypothesis, man is a kind of animal capable of adjusting interests and pursuing goodwill and cooperation and always tends to form political communities. The citizens of a state are created equal and directly participate in and manage affairs of the state according to the principle of fairness and justice. The political man hypothesis reveals the inseparability of man and politics in a class society where social interests are highly differentiated and has made positive contribution to solving the mystery of human nature. The long-standing theory of human rights in Western countries is derived exactly from Aristotle's doctrine of political man.

(To be continued)

Table 2. Continued

Hypothesis	Description
Moral man hypothesis	In the book *The Theory of Moral Sentiments*, Adam Smith held that every person has moral sense and a specific expression thereof is that people have compassion and sense of justice. Man's behaviors show an altruistic tendency and are in pursuit of the maximization of collective interests. The doctrine of moral man presented by Adam Smith has much in common with the doctrine of good human nature presented by Mencius in the pre-Qin period in ancient China. In the traditional Chinese society, morality, as part of the human nature, was the basis for the top-level design and institutional arrangements of society and the moral man hypothesis clearly had its influence.
Social man hypothesis	Based on the Hawthorne experiments, Professor Elton Mayo of Harvard University, a management scientist, founded the human relations school of management and proceeded to propose the social man hypothesis in the book *The Human Problems of an Industrial Civilization*. He held the view that a social man is a man who is in social relationships, with social demands, and has not only the motive to pursue personal remuneration and income but also the demand for friendship, sense of security and sense of membership. The social man hypothesis emphasizes that human relationships and membership of organizations are more effective in stimulating human behavior than financial compensation. The transformation from the economic man hypothesis to the social man hypothesis is undoubtedly a big step forward in management thoughts and management method.

(To be continued)

Table 2. Continued

Hypothesis	Description
Cultural man hypothesis	In his masterpiece *An Essay on Man: An Introduction to a Philosophy of Human Culture*, Ernst Cassirer, a German philosopher and the founder of cultural philosophy, put forward the idea of "cultural man". In 1981, William Ouchi, a professor at UCLA, published *Theory Z: How American Business Can Meet the Japanese Challenge*, the ground-breaking work on corporate culture theory. In this book, he presented the cultural man hypothesis of human nature and held the view that psychology and behavior of man are ultimately determined by values and other cultural factors. The cultural man hypothesis reveals the cultural nature, an underlying nature, of man, reaches deeper inside human nature, and has profound influence in reality.

Source: Compiled by the authors based on relevant materials.

Apparently, the above theories on human nature each unravels one aspect of human nature. For instance, the economic man hypothesis highlights man's egoism; the political man hypothesis highlights man's social nature; the moral man hypothesis highlights altruism in human nature; the social man hypothesis highlights man's non-economic sociality; the cultural man hypothesis highlights man's cultural-embedded nature. Although there are justifications for their existence, these hypotheses of human nature draw conclusions based on over-generalization of certain behaviors of man and are inevitably partial in theory and misleading in practice. As a result, they are seldom applied. These hypotheses of human nature have exerted on the society great positive influence and, at the same time, certain negative effect. Therefore, reflection is necessary while credit is given to them.

Human nature hypothesis of the law

Man is the logical starting point of social rules, and human nature lies at the core and serves as the soul in the building of social rules. Any institutional design has in-depth thinking about human nature lying behind it. The law and the rule of law in any times are based on the valuation of human nature and different valuations results in different methods of social control. Only laws that conform to human demands would be observed by people while those that deviate from human nature would be no more than a piece of waste paper. An important source of justifications of laws is whether they are in line with human nature. Therefore, human nature is where we are to find justifications for the necessity and inevitability of data rights legislation. As Oliver Wendell Holmes Jr. once said, law found its philosophy from the needs of human nature (Bernard Schwatz 1989, p. 134). Analytical jurisprudence, without attaching importance to human nature, will not reach the height of legal philosophy. In our people-oriented world today, it is all the more important for us to use human nature as the measurement of the merits and demerits of law. A good law should be well-grounded in human nature, and the values it pursues and the legal order it produces should both be in line with human nature and contribute to the survival and development of mankind.

Existing moral principles and laws are all established on the basis of human nature. "The economic man hypothesis is the human nature basis of the civil law and the premise of the civil law's regulation of the behaviors of social actors" (Yi Jun 2006). Philosophers, including Mencius and Xunzi in ancient China, Plato and Aristotle in ancient Greece, as well as Thomas Hobbes and Jean-Jacques Rousseau in the modern times, have all offered their unique insights into the relationship between laws and human nature (see Tables 3 and 4). Understanding human nature is the key to understanding man. Some people perceive human nature from the perspective of the natural aspect of man; some approach human nature from the perspective of the social nature of man; some view human nature from the perspective of ethics; and some analyze human nature from the perspective of class. Such differences in perspectives are bound to result in different conclusions about human nature. Different theories of human nature inevitably give rise to different views on law and different views on law will mirror the different theories of human nature. "Law is created by man and consequently connected with human nature in one way or another. Law is simply a product of the development of human nature"

(Zhuo Zeyuan 2001, p. 85). As Gustav Radbruch put it, what is important about the style of a legal age is nothing better than its view about man which determines the direction of the law (Gustav Radbruch 2001, p141). The human nature hypothesis of law is different under different historical conditions and different human nature hypotheses lead to different characteristics of law at different stages.

Table 3. Thoughts on the Human Nature Basis of Law in Ancient China

Representative Figure	**Basic Idea**
Xunzi	Law is a derivative of rites and righteousness (*li* and *yi*) a set of social system devised to ensure proper implementation of the two in people's behaviors.
Guan Zhong, Wang Chong, Lv Wen, and Bai Juyi	Law is a derivative of moral principles and a supporting means for the achievement of moral rules and rites. They generally believe that the law, though absolutely necessary, should not be too much or it would do more harm than good. They advocate "conciseness of laws and regulations".
Guan Zhong and Xunzi	Law has close relationship with its maker and is both the product and expression of the human nature of its maker. The monarch and sages should be the makers of the law because their human nature is good and in line with natural justice. Therefore, they are the model and defender of moral principles in the country and are capable of making out a set of detailed rites and laws according to moral principles.
Confucius	Human nature is the moral character of man and its core is "benevolence" (*ren*), that is, benevolent persons have caring and loving hearts and persons in power adopt beneficent political strategy, and the law is an arrangement for using compulsory measures to achieve benevolent rule based on that need.

Source: Yan Cunsheng, 2016. *Foundation of Law from the Perspective of Human Nature.* China Legal Publishing House.

Table 4. Western Thoughts on the Human Nature Basis of Law

School	Figure	Basic Idea
Natural Jurisprudence	Aristotle Marcus Tullius Cicero Hugo Grotius Thomas Aquinas John Rawls Thomas Hobbes	Man is the combination of rationality and sensibility with the former making man act virtuously and the latter making man act evilly; Rationality and sociality are what distinguishes man from other animals and the essence of human nature; and law is the very social system that reflects and actualizes such nature; natural law is the law of morality and the law must be moral.
Philosophical Jurisprudence	Immanuel Kant G. W. F. Hegel Gustav Radbruch	Early philosophical jurisprudence inherited the basic tradition of natural jurisprudence and likewise sought the foundation of the law from the morality of man and adopted the concept of the natural law. However, instead of treating the natural law as something in real existence, it construed such law as the idealistic law or philosophical law, that is, principles of law; late philosophical jurisprudence also connected law with human nature but made differences by adopting the viewpoint of development to conduct dynamic analysis on human nature. It held the idea that human nature was developing and changing, human nature or human archetype varies in different times and the law, based on human nature, thus also differs with times.

(To be continued)

Table 4. Continued

School	Figure	Basic Idea
-	Adam Smith David Hume	Man is egoistic in nature. However, because people must live in society and their success is dependent on interaction and co-operation with others, this process enables them to set up friendship with others and thereby develop compassion and sympathy towards others and then nurture various virtues. These virtues are not equal to one another and the superior would further develop into perfect human nature. The inferior is the justice. It is the basis on which social order relies and the maintenance thereof is thus inevitable. The way to maintain it is to punish wrong-doers and the law assumes this task. What man is conscious of is all man has. Man has two kinds of consciousness, pleasure and pain. Accordingly, what man does is to avoid pain and seek pleasure. Maintenance of social stability and prosperity requires compliance with some rules and political power and the law then results.
Utilitarian jurisprudence and analytical jurisprudence	Jeremy Bentham John Austin	Based on the perception of human nature and making use of the nature that man avoids pain and seeks pleasure, the law adopts the two methods of reward and punishment to cause people to do the things in line with the moral requirement, that is, the things conducive to the maximal well-being of the vast majority of people. The law is rooted in the utilitarian nature of man.

(To be continued)

Table 4. Continued

School	Figure	Basic Idea
Social Jurisprudence	Roscoe Pound	Although the law is generated based on and for people's pursuit of utility, it is not focused on transient utility of individuals and, instead, on the social benefit inclusive of various interests. The law is intended to use such benefits as criteria for measuring and regulating other interests.
Jurisprudence of Economic Analysis	-	Man is in nature the "rational agent maximizing self-satisfaction" and aims to pursue utility. The law, based on this theory and with benefits as its value orientation, regulates people's activities by way of increasing or decreasing their transaction cost to cause them to choose behaviors that benefit society.
Political Liberalism	Friedrich August von Hayek	The law, in nature, is a kind of social rules giving rise to social order. Social order is spontaneous and, as a result, the law as the social rules is formed spontaneously through interaction among individuals rather than formulated by man consciously.
-	Karl Marx Friedrich Engels	Man is a kind of animal of social practicality enjoying certain freedom and the law is the rule of man's activities commensurate to such nature. The law is the code of conduct formulated for people by the manager in society based on such a perception and reflects the collective will of the vast majority of society.

Source: Yan Cunsheng, 2016. *Foundation of Law from the Perspective of Human Nature*. China Legal Publishing House.

People's understanding of things is different as a result of the change of times and cultural differences. However, such difference is mostly just in words while the basic connotation or approach are very similar. This is especially true in studies of the human nature basis of the law. In their discussions on the composition of human nature and the relationship between the different elements, both Chinese and foreign scholars viewed man as a combination of rationality and sensibility with the former making man act virtuously while the latter making man do evil things. They all regarded human nature as consisted of the natural dimension of inherent traits and the social dimension of the acquired social nature. They had basically the same perception of the law, regarding it as the code of conduct and instrument of governance in society though there are discrepancies regarding the origin, nature and some other aspects of law. All the attempts to understand the human nature basis of the law in history are highly valuable inspirations for us. We should inherit them critically and move forward with relevant studies.

It needs to be noted that an insight into the essence of legal systems can be gained only when we see clearly the image of man that lies behind the law. Similarly, only when the image of man behind the law is sorted out based on logical rules, can we understand why man have different images in different jurisdictions. In jurisprudential research, we attach importance to the objective evaluation of legal phenomena, but not the analysis and examination of the image of man behind the law; we emphasize the technical analysis of legal rules, but not the spirit and rationale at the intersection of rules and humanity; we value grand legal systems but not careful analysis of the harmony and coordination between the development of the systems and the evolvement of human nature. As such, analytical jurisprudence is at most a matter of rules or techniques, and will never reach the height of legal philosophy and set out the fundamental legal principles that are lasting and all-encompassing. As we gradually go deeper into the theoretical study of data rights, we definitely have to reach into the depth of human nature, an issue of ultimate significance. The data rights system, as a set of rules governing data behavior, must base its authority, effectiveness and reasonability on human nature. For legal research and legislative activities, it is necessary to have some assumptions about what laws set out to govern. This is the basis on which we create systems, norms and laws. Similarly, legislation on data rights also needs to be based on assumptions about man, which is the object it intends to govern. Without such basis, the data rights law may be rendered useless and can even become unjust law.

Data Man Hypothesis and Altruism

Data changes, redefines, and connects the world and reshapes everything in our world. Soon enough, data will become the form of existence for all persons and things; and data, instead of what we do, will be the tags of our personality. The relations of production throughout society will be marked by data power and data relations.

> Datamation is more than a technological system and more than turning everything into bits and bytes. It reshapes people's way of production and life. It is a social system that continuously renews itself, and, more importantly, it renews or reshapes the social life of mankind. (Qiu Zeqi 2016, p. 184)

In a sense, man exists in two forms, natural man and data man; and has two kinds of technologies for life, biotechnology and data technology. Man as a natural being is being transformed by genetic technology, which is part of the technology for life. Man as a data being, or sociological being, is preconditioned on certain technology and relationships therewith. Social interaction relies on technology, a very basic part of which is data technology. We now rely heavily on data, and a data-oriented paradigm revolution is quietly under way in sociology with man at its center. This revolution will bring human society into an age where powers and rights are restructured and privacy and sharing compete and collaborate. This will profoundly change the image, as well as the connotation and denotation of man. In the future, it is likely that the human society will be a society of natural men, robots and gene-edited men. Here, we refer to all their categories of man, which are all data-based, collectively as data man.

Data man hypothesis

Man in legal terms, or, the imagined or realistic image of man as depicted by the law, has been the hotspot of attention in both Chinese and foreign academia.[1] In recent years, as the legal reality changes, Chinese scholars have been conducting more in-depth studies of man in legal terms and the legal concept of man is turning from "man of status" to "man of equality and freedom" (Yu Zhong 2009) in the constitutional sense, from "abstract man" to "concrete man" (Xie Hongfei 2002) in the realm of civil law, from "economic man" to "ecological man" (He Xiaorong & Chen Quansheng 2009) in terms of environmental law, from "atomized man" to "socialized man" (Zhu Xiaozhe 2002) in terms of social law, and from "person of ethics" to "person of science" (Shen Zhai 2011) from the perspective of jurisprudence. These studies have probed into the changes in the image of man in branch laws but have not revealed the entire process of the evolution of man in general legal terms and, therefore, cannot address some difficult issues encountered in the building of rule of law. We are of the opinion that man in legal terms is undergoing a transformation from "economic man" to "data man". Meanwhile, the form of human rights is undergoing a digitalization process and accordingly, our approach to human rights should change to be based on "data man". This makes it necessary to establish the new concept of digital human rights, establish corresponding human rights protection mechanisms and provide necessary legal support (Ma Changshan 2019).

The economic man, political man, moral man, social man and cultural man hypotheses are undoubtedly insightful, but they fail to reach deeper into human nature. Man is a combination of multiple facets and our understanding of it must be comprehensive and holistic. What we pursue is not being incisive but partial, but insights into all aspect of the topic. We should neither deny the said hypotheses of human nature nor treat them as eternal truth. Instead, we should regard human nature hypotheses as an open system that is constantly evolving and interpret the rationality and necessity of human behaviors from a broader perspective. This is because "in the big data era, all social relationships can be represented with data in

1 For instance, *A Legal Person* by Gustav Radbruch (Germany), *Peron in Private Law* by Hoshino Echi (Japan) and *Discipline and Punishment* by Michel Foucault (France) have all provided detailed analysis and study of the changes in human image in law and an illustration of the characteristics of the evaluation of "person" in law.

a world composed of data, and man is the sum of related data" (Li Guojie 2014). All social relationships are in essence data relations closely bound up with privacy protection and the altruistic sharing of data. Personal dependence is replaced by material dependence[2] and the evolution of mankind, technology and data provides a new realistic possibility for liberalizing people from the personal dependence in modern society. As Karl Marx predicted, human society would take three main forms in succession: It will move from a society featuring personal dependence to one featuring material dependence, and then to one where people are free and develop in an all-round manner. However, modern technology represented by data technology is changing the track of human society, bringing a dependence on data before people are completely free from their dependence on persons and on materials. Data has penetrated every corner of social life, quietly shaping and reshaping the social pattern and organizational relationship on which human existence relies, transforming the pattern of human cognition, behavior, social structure and resource allocation, and leading mankind into the era of digital civilization.

Countries today are changing rapidly from "countries on wheels" to the "countries in cyberspace" and this change requires changes in the "rules of the game" in people's social life and laws will have to change too (Laura E. Quarantiello 1999). In this era, law and algorithm, ethics and technology, as well as rules and morality are jointly pushing for a new order and legal scenarios are undergoing profound changes. When dealing with the nature of data man, our current knowledge and theoretical model, as

2 The issue of human development is an important part of Marxist philosophy on man. In his *Economics Manuscript in 1857–1858*, Karl Marx divided the progress of human development into the stage of human dependence, the state of material dependence and the stage of comprehensive development of human freedom. "Relationships of personal dependence (which were at first quite spontaneous) are the first forms of society in which human productivity develops, thought only to a slight extent and at isolated points. Personal independence founded on material dependence is the second great form: in it there developed for the first time a system of general social interchange, resulting in universal relations, varied requirements and universal capacities. Free individuality, which is founded on the universal development of individuals and the domination of their communal and social productivity, which has become their social power, is the third stage. The second stage creates the conditions for the third."

well as ethical and legal frameworks are clearly lack of explanatory power and vitality. In this connection, it is imperative to build a new dimension of good law so as to overcome the plight faced by the rights-first principle and return to the obligation-based approach to law which will resolve the problem of dysfunction of rights caused by the rights-based approach. The data man hypothesis provides a theoretical prerequisite for creating the dimension of good law and adds to the reasonability of the human nature hypothesis of law in the big data era.

Data man is the brand-new display of human nature in the big data era. History has proved that each step forward that human nature moves had unprecedented impact on legislation and the value pursuit thereof. In the age of private law, man in law is the economic man. Then, social law came into being on the basis of reflections on the egoism of the economic man[3] and the discovery of the sociality and altruism in human nature. It is undoubtedly a significant turn in the history of jurisprudence, but it is by no means the last turn because human nature will continue to evolve and improve with time. At present, global data security crises happen once and again as tension grows between man and technology, man and economy, as well as man and society. In this context, mankind again discovers that the social man hypothesis, among others, is no longer sufficient to resolve the conflicts between man and data and it is necessary to challenge and go

3 Economists have gradually realized that the economic man hypothesis, which represents a model of definitional thinking, is facing severe challenges in our time of intelligent development and informatization and that it cannot explain the altruistic behaviors existing in reality, which directly proves the inadequacy of this egoistic hypothesis. "We should frankly admit the limitations and incapability of the economic man hypothesis". We "don't have to deny but just have to go beyond the economic man" (Yang Chunxue 2005). From the perspective of economic philosophy, the doctrine of rational egoism is in a dilemma when it attempts to explain issues concerning contemporary economic behaviors and encounters challenges due to imbalance, information asymmetry and frequent occurrence of uncertainties of the market economy in the twentieth century. In addition, it is just because human being is not completely egoistic and is full of altruistic feelings for relatives, friends and even strangers that mankind has survived, thrived, and created glorious civilizations. So to speak, human development would not have achieved what it has achieved today without the altruistic behaviors among humans.

beyond existing barriers and limitations through deeper reflections. Data man is what we came up with after such reflections and it is a new display of human nature in the big data era.

By proposing the data man hypothesis,[4] we go beyond the traditional boundary between the good and the evil, breaks away from the traditional shackles restricting data sharing and emphasizes the altruism in human behaviors and relationships and in our form of existence. Data man, altruism and sharing as its basis, pursues, creates, and realizes the value of data following the basic principle of data value maximization. Its basic connotation is the balance between lawful protection and reasonable use of data. Different from the economic man who is egoistic in nature, the data man advocates the spirits of sharing and altruism. The data man hypothesis not only affirms the rationality in the pursuit of profits by various stakeholders but also stresses the necessity of cooperation and sharing, which conforms to the requirement of data power development and the reform of data relations. Therefore, we hold that the human nature hypothesis of data philosophy should be the data man hypothesis which embodies the unification of data protection and data use. We take this hypothesis as the starting point of our analysis of, and the premise for logical reasoning in, data rights theory.

The base point of the law is individuals whose demands and expectations of the law change constantly. "Each social transformation gives rise to changed demands of man and each change of the times causes people to have different expectations of the law. Therefore, the history of the development and evolution of the law is, to a great extent, the history of the constant development and change of the image of man in law" (Hu Yuhong

4 The emergence of the data man hypothesis is in one way or another necessary and inevitable. Firstly, it may change the structure of human nature from one centered on the economic man or the social man to one that is centered on the data man and pursues dynamic balance. Secondly, it enables us to review the existing rights system, create an institutional system that is suitable for the development of the digital society, build the data rights system on the basis of a multi-faceted human nature system, and reinforce the basis for the regulation of people's data behaviors and for a better life for mankind. Thirdly, we will not be able to build a data rights theory that is comparable to the system of economic theories if we cannot achieve breakthroughs in the theory and philosophy of data man.

2008, p. 16). The legal man model provides a sketch of man in law, which is the image of legal man produced from generalization and categorization of man in law (Wu Xianjing 2010). At present, data security risks are getting increasingly prominent, cases of data rights disputes are more frequent and the digital civilization is in the making. Against such a background, it is necessary and inevitable that the image of a legal man evolves toward the data man. The data man is set in the legal scenario represented by the rise of the data rights law which is the law regarding the ownership, rights, use and protection of data and mainly aimed at making the best use of data and resolving various conflicts and disputes. The emergence of issues related to data security and data ownership is significant to the data rights law in that they provide new legal facts which have to be tackled with the data rights law. Within the scope of the law, data rights are not only about the distribution of data rights and interests but also how people use and protect data. These two types of relationships are beyond the coverage of the traditional legal man model. At a time when data security crises spread around the world and when the data rights law is emerging as it should, we need to rethink about our traditional understanding of man in legal terms. How to build the image of man in the law and how the legal man model will involve are the theoretical questions our research on the data rights law needs to answer. Human nature lays the philosophical foundation for the data rights law and provides us with a way of expression for the data rights law. Our original intention is to expound the data rights law, a new historical phenomenon in the legal world, based on the fundamental research paradigm formed by man in the law and the legal man model; and also, we will expound the basic spirits, basic principles and basic system of the data rights law through comparison between the man in the data rights law and the man in other laws.

Of course, any model may bring the problem of oversimplification the issue at hand and neither the economic man nor the data man can cover all aspects of man in law. In fact, man has multiple images in modern law and in the future, the data man will probably become a major facet of the image of man in law while other facets of it will be merely modifications or supplements to it. The shift of the legal assumption of man from the economic man to the data man means that the law requires people to use a brand-new way of thinking in life. Since the transition from the economic man to the data man is a choice we make at our own initiative, what need to be done next is to bring the data man from theory to practice.

Data man and altruism

The word "altruism" was first proposed by Auguste Comte, a French philosopher and ethicist of the nineteenth century. Starting from the instinct and nature of humanity, he illustrated the rationality of altruism. "Just as there are rational requirements on thought, there are rational requirements on action, and altruism is one of them" (Thomas Nagel 1978, p. 3). Altruism has been studied in such fields as biology, sociology, psychology and economics, and defined from these different perspectives. Human is a social animal and cannot act completely in an egoistic manner in order to maintain and enhance cooperation. In any age, therefore, altruistic spirit is necessary and advocated in social, cultural and institutional development, and altruistic behavior is regarded as a good and important value. We call this value altruism. Altruism as a school of thought, matured in ancient times, was predominant in the Middle Ages, and remained influential in modern times. Its representative figures include, among others, Confucius, Mozi, Jesus and Immanuel Kant. So far as the human nature is concerned, they believed that the purpose of each individual's behavior can be selfless and altruistic. Plato's Utopia, Jean-Jacques Rousseau's social contract, and Peter Kropotkin's mutualism all stress that human is good in nature if not corrupted.[5] The injunction that "we ought to become better men" resounds unabatedly in our souls (Immanuel Kant 2003, p. 33). The traditional Chinese culture, especially Confucianism, emphasizes group effect and altruism. According to Mencius, for example,

5 Karl Marx and Friedrich Engels repeatedly pointed out that capitalism and all previous social forms were against human nature. This indicates that human nature, in their minds, was originally the fine and kind attribute of man and has been alienated by private ownership and class oppression. To construe human nature as good is in line with their original intention.

everyone is endowed with altruism in their nature and everyone has the power to benefit others.

The altruistic behaviors of human beings are the result of biological evolution and social development combined. Cooperation is so important to mankind that "in civilized society he stands at all times in need of the cooperation and assistance of great multitudes, while his whole life is scarce sufficient to gain the friendship of a few persons" (Adam Smith 1997, p. 13). Cooperation penetrates all dimensions, all fields, and all regions of our social and economic life and runs through the development of human society (Huang Tao 2009). In *The Wealth of Nations*, Adam Smith used the examples of making pins to illustrate the significance of the division of labor and some examples to explain the significance of cooperation:

> The woollen coat which covers the day-labourer, as coarse and rough as it may appear, is the produce of the joint labour of a great multitude of workmen. The shepherd, the sorter of the wool, the wool-comber or carder, the dyer, the scribbler, the spinner, the weaver, the fuller, the dresser, with many others, must all join their different arts in order to complete even this homely production. (Adam Smith 1997, p. 11)

Herbert Simon defines the cooperation spirit as social tolerance, sympathy, readiness to help others, passion, morality and other virtues. Through these qualities, an individual sacrifices its fitness for survival. But because such altruism increases the average fitness for survival of whole society, the society in turn encourages such acts of altruism (Wang Dingding 2005, p. 199). Based on an introduction to the latest research findings of Herbert Gintis, an American economist, and others, Wang Dingding and others pointed out that the cooperation order of mankind has always been in existence and omnipresent. For each individual, cooperation is better than non-cooperation. Therefore, cooperation is not against the basic principles of biology and economics. All selfish individuals wish to cooperate rather than not. Cooperation means the coexistence of egoism and altruism (Wang Dingding 2005, p. 204). Cooperation lies at the very bottom of the foundation of the composition and existence of human society. As a result of the division of labor and cooperation, man's behaviors are fulfilled by means of and through others. So to speak, altruism is an effective way to fulfill purposes. Cooperation produces joint forces. "The question here is not only to enhance individual productive forces by co-operation, but also to created a new productive force which is collective inherent" (Central Compilation and Translation Bureau 1972, p. 362).

The big data era requires the establishment of the concept of altruism. The structure of relationships in the digital society determines that such a society is inherently decentralized, flat, and borderless, and that its basic spirits are openness, sharing, cooperation and mutual benefit. That means such a society and such an era are bound to be people-oriented with altruism as their core value. Huge cooperation surplus gives birth to an altruistic spirit and altruism may lead people out of the prisoner's dilemma. Egoism and altruism form a dialectical unity. Altruism should come prior to egoism and is the prerequisite for better egoism.[6] Jack Ma once said in a speech that "mankind is heading from the IT age to the DT age" and that what lay at the core of this age is altruism. According to him, one should "believe that others are more important, cleverer, and more capable than you; and that you cannot succeed without others' success." Altruism and sharing are better than egoism and exclusivity; and altruism is the core of the future.

The evolution of human nature is bound to bring about changes in the value of the law. Data man represents a brand-new version of human nature in the big data era. It means that our "self" evolves into a greater self which is an integration of man and data, and that the altruistic spirit not only prevails in physical world but it also brings order to the virtual space. The traditional order is centralized, hierarchical and exclusive, while the new order will be decentralized, flat and open. This determines that the essence of the data man is altruism and sharing. Human nature is always marked with the characteristics of the times and will inevitably drive the evolution and development of the value of the law as the wheels of history move ceaselessly ahead. The change in human nature in the big data era, which is represented by the data man will certainly and ultimately bring about the change in the values of security, sharing and altruism of the law.

6 American economist Milton Friedman, winner of Nobel Prize in economics, once aptly commented that before reading *The Wealth of Nations* he had no idea what egoism was, and that it was not until after reading *The Theory of Moral Sentiments* that he understood that altruism meant egoism with a clear conscience.

Possibility of altruism

In *The Theory of Moral Sentiments*, Adam Smith clearly pointed out the altruistic nature of man at the very beginning, stating that:

> How selfish so ever man may be supposed, there are evidently some principles in his nature, which interest him in the fortunes of others, and render their happiness necessary to him, though he derives nothing from it, except the pleasure of seeing it. (Adam Smith 2015, p. 5)

> The capacity of his stomach bears no proportion to the immensity of his desires, and will receive no more than that of the meanest peasant … They consume little more than the poor, and in spite of their natural selfishness and rapacity, though they mean only their own convenience, thought the sole end which they propose from the labors of all the thousands whom the employ, be the gratification of their own vain and insatiable desires, they divide with the poor the produce of all their improvements. They are led by an invisible hand to make nearly the same distribution of the necessaries of life, which would have been made, had the earth been divided into equal portions among all its inhabitants, and thus without intending it, without knowing it, advance the interest of the society, and afford means to the multiplication of the species. (Adam Smith 2015, p. 234)

> There is, in man's nature, a secret inclination, and motion, towards love of others. (Francis Bacon 1983, p. 36)

Altruism is not an illusion. It is both necessary and possible. In modern society, altruism exists obviously in three circumstances: the willingness to spend one's own time, energy and wealth in exchange of certain immediately visible interests of others, certain future interests of others and certain actually void interests of others (Cheng Enfu 1997, p. 151–161).

Altruism is good for the all-round development of people. According to Abraham Maslow's hierarchy of needs, those who are at a lower tier in the hierarchy of needs tend to show egoistic behaviors while the needs at higher tiers can only be satisfied through cooperation and sharing. A certain degree of altruism is therefore necessary for the satisfaction of such needs. "The higher one is in the hierarchy of needs, the more he or she will reveal the natural inclination to share" (Wang Tianen 2018). Therefore, the higher the level of needs, the more needs to share and be altruistic to meet them. After the needs at the low tiers are satisfied, one will gradually move up the ladder to the level of self-actualization and by then, there will be chance and possibility to resolve the conflict and tension between egoism and altruism. Thus, when only the most basic material needs are pursued, it is reasonable for one to seek the maximization of personal interests. However, once he/she moves up the hierarchy of needs, egoism and altruism will no longer compete with each other. Instead, it will feel as if egoism becomes part of altruism.

Human society needs altruism. Since ancient times, people have been depending on one another for survival and no man is an island. Just as Karl Marx put it, "only in the collective can individuals acquire the means to develop their talents in an all-round way". In summarizing his achievements, Isaac Newton once said that "if I can see a bit farther than some others, it is because I am standing on the shoulders of giants." This implies that altruism among individuals (including, among others, classmates, friends and co-workers) is absolutely necessary. As the division of labor gets more refined and chains connect people more closely than ever, individual's interests are actualized through the satisfaction of the needs of others, society and the nation. If everyone pursues only the maximization of their personal interests and turn a blind eye to the interests of others, we will find ourselves caught in the Hobbesian jungle. Mutual harm in society is in essence the result of the short-sightedness of excessive egoism and, if not regulated, it will evolve and lead to a mutual-harm society. In contrast, if everyone is willing to transfer part of his or her own interests for the interests of others, a society of "all for one and one for all" will become possible. In a digital society, we must do more to guide people towards altruistic behaviors so as to ensure the healthy, orderly, harmonious and sustainable development of society.

Problems in global data governance, while posing unprecedented crises and plights to data security, serve to prove the cooperation and altruism strategy necessary and possible if we are to get rid of such crises and plights. According to Martin Nowak, a biologist at Harvard University, "cooperation is the architect of creativity throughout evolution, from cells to multicellular creatures to anthills to villages to cities." When getting prepared for the new challenges of global governance, mankind must find new cooperation models and altruism should be the basis of cooperation. As for countries, only when they cooperate with one another, observe the principle of data interests transfer and seek common grounds or balance between the respective data interests of different countries and nations and the interests of the data community with a shared future for mankind, can it become possible for all stakeholders to maximize their data interests. Of course, as actors in the international community, all parties are, as far as data interests are concerned, similar to the economic man that seeks maximization of interests for some time. There will not always be common ground or balance and betrayal of cooperation will be nothing uncommon. In response to this, it is necessary that we formulate a set of effective international rules for data governance to deal with such situations and maintain long-term and continuous international data cooperation.

If human nature cannot be anything but evil, those who design the system are certainly evil too. Yet those who are evil will not be able to create any good system. Nonetheless, it is absolutely possible for us and we are definitely able to abandon the evil in us, get rid of the bestiality in human nature, and amplify what is good. Or at least, we can avoid the possibility and tendency of doing evil things. Man's sociality is the soil where altruism grows, and the need for cooperation, in particular, provides direct motivation for altruism. "A person that has experienced the process of socialization possesses not only the innate egoistic motives but also the altruistic motives formed through subsequent value internalization and the subsequently formed altruistic motives restrain and remodel the egoistic motives" (Guo Jing 2005). History shows that mankind has gradually reduced elements such as brute, greed and selfishness in it and made his altruistic mentality, inner law and the idea of sharing the theme of life along with the development of society and the progress of civilization and thereby taken the road of development dominated by altruism. In human society, it is an ideal that everyone takes altruism as the code of conduct. When data resources and products are abundant and can be distributed according to needs, the ideas of equity and sharing will gain popularity, data labor will become the means towards a happy life, altruism will grow greatly and egoism and altruism will form a perfect unity in man. With the change of the times and the development of society, the value of altruism will become increasingly prominent and altruism, as the blossom of civilization, will surely be in full bloom.

According to Thomas Aquinas, the law is for the purpose of common good. When designing the data rights system, we must take into consideration the altruism in human nature, do what we can to encourage the good in human nature while oppressing the possibility of man doing evil things. Altruism is the human nature basis of the data rights law and is what the formulation and the implementation of the data rights laws start and end with. As the legal system governing the ownership, rights, use and protection of data and the basic norm governing the data-related behaviors and maintaining data order, the data rights law should aim to realize balance and coordination between effective protection of data rights and making the best use of data, and safeguard public interests and public security while promoting the free flow and sharing of personal data. In this regard, citizens' transfer of data rights, to a certain extent, is crucial to the realization of balance and coordination between law-based protection and reasonable use of data. That is, the legislation on data rights is intended to promote the flow and use of data rather than to impose restrictions on data by spreading the dense net of justice. As Gustav Radbruch once said, the concern of legal system was not about making people fix their eyes at all times like guards but enabling them to occasionally and blithely look up at the bright stars, flowers and trees in full bloom as well as necessity of unconstraint and virtues (Gustav Radbruch 2001, p. 9). Altruism is the human nature basis or dimension of the data rights law, meaning that the data rights law starts with altruism, conveys the requirements of altruism, takes altruism as its main content and the ultimate objective of altruism, that is, sharing, as the ultimate value it pursues and primarily aims at modeling and enhancing the altruism in man. Of course, this does not mean that the data rights law does not pursue other values such as security, efficiency, benefits. The key here is that these values should not take the place of altruism as an objective.

With the idea of sharing gaining popularity among people, altruism that is hidden in human nature is gradually coming out. In a certain sense, the data rights law plays the role of a midwife for altruism, helping nurture of the altruistic spirit. Human being can develop true altruism (Holmes Rolston 2000,

p. 465). The formulation of the data rights law indicates that mankind has gained further understanding of the relationship between man and data. It makes people realize the necessity of making best efforts to increase the data well-being of society according to the principle of transfer that is the best for increasing the overall interests of society. For society, it is righteous to create a system with a view to increasing the content of altruistic human nature, inspiring the altruistic spirit among people and then further harmonizing the relationship between man and data. It is well-grounded and fully reasonable to base the data rights law on the data man hypothesis of human nature because this hypothesis not only describes the new human nature that relevant parties should naturally present as is determined by the sociality, altruism, and sharing nature of the data rights law, but also provides guidance for the science-based making and effective implementation of the data rights law by mitigating or overcoming the plight of data security in data governance. This is both what is inevitable as society develops and what is around the corner as mankind continues to make progress.

The Data Rights System and Data Rights Legalization

Remixing[7] is a force that pushes for changes that are bound to happen. It has unprecedented impact on the current legal rules, rights structure, and ethical standards. It highlights the defects in the current supply of legal system products and even overthrows people's established understanding of the law. Therefore, in the age of remixing, in order to establish the basic legal principles, institutional rules and ethical norms, an important premise is that we must grasp the essence of social structure, reconstruct the model of social relationship and expound the human nature basis of

7 Remixing is the "rearrangement and reuse of the existing things" (Kevin Kelly 2016, p. 240). Remixing involves the coexistence and opposition of chaos and order, interchangeable internal structure and movement process. It is not the rigid mixture of old methods and new methods but the reconstruction of modes for integration and arrangement of components.

law. Mankind is entering a new age where it needs to rebuild its laws to regulate the virtual world. The traditional mechanism for the generation of laws can no longer meet the needs of the legalization of the virtual world. This is an era where the systems of rules in the virtual world and the physical world adapt to each other and where laws are created and reformed in diverse forms. The digital civilization provides the motivation for innovations towards the establishment of the data rights law system and the data rights law provides the existential basis for enhancing the order of digital civilization. As human society moves from agricultural civilization to industrial civilization and then to digital civilization, the law transitions from the law of persons to the law of things, and then to the law of data.

Personality of data man

We are in a world surrounded by data men. We cannot turn a blind eye to them when they enter the field of life of human beings in modern times. The twenty-first century is a digital, networked and intelligent age. The data power and data relations in this age inevitably require the legal principles and legal system to be different from those targeting at the assembly lines in the nineteenth century and the automated systems in the twentieth century. The traditional legal system, in particular the system of legal subjects, has been or is facing unprecedented challenges. Scientific and technological progress reshapes our understanding of the law and changes our legal rules. It forces us to reexamine our personality system based on our social reality and from the perspective of the theory of law[8] and ponder whether it is necessary to grant legal personality to

8 Personality generally refers to the subject qualification that man born and living as human being possesses and distinguishes man from other species and forms in essence. It was initially a philosophical concept. Later in the theory of law, personality, after evolution and expansion in concept several times, is eventually determined as the interests in personality inherent in man as confirmed by the law. That is, personality is the qualification of man to independently enjoy rights, assume obligations and achieve freedom with dignity and thus generates various specific rights of personality. It is the basis and premise for man to enjoy other civil rights and perform civil conducts.

data man. Legal rights must be based on personality or they would otherwise conflict with social welfare (Robert Morrison MacIver, trans. Chen Qitian 1946, p. 180). The study on the rationale behind whether data man should have legal personality is the core content of adjustments to the law in the future. As data man becomes more socialized, it is necessary to study its legal status so as to fill the gap between social development and the law.[9] Citing the example of personal injury caused by a driverless vehicle, David C. Vladeck, a professor of law at Georgetown Law School, presented the questions of how our laws should deal with robots and how to assign liabilities for the consequences of their behaviors. According to him, the legal status of robots is an issue that legislation has to address (David C. Vladeck 2014, p. 129–150). With the development of intelligent robots, our constitution and laws may need to be modified or rewritten (Phil Mcnally & Sohail Inayatullah 1988, p. 119–136).

At present, technology is advancing at exponential rate, and the future is full of uncertainties and risks. We need to be cautious. In his book *The Question Concerning Technology*, Martin Heidegger pointed out that modern technology was no longer neutral and it, as *Gestell* [literally "enframing"], controlled and dominated the whole life of modern man or had become the historical destiny of modern man. The development of biotechnology and

9 The *New Generation Artificial Intelligence Development Plan* promulgated by the State Council points out the necessity of studying relevant legal issues and establishing accountability system, clearly makes it the strategic objective to "set up the system of laws and regulations, ethical norms and polices on artificial intelligence" and proposes to "formulate the laws, regulations and ethical norms for promoting the development of artificial intelligence" as one of the measures for guaranteeing the healthy and rapid development of artificial intelligence. In addition, it particularly states the necessity to actively participate in global governance of artificial intelligence, intensify study of robot alienation and security regulation as well as other major internationally common issues on artificial intelligence, deepen the international cooperation in laws, regulations and international rules on artificial intelligence, jointly cope with global challenge and optimize the allocation of innovation resources. It is imperative to get in line with internationally accepted practices and participate in global dialogue in respect of the specifications, standards and regulating methods for the development of artificial intelligence, enhance the study on the laws and regulations relating to artificial intelligence, specify the rights, obligations and responsibilities relating to artificial intelligence and take the study on the legal status of artificial intelligence as the focus and core.

intelligent technology are substantially changing man, mending it, transforming it and recombining its elements. Man–machine interdependence, man–machine interaction, man-machine combination, man–machine collaboration and man–machine integration are becoming the general trend. American futurist Ray Kurzweil asserted that "this impending merger of biological intelligence with the nonbiological intelligence that we are creating" (Ray Kurzweil 2015). When man and machine are getting increasingly symbiotic or integrated, the question is whether this partnership is a man or a machine. Probably there is no definitive answer to this question. If data man is man in a certain sense, the issues to be addressed include whether or not it enjoys human rights and other basic rights, whether it possesses personality and dignity just as a natural man does and whether it ought to be identified as a subject of legal relations or moral relations and assume corresponding consequences of behaviors. There are many such issues and new issues are emerging continuously. In the book *Robots*, John Jordan said that we should now immediately start a real discussion: "What is our identity in contrast to these machines?" (John Jordan, trans. Liu Yuchi 2018, p. 163). A new understanding is required as to what man is, what man's nature is, and what value principles are to be followed when dealing with interpersonal relationships and man–machine relationships (Sun Weiping 2017)? Ray Kurzweil even predicted that robots with self-awareness and consciousness will appear in 2029 and become common in the 2030s. They will have various subtle emotions similar to those of man (Ray Kurzweil, trans. Sheng Yangyan 2014, p. 195). It seems inappropriate for us to deem such data man as a robot since it no longer feels like machines. Since discussions on the legal personality of data man has important theoretical significance and practical value, the academia has presented ideas such as e-personality, virtual personality and limited personality. It needs to be noted that relevant research should "reserve necessary system space for the growth of emerging technology" (Wang Liming 2018).

Although these are just postulations, we should probably take precautions and treat this last major legal issue of mankind with prudence.[10] In

10 Stephen Hawking, a famous physicist, once stated that "the success in creating artificial intelligence could be the biggest event in the history of human civilization and also could be the last event" and "the development of artificial intelligence could spell the end of the human race" (Sun Weiping 2017).

analyzing the significance of legal personality, Hoshino Echi, a Japanese jurist in civil law, stated that even beings other than human being, will be acknowledged if they are suitable for acting as subjects of rights and obligations in private law (Hoshino Echi 2004, p. 21). Israeli historian Yuval Noah Harari was of the opinion that "the law of human race has come to recognize such entity of intersubjectivity as a corporation or a nation and call it 'legal person'. Toyota or Argentina has neither body nor mind. But both are bound by the international law, can own land and money and may become plaintiff or defendant before courts. Algorithm may also obtain such status probably soon after" (Yuval Noah Harari, trans. Lin Junhong 2017, p. 293). While a heated debate is going on in the academic circle, legislature is not left behind and has also come to the fore. In 2017, the European Parliament's Committee on Legal Affairs proposed "creating a specific legal status for robots in the long run, so that at least the most sophisticated autonomous robots could be established as having the status of electronic persons responsible for making good any damage they may cause, and possibly applying electronic personality to cases where robots make autonomous decisions or otherwise interact with third parties independently" (European Parliament's Committee on Legal Affairs 2015). Russia followed closely by proposing in Article 1 of the *Grishin Law* that robots be granted the legal status of "robot-agent" and stated that a robot-agent is supposed to possess independent property and assume liability for its own debts with such property and may receive and exercise civil rights and undertake civil obligations in its own name (Zhang Jianwen 2018). Worldwide, countries accept data man as legal subjects mainly in two ways. Some countries use legislation. Saudi Arabia, for instance, grants robot Sophia nationality of Saudi Arabia through legislation. In other countries where no legislation is in place for this purpose, policies are issued to support the development of robots and grant robots corresponding legal status. So far, China has not granted data man any legal status in any of these ways and the subjects of crimes, in principle, remain to be natural persons who have reached the age for taking criminal liability and have the capacity for criminal liability. For example, Article 2 of the *General Provisions of the Civil Law* provides that "civil law regulates personal relations and property relations among natural persons, legal persons and non-legal-person organizations which are civil subjects of equal status".[11]

The structure of the rights system is always changing. The complexity of social evolution is attributed to the differences in the legal personality, status, capacity, rights, qualifications and responsibilities which are conferred under the law to different subjects. The expanded scope of the subjects of legal relations reflects the dynamic changes in the basic idea and value of the law. As far as the evolution process of the law is concerned, we seem to have no reason to doubt it that the scope of the subjects of legal relations will expand to cover data man or any other new species in cyberspace, but this will depend on the needs of the legal system and social system. In the history of the concept of the subjects of legal relations, the emancipation, the affirmative action, feminism, labor organizations, legal person system, legal disputes concerning embryos, persons in vegetative state and gene-edited babies, as well as the new types of claims for rights arising out of public interest litigations and class actions, have all been making breakthroughs in the modern theory on the subjects of legal relations. This proves that the concept of legal personality evolves with time and has its flexibility (Yu Chengfeng 2017). The concept of the subjects of legal relations have gone through changes which first allowed human to be treated as non-human, and now non-human to be treated as human. This is a process towards openness and inclusiveness.[12] Just like mouse, religious

11 Although legal persons and non-legal-persons are not natural persons, they are not independent of the "personified" entities of natural persons and thus have the attributes of natural persons.

12 For example, the U.S. Federal Court has tried a case filed in the name of the Byram River against a shore-side company for causing pollution; and Sierra Club Law Protection Foundation and Hawaii Audubon Society once filed a complaint on behalf of Palila, a bird species which had only a few hundred of them left. Judge Williams Douglas stated in his paper *Should Trees Have Standing? Towards Legal Rights for Natural Object* that since law can confer legal standing to nations, corporations, infants, persons without capacity for conduct, autonomous cities and universities, etc., that cannot speak or have no consciousness and assign them protectors or agents, why cannot law confer legal standing to natural objects? An old woman in Italy left a will and gave as gift 50 percent of her property, that is, estate valued at more than €1 million, to her favorite dog, making the latter the first dog worth more

heterodoxy and witch, which were brought before courts as defendants at some points in history, data man will probably have a part to play in the new rules in the capacity of defendant, plaintiff or even judge, lawyer or notary in the future. On the ground that animals have certain rights, some people contended that data man should be respected since it has consciousness and feelings and it is getting harder to distinguish between data man and natural man. As French Enlightenment thinker Jean-Jacques Rousseau stated in the *Discourse on the Origin and Foundation of Inequality among Mankind*, animals should enjoy the rights endowed by nature and mankind also has the obligation to maintain such rights. Jeremy Bentham, the founder of utilitarianism, was among the advocates of animal rights. In the script of a speech on the necessity of expanding the legal rights of animals, he wrote: "the day may come when the rest of the animal creation may acquire those rights which never could have been withheld from them but by the hand of tyranny." Referring to claims of animal rights, we may deduce the legitimacy of rights for data man.

In the future, the scope of the subjects of legal relations is likely to extend beyond the boundary of man in biological sense and species may not be the primary barrier to being granted rights. Legal systems should follow the evolution logic of rights holders, "an open attitude should be developed towards the status of robots as rights holders and it should be denied that difference in species constitute a technical difficulty for statutory rights" (Zhang Yujie 2017). In the future, legal order is very likely to have a new personality rank for participation in legal processes through creating various types of legal personality masks so that data man or other man can all take a node in the bundle of rights in legal relations and become distributed nodes in the legal relationship network in the future legislative

than €1 million in Italy to date. Similar examples included shepherd dog Gunther IV worth £224.6 million, chimpanzee Luka worth £53 million and cat Tomasino worth $15.66 million. All these examples illustrate that subjects in civil relations is no longer limited to natural persons and many objects that are not natural persons are gradually accepted as person in law based on the need of law makers and receive the status of subjects in civil relations and show a growing trend toward "non-human treated as human". This has also provided space of interpretation for granting legal status in civil law to such humanoid as data man.

consideration and legal practice. "Although it may have great impact on the old legal dogmatism, it plays positive functions that help adapt to social development" (Zhou Xiang 2019). The development of data man is inevitable and legal rules that govern the development of data man are also necessary. Regulation over data man relies on adjustments to the legal system and institutional arrangements of the law, which will keep evolvement in this regard within a reasonable range. All indicate that it is time to appropriately regulate data rights and data man, and to establish and improve the order of relevant laws and moral standards.

Institutional system of data rights

People always make necessary institutional designs based on their own needs. The institutional system of data rights is important basis and principle for the protection of the rights and interests of data resources. Therefore, it is imperative that we build an institutional system and a set of operating rules for such a new type of rights and interests as data rights. So far, there is not yet any common theory concerning the data rights system in the academia or the community of practitioners, and disagreements remain on some specific issues. Yet still, people are clearly aware that there are problems in the existing legal system of data rights in terms of its theoretical basis, structure, application in practice, and other aspects; and that small modifications and revisions will not do. Under the background that a new round of technological revolution and industrial transformation is in the making, new efforts have been launched to amend laws regarding the extraterritorial data protection system. We should study the overall design of the data rights system. This is because analysis of specific types of data rights, no matter how careful and detailed it is, would eventually produce no more than delicate components that cannot be assembled. Therefore, we need to consider creating an institutional data rights system in line with the trend of modern social development. In contemporary society, the disorder and lack of rules in data rights relationships directly requires a sound data rights system to be put in place. The clear separation between the ownership of data and the use of data is the basic reason for establishing data rights sharing system, while mutual benefit is the realistic foundation for the sharing system to stand on its own.

The legal system coordinates between the ideal and reality of society or, to put it another way, it belongs to the gray area between the standard world and the real world. This is especially true for the data rights system. Its significance lies not only in safeguarding and actualizing justice but also in creating order, that is, minimizing data transaction cost and improving the efficiency of data resource allocation with institutional arrangements which combine the relationships and rules of data rights and, meanwhile, effectively integrate, adjust and protect data rights relationships. To this end, we need to create an institutional system centering on data rights. The first part of this is the system of data rights legalization. It makes legal provisions and descriptions regarding, among other things, the connotation, denotation, realization procedure, loss process and remedy of data rights by establishing a system so that legal basis is laid for the realization of data rights. The establishment of the system of data rights legalization can contribute to the transformation from due data rights to statutory data rights and actual data rights. Data rights, as part of the fundamental rights for human survival and development, represent well-justified claims for interests and they should conform to the realistic requirements of relevant systems and value orientation. This is the path towards statutory data rights. The second part of this system is the data ownership system. Data ownership, which grants complete domination over data, constitutes the core of the data rights system. It mainly includes the rights to control, use, earn from, and share data, and these four functions may be separated under certain conditions. The data ownership system defines data as belonging to a certain owner on the institutional level and put the data in the complete control of this owner. The data ownership system breaks the limitation of the traditional idea that properties are tangible and at the same time it moderates the closed and exclusive structure of traditional ownership and the principle of one ownership for one object. Thus, it helps protect the rights and interests of data rights holders but also promote the sharing and use of data across society. The third system is the system of usufructuary rights of data. The usufructuary rights of data is generated in order to resolve the conflict between the ownership of and demand for data and is the right to the use plus the right to earnings over data owned by other persons under certain conditions. It is a kind of right over data of others and also a kind of restricted data ownership. The usufructuary rights of data grants domination over the use value of data and they cover three functions, namely, the right to control, the right to use and the right to earnings. The system of usufructuary rights of data is the result of our move from domination-centered data rights to use-centered data rights. It can help us better realize the value of data rights and serves as a method to actualize ownership. The fourth system is the system of usufructuary rights of public data. The usufructuary rights of public data refer to the whole of rights, which has the nature of public law, that administrative institutions set on the public interest data they provide or manage in order to ensure and increase public welfare. It is a kind of transferred usufructuary rights of data. What is transferred is public data and the holders of such rights can be governments and other administrative institutions, as well as the general public. For the administrative institutions represented by the government, the usufructuary rights of public data include the right to collect data, the right to plan data development, the right to grant permission to use data, etc. For the general public, the usufructuary rights of public data include the right to informed consent over data, the right to modify data, the right to be forgotten of data, etc. The fifth system is the sharing system. Data rights are, in nature, the rights to share and the central concern of the sharing system is the balance between the data rights and interests of individuals and the public interests over data. The sharing system corrects the preference to private interests over public interests in our previous approach to data and instead proposes and advocates a new approach which pursues balance between private interests and public interests. Meanwhile, balance between personal rights and interests and public interests also constitutes the fundamental issue of innovations in and arrangements of the data rights system. The sharing system, with fair distribution of private interests and public interests as the core principle, provides value basis for solving the conflicts between different stakeholders and data rights holders. These five major dimensions constitute the personal data protection system established for the value objectives of making the best use of data and ensuring data security. However, the protection of personal data should involve not only the protection of personal rights. It should go beyond consent or informed consent to take an open, inclusive and friendly attitude that facilitates industrial development and social justice, maintain the flexibility of relevant rules and make better (rather than more) use of the bottom-up and distributed rule-making mechanism so as to set up a system that better serves the specific value objectives and better meets the practical needs of data protection.

At present, issues concerning data rights mainly fall into two categories: ownership and use. Accordingly, the data rights system may basically be composed of two parts, each dealing with one category of issues. It is not an issue of simply unifying the legal system for data use. It is, instead, a reform of traditional values. Moving forward along the logical line we envisaged, we will definitely reach a new approach towards data rights and new ethics and produce new operating mechanisms for data rights. "According to the basic principles of legal system building, the combination of legal norms is always constrained by the concepts of specific systems. Different legal norms must be coordinated and complementary and must not have any conflict and contradiction" (Xia Xiaoxiong 2019). This is an important point in the building of the institutional system of data rights. For lawmakers, the concept of functionality, general principle and typing structuring are important to the structure of the data rights system. Therefore, on the basis of systematic transformation, the concept of functionality, norms in principle, type-based distinction and other relevant "instruments" should be effectively applied to construct and make proper arrangement of the data rights system and optimize the internal logic and system correlation of data rights norms.

Current studies are not yet sufficient to produce specific proposal for a matured data rights system, but they have a bright future and can definitely contribute to the establishment of the data rights system. Today, as data rights disputes arise frequently and in large numbers, it is necessary to specify, among other things, the nature, status and content of data ownership,[13] data rights,[14] data use[15] and data protection.[16] Moreover, there are realistic materials available for relevant analysis, study and reflections. In China, in-depth research and discussions concerning the data rights system have been conducted from different perspectives and on different levels in all circles of society. At the level of legislation, relevant provisions can be found in branch laws, but none of such laws carries data protection in its name. Taking data as a kind of basic strategic resources of the country, more efforts need to be made to make overall considerations for the system and produce comprehensive strategic

13 Data ownership is the logical starting point of the protection of data rights and the precondition for establishing data rules. Ownership is different for data of different types or at different stages of its lifecycle. Data boundaries, including the boundary of open government data, the boundary of commercial use of corporate data and the boundary of privacy of personal data, should be clearly defined through legislation.

14 Data rights constitute an important part of data rights legislation and a law that has nothing to do with rights is not likely to get people interested in it. Legislation should grant data rights holders rights such as the right of data access to data, the right to correct data, the right of data to be forgotten, the right to data portability, the right to use data, the data *jus fruendi* and the right to data relief. It should contain not only provisions on the rights of data owners such as the right to control data, the right to use data, and the data *jus freudi* but also provisions on the rights of others to use data such as the usufructuary rights of data, the usufructuary rights of public data, and the right to share data.

15 The value of data lies in it being in use. The principle of making the best use of data shall be taken as the premise to develop the value of data through commercial use, administrative use and civilian use and generate the data use model that combines three chains, namely the whole industry chain, the whole governance chain and the whole service chain. Data rights regulation is intended to safeguard public interests and public security while promoting the free sharing of personal data. To this end, citizens are required to transfer part of their data rights. Legislation seeks to lay down specific criteria for balance between legal protection and reasonable use of data.

16 The responsibility for protection is part of the responsibility of laws, regulations and rules. If a law has no provisions on the responsibility for protection, the rights and obligations it provides for will be of no avail. Intensified security governance is required for data collection, storage, transmission and use in order to prevent attacks on, as well as leakage, theft, tampering and illegal use of data. In addition, data has a bearing on state security and national interests and separate protection of data sovereignty at national level is necessary.

design. The modernization of the legal system of data rights is by no means improvements in some individual aspects. It requires adjustments made in a holistic manner at the bottom of the data rights system, so that the system becomes one that is well balanced and coordinated with synergies between its different parts, smooth internal logic, and the ability to adapt to the external practical demands. In addition, active efforts should be made to absorb the fruits of the development of the legal civilization of mankind and make good use of the useful experience, elements and mechanisms of foreign data rights systems so as to make the data rights system an important part of the legal system under new historical conditions.

Moderation of data rights legalization

The principle of data rights legalization is regarded as "one of the important pillars of the property law" (Xie Zaiquan 1999, p. 40). Same as laws in many other areas, the data rights law also needs to comply with some basic principles.[17] Although there is likelihood that these principles will not be expressly referred to in the data rights law that will come into being in the future, "they will serve as the basis for the legislation and have their influence on the law in terms of legal adaptation and legal interpretation" (Hu Xuyu 2006). The principle of data rights legalization plays a role that no other principle can replace in confirming ownership and adjusting data use, and it holds a central position in the data rights system. It is fair to say that the doctrine of data rights legalization would be impossible if the concept of data rights does not exist, and thus would be impossible to build the system of data rights law. In addition, in building the institutional system of data rights, we need to combine theoretical and practical efforts. A sound theoretical system provides the guiding philosophy and values and specify the basic principles and goals. Without it, the data rights system would lose its soul and become disoriented. The building of the data rights system is a complex and systematic project. It

17 "Legalism" refers to the legislationism which requires strict adherence to the provisions of the law. In this regard, what comes first is the "statutory crime and punishment" in criminal law and the "numerus clausus" in civil law.

requires both a theoretical system that provides guidance and clear operational mechanisms that provide the operational framework and practical content. While clarifying the theoretical system and operating system, we should also work to summarize specific working methods in the practice of building the data rights system and formulate relevant rules to institutionalize matured experience in a timely manner. The point here is to form effective institutional supply and support data rights legislation with sound methodology.

The key to realizing data rights lies in the move from due data rights to statutory data rights and then to actual data rights. Statutory data rights mean that the types and content of data rights must be prescribed by law instead of any other normative document. Statutory data rights types mean that all types of data rights must be prescribed by law and the parties concerned are not allowed to set up any type of data rights beyond those prescribed by law or change the types of data rights prescribed by law through agreements. The purpose is to determine through legislation which types of rights are data rights and which are not. As for statutory data rights content, the meaning here is twofold: For one thing, the content of data rights must be prescribed by law and relevant parties are not allowed to stipulate data rights otherwise through agreements; and for another thing, the parties concerned are not allowed to make stipulations not in conformity with the mandatory provisions concerning the content of data rights legalization (Long Rongyuan & Yang Guanhua 2018). However, while laying down mandatory requirements and direct provisions in respect of the types, content, mode of acquisition and other aspects of data rights, we should also uphold some basic values and ideas when doing the design of the data rights system construction.

Separation between ownership and the right to use. With the coming of the digital, networked and intelligent age, our ownership system[18] is facing

18 The answer to the significance of ownership in law can be found in a historical allusion from *The Book of Lord Shang*. It is a story that Shang Yang told to king of Qin, which reads: "A rabbit ran and hundreds of people chased after. It was not because that the rabbit could be divided into hundreds, but because its ownership was not determined. There were a lot of rabbits on the market but no thief dared to take it. It was because the ownership of the rabbits was determined." In this story, Shang Yang

unprecedented challenges. In an industrial economy, the right to domination and the right to use within the framework of ownership are merged (Jiang Qiping 2012). As Mathew Ingram once wrote, the digitization of music and video had brought much convenience for mankind and now, with its Lending Library, Amazon has brought this trend into the book industry. But this may not always be a good thing. Physical media would gradually disappear; besides, it changed the relationship between users and the purchased content. What we bought would not be ownership of the content but rather the short-term right to use. What he pointed out here is an important phenomenon: in the digital age, ownership (actually the right to domination which is part of ownership) is separating from the right to use.[19] At present such a separation can be found extensively in practice. Although people are still working to figure out the proper legal structure of data ownership, reality has proved that data ownership is not important as opposed to who has the right to use data and what value can be created. "The entire global economy is tipping away from the material and toward intangible bits. It is moving away from ownership and toward access. It is tilting away from the value of copies and toward the value of networks. It is headed for the inevitability of constant, relentless, and increasing remixing" (Kevin Kelly 2016, p. 242).

---

wanted the king of Qin to think why one rabbit in mountain was chased by hundreds of people while no one dared to touch the rabbit in the cage. The answer lies in the ownership. The reason for hundreds of people to chase after the rabbit in mountain was because its ownership was not definite; but for the rabbit in the cage, its ownership was definite and anyone who took another's rabbit at his own discretion would be deemed as committing tort. This allusion illustrates the basic function of ownership in determining social order. In general, the social order of property guaranteed by ownership is the foundation of social order and the governance of a country should start with the establishment of definite ownership (Sun Xianzhong 2019).

19 As early as in 2000, Jeremy Rifkin wrote in *The Age of Access* that: "The very thought of leaving markets and property behind – of advancing a conceptual change in the structuring of human relationships away from ownership and toward access – is as inconceivable to many people today as enclosure and privatization of land and labor into property relationship must have been more than half a millennium ago. [However], it is likely that for a growing number of enterprises and consumers, the very idea of ownership will seem limited, even old fashioned, 25 years from now."

Data ownership is a type of complete and adequate data rights, while all other data rights are incomplete and inadequate, as they are the result of some powers and functions of data ownership spinning off from it. Data rights are of value in nature. This converts data rights holders' domination of data into domination of value and makes it possible for people to use data in more ways and at a higher efficiency. To clarify data ownership is not the end in itself but a means to facilitate data use in an institutional manner so as to stimulate and bring into play the initiatives of data users and create more data value. The use-oriented separation between rights and functions is getting increasingly common and this trend is bound to undermine central position of ownership in the data rights system. In the meantime, the center of data rights will inevitably shift from ownership towards rights over the data of others and the data rights system is expected to undergo a shift from possession to use and from ownership to the right to use. The absoluteness of ownership will be restricted more and more by public interests and public law of the state. As for the relationship between the rights over the data of others and data ownership, the former will surely have some priority over the latter, the legal status of data users will be reinforced so as to push the right to use data towards those who can make more effective use of data. The data rights system is an important institutional factor that promotes the development of the digital economy, having substantial influence on the arrangements concerning ownership and utilization and the balance between efficiency and fairness. For the data rights system, obviously, an overemphasis on ownership may hinder data use and efficiency; an overemphasis on efficiency may undermine ownership and jeopardize fairness; an overemphasis on rights over data of one's own would oppress rights over the data of others; and an overemphasis on rights over the data of others would restrict rights over data of one's own. Therefore, the crux of the principle of data rights legalization is to balance between ownership and use, efficiency and fairness, and rights over one's own data and over data of others, and to give rise to new data order.

According to British jurist Henry Maine, there are three ways to coordinate between law and society, namely, legal fiction, equity, and legislation

(Henry Maine 1995, p. 15). These three are in general reflected in overcoming the limitations of property law legalism.[20] For the emerging data rights, "the best approach is making laws as soon as possible" to reveal the true features of data rights and achieve the unification of the substantial requirements and legal provisions of data relations. Data rights legalization serves as an important principle of data rights law and rigid application will make it unable to adapt to the needs of development. Because it is impossible to anticipate at the time of legislation the needs of social development in the future so as to create an inclusive data rights system, and strict compliance will unavoidably render the statutory data rights system disconnected with society. In particular, due to the limitations of data rights legalization, some new forms of data use, once they arise in practice, are not likely to be incorporated in a timely manner and the data rights disputes thus resulted will be difficult to handle and may cause social anomie and disorder. Data relations will get increasingly complicated and the data rights system will not be able to provide for all types of data rights in detail. Therefore, we cannot rely completely on legislation for the recognition and establishment of data rights. This means that the provisions we formulate following the principle of data rights legalization should contain clear statement of this principle and, meanwhile, take into account the enforceability and openness of it, so that there can still be some flexibility with which the system may keep up with changes in the real world. No system is closed or supreme, and the data rights system is no exception.

20 Legal fiction is intended to achieve the coordination between law and society mainly through interpretation of provisions of the law. In civil law countries, the method of equity is manifested as the role of general principles in guiding specific norms and the application of these principles as general provisions of civil law plays the role of overcoming the limitation of statutes. When any new type of rights arises in social development, timely recognition thereof in law can mitigate the rigidity of the statutory system of property law (Yang Yuxi 2002).

Bibliography

Bacon, F. 1983. *The Essays of Francis Bacon*. Trans. Shui Tongtian. Beijing: The Commercial Press.

Central Compilation and Translation Bureau. 1972. *Complete Works of Marx and Engels (Vol. 23)*. Beijing: People's Publishing House.

Central Compilation and Translation Bureau. 1979. *Complete Works of Marx and Engels (Vol. 46)*. Beijing: People's Publishing House.

Central Compilation and Translation Bureau. 2009. *Collected Works Marx & Engels (Vol. 1)*. Beijing: People's Publishing House.

Chen, Zhonglin. 2001. "Freedom, Human Rights, Rule of Law: Interpretation of Human Nature." *Modern Law Science*, 3rd Issue.

Cheng, Enfu. 1997. *Analysis of the Western Theory of Property Rights*. Beijing: Contemporary China Publishing House.

European Parliament's Committee on Legal Affairs. "Report with Recommendations to the Commission on Civil Law Rules on Robotics, (2015/2103 (INL)." <http://www.europarl.europa.eu/sides/getDoc.do?pubRef=-//EP//NONSGML+REPORT+A8-2017-0005+0+DOC+PDF+V0//EN>.

Feuerbach, L. A. 1984. *A Selection of Feuerbach's Philosophical Works (Vol. 1)*. Trans. Rong Zhenhua, et al. Beijing: The Commercial Press.

Gao, Chengjun. 2014. "Differences between Chinese and Western Legal Cultures from the Perspectives of Human Nature Hypotheses." *Journal of Gansu Political Science and Law Institute*, 4th Issue.

Gustav Radbruch, G. 2001. *Aphorism of Legal Wisdom*. Trans. Shu Guoying. Beijing: China Legal Publishing House.

Guo, Jing. 2005. "The Humanity Value of Reciprocal Altruism." *Journal of Dialectics of Nature*, 11th issue.

Han, Dongping. 2016. "Solving the Mystery of Man: Deconstruction and Reconstruction of the Definition of Man." *Wuhan University Journal (Humanity Sciences)*, 6th issue.

Harari, Y. N. 2017. *Homo Deus: A Brief History of Tomorrow*. Trans. Lin Junhong. Beijing: CITIC Press.

He, Xiaorong, and Chen Quansheng. 2009. "Observation of the Theory of Environmental Rights from the Perspectives of 'Ecological Man'." *Journal of Fuzhou University (Philosophy and Social Sciences)*, 1st issue.

Hoshino, Echi. 2004. *Person in Private Law: Focusing on the Civil Law and the Property Law*. Trans. Wang Chuang. Beijing: China Legal Publishing House.

Hu, Xuyu. 2006. "Value Evolution and Rationality Analysis of Numerus Clausus: Whether or Not the Formulation of the Property Law of China should Observe the Numerus Clausus." *Legal Forum*, 2nd issue.
Hu, Yuhong. 2002. *An Introduction to the Methodology of Jurisprudence*. Jinan: Shandong People's Publishing House.
Hu, Yuhong. 2008. *Statement of Philosophy of Law of "Individuals"*. Jinan: Shandong People's Publishing House.
Huang, Tao. 2009. "From Economic Man Hypothesis to Cooperative Man Hypothesis." *Reform of Economic System*, 2nd issue.
Hume, D. 1996. *A Treatise on Human Nature*. Trans. Guan Wenyun. Beijing: The Commercial Press.
Information Society 50 Forum. 2016. *The Future has Come: the Internet Plus Reconstruction and Innovation*. Shanghai: Shanghai Far East Publishers.
Jiang, Qiping. 2012. "Data Ownership Requires the Separation the Right of Domination from the Right to Use." *China Internet Week*, 5th issue.
Jordan, J. 2018. *Robots*. Trans. Liu Yuchi. Beijing: China Renmin University Press.
Kant, I. 2003. *Religion within the Bounds of Bare Reason*. Trans. Li Qiuling. Beijing: China Renmin University Press.
Kelly, K. 2016. *The Inevitable*. Trans. Zhou Feng et al. Beijing: Publishing House of Electronics Industry.
Kurzweil, R. 2014. *How to Create a Mind*. Trans. Sheng Yangyan. Hangzhou: Zhejiang People's Publishing House.
Kurzweil, R. 2015. *The Singularity is Near: When Humans Transcend Biology*. Trans. Li Qingcheng. Beijing: China Machine Press.
Li, Guojie. 2014. "Data Sharing: Premise for the Modernization of the State Governance System in the Big Data Age." *China Information Weekly*, August 25.
Long, Rongyuan, and Yang Guanhua. 2018. "Study on Data Rights, Data Rights System and Data Rights Law." *Journal of Law and Technology*, 5th issue.
Ma, Changshan. 2019. "The Fourth Generation of Human Rights and Its Guarantee under the Background of Intelligent Society." *China Legal Science*, 5th issue.
MacIver, R. M. 1946. *The Modern State*. Trans. Chen Qitian. Beijing: Zhonghua Book Company.
Mcnally, P., and Inayatullah, S. 1988. "The Rights of Robots." *Futures*, 20th issue.
Maine, H. 1995. *Ancient Law*, Trans. Shen Jingyi. Beijing: The Commercial Press.
Nagel, T. 1978. *The Possibility of Altruism*. Princeton, NJ: Princeton University Press.
Qiu, Zeqi. 2016. Towards a Digitalized Society. In Information Society 50 Forum, *Future Has Come: Reconstruction and Innovation in the "Internet Plus" Era*. Shanghai: Shanghai Far East Publishers.
Quarantiello, L. E. 1999. *Cyber Crime: How to Protect Yourself from Computer Criminals*. Trans. Wang Yong. Nanchang: Jiangxi Education Publishing House.

Rifkin, J. 2017. *The Zero Marginal Cost Society: The Internet of Things, the Collaborative Commons, and the Eclipse of Capitalism.* Trans. Expert Group of CCID Research Institute. Beijing: CITIC Press.

Rolston, H. 2000. *Environmental Ethics: Duties to and Values in the Natural World.* Trans. Yang Tongjin. Beijing: China Social Sciences Press.

Schwartz, B. 1989. *A History of American Law.* Trans. Su Yanxin. Beijing: China University of Political Science and Law Press.

Shen, Zhai. 2011. "From Person of Ethics to Person of Science: On the Change of Man in Modern Chinese Law with Civil Law as an Example." *Pacific Journal*, 8th issue.

Smith, A. 1997. *An Inquiry into the Nature and Causes of the Wealth of Nations (Vol. 1).* Trans. Guo Dali, et al. Beijing: The Commercial Press.

Smith, A. 2015. *The theory of Moral Sentiments.* Trans. Jiang Zhiqiang, et al. Beijing: The Commercial Press.

Sun, Weiping. 2017. "Reflection on the Value of Artificial Intelligence." *Philosophical Researches*, 10th issue.

Sun, Xianzhong. 2019. "Six Issues in the Study of the Ownership of Private Economy." *Journal of Law and Economics*, 5th issue.

Vladeck, D. C. 2014. "Machines without Principles: Liability Rules and Artificial Intelligence." *Washington Law Review*, 89th issue.

Wang, Dingding. 2005. *Lectures on Foundations of Institutional Analysis.* Shanghai: Shanghai People's Publishing House of Shanghai Century Publishing (Group) Co., Ltd.

Wang, Liming. 2018. "New Challenge to the Civil Law in the Age of Artificial Intelligence." *Oriental Law*, 3rd issue.

Wang, Tianen. 2018. "Information Civilization: A Key to a New Understanding of Development." *Social Sciences in China*, 6th issue.

Wu, Xianjing. 2010. "Theoretical Implications of Person of Ethics and Its Significance to the Environmental Law." *Law Review*, 4th issue.

Xia, Xiaoxiong. 2019. "Modernization of the Company Law: Institutional Reform, System Reconstruction and Spirit Remodeling." *Northern Legal Science*, 4th issue.

Xie, Hongfei. 2002. "Man in Modern Civil Law." *Peking University Law Review*, 2nd issue.

Xie, Zaiquan. 1999. *On the Property Rights under the Civil Law.* Beijing: China University of Political Science and Law Press.

Yan, Chunsheng. 2007. "Morality: Human Nature Dimension of Law – On the Relation between Law and Morals." *Science of Law (Journal of Northwest University of Political Science and Law)*, 1st issue.

Yan, Cunsheng. 2007. "Morality: Humanity Dimension of Law – On Law and Morality." *Science of Law (a journal of Northwest University of Politics and Law)*, 1st issue.

Yan, Cunsheng. 2016. *Foundation of Law from the Perspective of Human Nature.* Beijing: China Legal Publishing House.

Yang, Lan. 2018. "How Marx Defined the Nature of Man." *People's Tribune*, 8th issue.

Yang, Yuxi, 2002. "On Numerus Clausus." *Journal of Comparative Law*. 1st issue.

Yi, Jun. 2006. "Methodological Individualism and Private Law." *Chinese Journal of Law*, 1st issue.

Yu, Chengfeng. 2017. "From Trial of a Rat to the Law on Artificial Intelligence." *Dushu*, 7th issue.

Yu, Zhong. 2009. "Change and Comparison: Person Depicted in the Text of the Constitution." *Studies in Law and Business*, 5th issue.

Zhang, Jianwen. 2018. "Contribution and Limitation of the Grishin Law: A Review of the Draft of the First Robot Law of Russia." *Journal of East China University of Political Science and Law*, 2nd issue.

Zhang, Yujie. 2017. "On the Rights and Risks of Robot in the Era of Artificial Intelligence." *Oriental Law*, 6th issue.

Zhou, Xiang. 2019. "Intelligent Robots as Rights Holder." *Law Science*, 10th issue.

Zhu, Xiaozhe. 2002. "Man in the Social Law." *Law Science*, 8th issue.

Zhuo, Zeyuan. 2001. *On the Value of Law*. Beijing: People's Publishing House.

CHAPTER 2

Rights to Data

The progress of science and technology constantly pushes people to explore the scope of rights. As such efforts intensify, people become more aware of their rights and the traditional scope of rights undergoes changes. A new thing, in particular, enters the field of legal relations. This is data. It is different from physical things and beyond human beings. Data can not only be regulated by law, but also give rise to a new form of rights. The question at hand is which meta concept to choose for the confirmation of rights to data. By proposing data rights, we remove the rights over data from their old position in a traditional system with personality rights and property rights as its logical starting point and give them a unique position in the rights system. Data rights include rights to data, rights to share, and data sovereignty. Data rights have the characteristics of private rights, public rights and sovereignty, which are manifested respectively as rights to data, data power, and data sovereignty. The first two are often in confrontation and competition, constantly seeking a balance. Rights to data can be divided into personal rights to data, corporate rights to data, and government rights to data. Based on this, it is necessary to clearly define different types of data, explore ways to create a reasonable structure for rights to data, and study the corresponding legal system for data protection.

Data Rights and Data Power

Right is a concept of law, while power is a concept of politics. By introducing the right–power paradigm, we make it easier for people to reach a minimum consensus on the basic concepts involved in the studies of legal issues concerning data, so as to have compatible concept systems, observation perspectives, and research methods for explaining and solving the legal issues concerning data (Wen Yuheng 2019). Human society is entering a new stage marked by data productivity. People have begun to reconsider the relationship between men and data, and think about the rights and powers related to data. Data is not only a right paradigm, but also a power narrative. Specifically, data is a new factor of production and a new resource for innovation. It also gives rise to a new form of organization, a new type of rights type and a new manifestation of power. Data use has become an important way people increase their wealth, and the protection of data rights and the limitation of data power have become an important feature of the digital civilization.

From number to data rights

Number: The origin of everything

Number is a concept formed before mankind started trying to understand the objective world. In human production activities such as gathering and hunting, the concept of number began to form as man compared different kinds of things. "People gradually realized that things share some common features and form units, and they also realized that things of different kinds also have something in common in terms of quantity, such as the corresponding relationship that can be formed between them in quantity. This abstract nature of quantity shared by things of different kinds is number." (Liu Hong & Hu Xinhe 2013) British philosopher Bertrand Russell generalized this abstract nature with these words: "It is only at a high stage of civilisation that we could take this series (series of natural numbers) as our starting-point." (Bertrand Russell 1982, p. 8). As early as in ancient Egypt, Rome and China, people began to use numbers to explain the rules and relationships in the world, and gradually started to use numbers for trade, counting, and statistics.

"The concept of number in human brain represents mankind's first attempts to pursue and think about the origin of the world." (Gao Jianping & Qi Zhiyuan 2019) This is the philosophical origin of Pythagorean School's dictum that "all is number". Pythagoras raised number to the position of the origin of all things in ontological terms, regarding number not as a qualitative rule, but an attribute penetrating all things and the common feature of all things. The substance of things will disappear, but number has no beginning and no end. It can be used to interpret everything, carry everything and control everything. That "all is number" takes number not merely as a way of calculation, but also a path that leads mankind to understand all things. That "all is number" represents man's pursuit of one thing that all things share in common, which is number. Number enables the human brain to generalize everything, understand the world, make plans proportionately, and build the world with in harmony. In Pythagoras's view, number is not only the origin of the real world, but also the origin of the virtual world created by modern science and technology, or the origin of the human spiritual world. In other words, number is the origin of all things in the world.

On our way from numbers to a complete virtual world, it seems that every step reflects the idea that "all is number". Number runs through every stage of the whole process, from counting to calculation, and to modeling, presentation, and ultimately storage and communication; and all the related things have their own number information. "Everything else shows that they, in nature, are an imitation of numbers." (Ru Xin 2005, p. 39) Items in the virtual world are stored in the form of digital information, which is convenient to read in digital form later. This seems to mechanically demonstrate Pythagoras's theory that number is the origin of all things on the computer, and also realizes the ideal that number serves as rules in modern digital world.

From data to big data

Data represents man's understanding of the causal relationships in the objective world. Data, in a sense, is the extension and expansion of the concept of number and an inevitable product of the development of human social science when it reaches a certain stage. "Information technology such as microelectronics, electronic communication and computer technology has led to a new round of technological revolution and gradually pushed mankind into the information society." (Zhang Xinbao 2015) At this point, the modern way of thinking centered on data came into being, and data became the core of the methodology that people use to understand the world. The word "data" comes from the Latin word "*datum*", which first appeared in the thirteenth century, meaning "something given". From a philosophical perspective, "data is the product of human cognitive activities, a subjective reflection of objective things, and a logical language for representing things and phenomena" (Liu Hong & Hu Xinhe 2013). In the field of computer, data generally refers to any material that can be processed by computer, including all kinds of words, numbers, charts, etc. It can be seen that data comes from the needs of keeping record of the objective world. Data is used as a tool in human practice. It goes beyond the function of representing features, breaks the barrier of time and space, and becomes the basis for our efforts to deduce the rules about how things move and change, ultimately helping us establish our modern society and civilization.

Big data contains man's understanding of the totality of relationships in the objective world. "Big data is a collection of data characterized by large quantity, multiple types, fast access, and high application value. It is rapidly turning into a kind of new-generation information technology and a model of service delivery, covering the collection, storage and connection of massive data from scattered sources and in diverse formats. The goal is to discover new knowledge, create new value, and bring out new capabilities" (State Council of the People's Republic of China 2015). Big data represents a new stage of informatization. It is no longer a new concept now. It ushers in a new era, constitutes a multi-dimensional infinite variable, and is about to transform the way people try to understand the world, shifting the focus from causal relationships to correlations. With big data, we will "examine the objective world with systematic methodology to reveal relationships between different parts, between a part and the whole, and between our systems and the environment. Data, as a tool with which human beings examine the world, describes objective things which constitute only the subjective part of the world, not the whole of it. On the contrary, big data helps people expand the scope of their cognition in time and space and extend their knowledge about the world from parts of it to the whole of it" (Gao Jianping & Qi Zhiyuan 2019).

As was pointed out at the Fourth Plenary Session of the 19th CPC Central Committee that it is necessary to improve the mechanism where the contributions of production factors such as labor, capital, land, knowledge, technology, management and data are evaluated in a market-based manner and remuneration is determined by contributions. This is the first time that the CPC Central Committee accepts data as a production factor that counts for contribution and thus income distribution. On the one hand, data, as a kind of resource, can promote global economic growth and social development just like land, labor, capital and other production factors; on the other hand, data, as a constructive force for social relations, lies at the core of our times and constitutes three essential elements of human activities in the natural world together with material and energy. Data has been transformed from a kind of symbol that describes things into something essential for all things in the world.

Big data is a collection of data, and more than that. Big data has become an important force that rebuilds our social order today, leading mankind into the era of digital civilization. Big data, inclusive as it is, will break the boundaries between countries, governments, organizations and the public. The biggest influence that big data has exerted on us is that it "created a common world for us all, a world we can only share in any case" (Bei Ke, Deng Zhenglai & Shen Guolin 2010). In the era of big data, the focus of competitions among countries has shifted from capital, land, population and resources to data. Countries will be divided into groups based on their data capabilities and a dramatic change will occur to the global landscape.

The proposition of data rights

As data gradually becomes a kind of resource, asset, and capital, a shift from data to data rights has becomes an inevitable trend as mankind moves towards the digital civilization. It is also the general trend that data be recognized as carrier of rights and powers and this recognition be institutionalized. Data order will become the top order in the future society. There are four new things about data rights: First, data rights involve a new type of objects; second, data rights are a new type of rights; third, data rights represent new natures of rights; and fourth, data rights contain new type of functions (see Table 5). Data rights are the precondition for establishing data rules and an important cornerstone for grasping the development opportunities of digitalization, networking and intelligent development, and handling the challenges of big data development in law, security and government administration.

Table 5. Features of Data Rights

Feature	Description
Object of right	Data is not an object in the sense of the civil law (i.e. not an object of property rights). It is neither a physical object in physics nor an intangible object as described in intellectual property rights. Data is an independent objective being and forms a digital world that is beyond the physical world and the spiritual world. The subjects of data rights are specific rights holders, including the specific objects that the data is about and those who collect, store, transmit and process the data (including natural persons, legal persons, and non-legal person organizations). The scope of the rights varies with the subjects. The objects of data rights are specific datasets. Data is a combination of a series of digits, codes, images and texts. Single digits or codes have no value and value can only be produced by combining, integrating and pooling them. Therefore, the objects of data rights should be specific datasets with rules and value.
Type of right	According to legal interpretation in the traditional sense, human rights can be classified into two types: personality rights and property rights. In the digital era, human beings leave digital footprints to varying degrees in various kinds of digital ecosystems. On the one hand, these data are the fragments of human behaviors, an important records of individuals' participation in social activities, and an important way to extend personality. Therefore, it is necessary to safeguard the human dignity of data subjects, and ensure that they enjoy the right to freedom, the right to fame, the right to privacy, and the right to information; on the other hand, data are also important social resources. Data have value and can bring economic benefits to data subjects, so it is necessary to grant data asset rights. Thus, data rights will contain both personality rights and asset rights.

(To be continued)

Table 5. Continued

Feature	Description
Nature of right	Data rights are a combination of public power and private rights. They include both data sovereignty that reflects national dignity, and the right to data that highlights personal well-being for individuals. Therefore, data rights should be analyzed not only as a kind of personal rights regulated by private law, but also from the perspective of state security regulated by public law. This is to say, data rights need both self-regulation of private law and the interference from public law.
Function of right	Property rights are exclusive as a kind of ownership, so there can never be two ownerships over one object and everyone has the obligation not to interfere with the rights holders' absolute domination over the objects of the rights. Data rights, on the contrary, are not exclusive. They are rights to be shared. This is manifested by multi-ownership of data, which is the core and essence of data rights. That data rights are for sharing in essence will be a milestone that rewrites the rules of human civilization.

Source: the authors

It should be pointed out that data rights have the features of private rights, public rights and sovereignty. In the realm of private rights, data rights are divided into personal data rights and corporate data rights according to who holds the data, and personal data resources and corporate data resources are respectively regarded as the objects of these two categories of the rights to data. In the realm of public rights, data rights show clear public and collective features. It is a kind of collective power with the state and government as the rights holder, and with the maximization of public interests as the value orientation. It is intended to vigorously maintain order for participation in public affairs and characterized by self-expansion. In the realm of sovereignty, data rights, manifested by data sovereignty, are important parts of and necessary supplements to state sovereignty. It enriches and expands the connotation and denotation of traditional state sovereignty, adapting it to the new situation of modern cyberspace governance and helping ensure the independence of state sovereignty.

"Whether a new right or power can be established, in the final analysis, depends on whether production activities can generate an increase in material wealth, thus making it possible to have new interest entities and realize interest requirements" (Dong Zhiwei 2001, p. 297). Data empower people. Data man will give rise to new rights and legal relations, such as rights to data, rights to share, and data sovereignty. Data rights here are not an independent rights system, but a kind of intended rights on the basis that the current legislations cannot fully regulate the data space. It is beyond the existing rights protection system, and disputes over data rights, once they arise, cannot be properly handled due to a lack of legal measures compatible to new data processing behaviors. Thus, a new type of disputes may come into being. When a new kind of rights relationship emerges, the traditional legal relations system will face insurmountable obstacles and find itself incapable of handling the new relationships. Thus, it is necessary to build a practical and effective system for the governance of data.

Rights to data

Rights to data is a new type of rights

The rights to data arise with the emergence of data and are highlighted with the development of big data. The rights to data have their constitutional dimension and civil right dimension. They are a new type of rights containing both personality rights and property rights. The subjects of the rights to data include the specific targets that data points to and those who collect, store, transmit and process the data. Different right subjects have different rights. The objects of the rights to data are specific datasets with rules and values, mostly personal data. The key point in the protection of the rights to data is personal data rights. Personal data rights are widely recognized in civil law countries and regarded as a fundamental right in legislation. Personal data rights are a kind of constitutional rights. Article 38 of *The Constitution of the People's Republic of China* provides the constitutional basis for personal data rights to become a fundamental right.[1] In addition, personal data rights emphasize the independence of individuals' personality and freedom of conduct, which is a civil right in line with the basic value orientation of the personal interests of private rights and the freedom of conduct enjoyed and realized by it. When taken as an asset, data is unique in that it is for general use, external, and non-exhaustible. Based on this, in the ideal state of pure academic deduction, the complete rights to data can be divided according to how it is used into multiple bundles of rights, such as the right to possess, the right to use, the right to earnings, the right to share, and the right to cross-border transmission. The right holders can have one or more bundles of these rights at the same time. For different bundles, the value of data as assets will be different (see Figure 1).

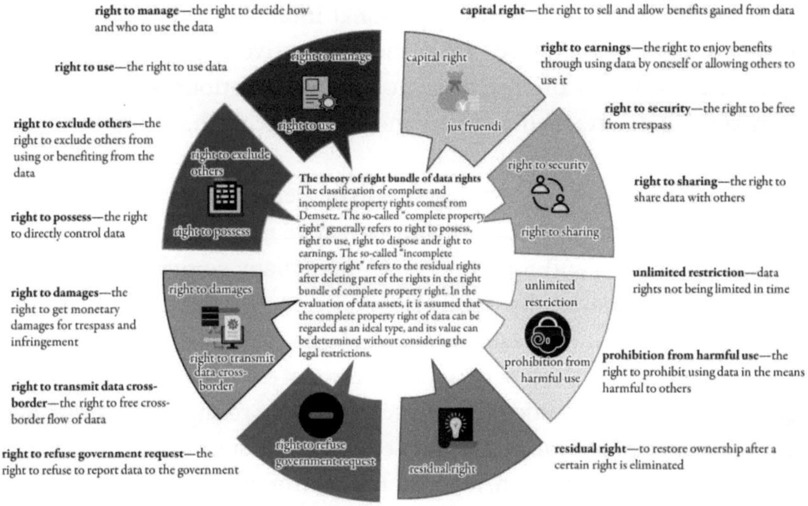

Figure 1. Bundles of the Rights to Data.
Source: Deloitte and Ali Research, "The Approach of Data Assets: Data Assets Valuation and Industry Practice", October 29, 2019. <https://www2.deloitte.com/cn/zh/pages/finance/articles/data-asset-report.html>.

1 According to Professor Lin Laifan, the content of Article 38 of *The Constitution of the People's Republic of China* is divided into two parts. The first part is "the inviolability of the personality and dignity of the citizens of the People's Republic of China", which is

Legal interests of rights to data

Rights are the meaning force that is granted by legal norms to a person to meet his personal interests, that is, the legal force for the person to enjoy specific interests (Hans Brocks & Wolff Dietrich Walker 2019, p. 276). Right is the most mature category in the legal system. It deeply reveals the internal relationship between rights and factual interests (Lv Zhixiang & Zhang Qiang 2019). The change of the status of rights shows that the relationship between state and individuals is led more and more by rights. According to the classical Western theory of rights, in the abstract sense, rights are related to freedom, interests and justice, and it is even safe to say that private rights equal freedom, interests and justice. Private rights refer to individual rights aimed at meeting individual needs, focusing on embodying and safeguarding personal interests, which is essentially private in nature. Therefore, "from the perspective of private rights, data rights are the rights of enterprises, other organizations and citizens to possess the data attached to them and the data they have acquired" (Lv Tingjun 2017).

In the past half a century, legislation on personal data protection has become one of the most remarkable legislative movements in the world. For the protection and use of personal data, many countries take a dual approach of regulation by public law and empowerment by private law (Cheng Xiao 2018). The *Data Protection Act* enacted by the State of Hesse, Germany, in 1970 is the first dedicated personal data protection law in the world, and a data protection committee was set up to supervise the storage and transmission of official documents within the state government, so as to prevent illegal acquisition, revision and destruction. In 1973, for the purpose of personal data protection, Sweden adopted the *Data Act*, which was the first law in the world that explicitly restricted the cross-border transfer of personal data. In 1974, in the face of severe abuse of personal data, the

similar to the basic constitutional value of German "human dignity"; the second part is "the prohibition of insulting, slandering and false accusation against citizens by any means", which expresses the protection of individual rights, equivalent to personality rights in the constitution. See Lin Laifan & Luo Zhengyan. 2008. "Personality Rights in the Constitution." *Jurists*, 5th issue.

Congress of the United States began to consider the protection of personal data, and finally adopted the *Privacy Act*. In terms of regional or global cooperation, in 1980, the Organization for Economic Co-operation and Development (OECD) issued the *Guidelines on the Protection of Privacy and Transborder Flows of Personal Data* on the basis of various national laws in this aspect. The purpose was to give recommendation for the protection of privacy and freedom of personal data. In the 1970s, the European Union began to call on its member countries to legislate on data, and constantly pushed the legislative work on personal data protection forward as technology and society make progresses. In particular, the *General Data Protection Regulation* implemented in 2018 redefines personal data authorization and grants data subjects the right to forget and delete their own data.

The system of personal data rights is a theoretical response to practical demands, so it will inevitably have to go from due rights to statutory rights and then to actual rights (Shi Pengpeng 2013). "The move of the personal data rights system from due rights to actual rights actually depends on the edification of due rights to individual cases to raise the awareness of individual rights holders, which can then develop into a consensus of the vast majority of people. On this basis, it is necessary to affirm claims of such rights in the form of legislation, and confirm such rights with corresponding systems" (Wen Yu 2019). With the advancement of datamation process, rules of personal data protection have been incorporated into fundamental and major laws such as amendment to the *Criminal Law of the People's Republic of China*, amendment to the *Law of the People's Republic of China on the Protection of Consumer Rights and Interests* and the *Cybersecurity Law of the People's Republic of China*. In the *General Provisions of the Civil Law*, which is a fundamental law, Article 111 stipulates for the protection of the right of natural persons to personal information, highlighting the principle that personal information must be acquired and used according to law. This is of great significance.

Social context of the rights to data

To understand the rights to data, we must first have an accurate understanding of the current social conditions at home and abroad. In recent years, Internet users around the world have been engaged in deal with the devil with large technology companies:[2] They submit their personal data and get services. For a long time, most Internet users are only aware of the superficial fact that they get services for free, not the other side of this fact that technology companies also get and use users' data for free. Personal data is not only put into commercial use, but also leaked, trafficked and abused on many occasions (Xi Po 2018). There are many such cases abroad and examples include Google Street View's privacy infringement since 2007, Sony's stealing game data in 2011, the PRISM incident of 2013, data leakage of three major credit card companies in South Korea in 2014, Anthem stealing 80 million pieces of personal information in 2015, the leakage of state information data in Turkey in 2016, Gmail and Yahoo!'s account sale in 2017, the Facebook Cambridge analysis incident of 2018, and the sale of the data of 159 million users of LinkedIn in 2019 (see Table 6). In China, there are also a number of data leakage incidents caused by e-commerce platforms, portal websites, and Internet finance platforms, including the leakage of email accounts and passwords, and even bank card information. People are highly concerned about such cases.

Personal data in the digital era is not only regarded as an important production factor, but also "the currency of today's digital market".[3] We are entering a new era of the right to use based on the idea of sharing. Kevin Kelly, a technology thinker, clearly points out that "I can pay for them (goods or services), but I won't possess them ... To some extent, the right to use has also become the right to possess" (Kevin Kelly 2012, p. 111). The same is true for data, but the unrestricted use of data will destroy the orderly life that we have been enjoying. Specifically, in the modern society represented by the application of big data technologies,

2 Deal with the devil describes a kind of mental disorder. One who suffers from this kind of disorder is so obsessed with something that appears to be valuable that he/she loses the reason or opportunity to see and understand other valuable things or spirits in life.

3 At Digital-Life-Design Conference 2012, Viviane Reding, European Commissioner for Justice, Fundamental rights and Citizenship, claimed that personal data had become the currency of today's digital market.

Table 6. Typical Data Security Incidents Abroad

Time	Case	Description
2007	Google Street View privacy infringement	Google faced a number of privacy-related lawsuits for illegally using cars and trucks to collect personal information such as e-mails and passwords from unencrypted private wireless networks. At one time, the lawsuits were the largest of their kind in American history. Google lost billions of dollars in them.
2011	Sony game data theft	The PlayStation Game Network (PSN) of Sony Corporation, Japan, was hacked, and data of 77 million online game users was stolen, including the users' names, residential addresses, email addresses, birthdays, passwords, password prompts, etc. It became the severest hack and data theft by that time.
2013	PRISM	Edward Snowden, a former employee of the National Security Agency (NSA) of the United States disclosed some secret documents of the agency's PRISM surveillance program to *The Guardian*. It was reported that NSA monitored the call logs of millions of users. The secret surveillance program known as PRISM was launched by the United States in 2007, which allowed NSA to directly enter the central servers of Internet companies to search for data and collect intelligence. Nine international Internet giants, including Microsoft, Yahoo!, Google and Apple, were covered by the program.
2014	Data leakage of three major credit card companies in South Korea	In the process of developing computer programs commissioned by credit card companies, a Mr. Park and other employees of credit rating companies illegally collected and disclosed 104 million pieces of personal information of people who held KB cards, Lotte cards or NH cards. In addition to personal information such as name, telephone number, residence and company name, it involved 5,391 pieces of sensitive credit information such as ID card number, loan transaction details and credit card approval tax exemption certificates, which accounted for more than half of all the leaked information. This is the largest incident of personal information leakage of credit card holders in South Korea.

(To be continued)

Table 6. Continued

Time	Case	Description
2015	Anthem theft of 80 million pieces of personal information	Hackers stole tens of millions of customers' information from Anthem, a US health insurance company, including their name, dates of birth, medical card information, social security numbers, addresses, e-mail addresses and employment information (including income), making it the largest leakage incident of health-related institutions in the United States.
2016	Personal information leakage in Turkey	Nearly 50 million Turkish citizens' personal information was involved, including a series of sensitive information such as names, ID card numbers, parents' names and addresses, which are packed by hackers with an IP address in Finland. People can download the data they are interested in a P2P manner.
2017	Gmail and Yahoo! account sale	A large number of Gmail accounts, Yahoo! accounts and PlayStation network accounts and passwords were publicly sold on the dark web by a supplier by the name suntzu583.The total number of Gmail accounts that were sold amounted to 4,928,888, which was divided into three parts, each containing information of 2,262,444 accounts, including emails addresses and passwords.
2018	Facebook Cambridge analysis incident	Cambridge Analysis, a data analysis company that provided data analysis services to US President Donald Trump during the 2016 presidential campaign, and its subsidiary Strategic Communications Lab stole and privately kept 50 million Facebook users' data which they used to manipulate the presidential election.
2019	Sale of the data of 159 million users of LinkedIn	Andrew, a hacker, put sensitive data of 159 million users of LinkedIn for sale on Pastebin. In order to prove the authenticity of the data, the hacker also released the login credentials of 100 users, including even that of well-known CEOs.

Source: Compiled by the authors according to relevant reports.

man-made risks have gradually replaced natural risks as the main threats to human survival. How to control risks and ensure security has become an issue of common concern for the development of modern society. We urgently need to establish an interest balancing mechanism to tackle the disorder resulted from the neglect of the rights of data rights holders and create a new social order.

Due to different backgrounds of individuals, data rights holders' claims for their own data interests differ greatly. Such interest differentiation is manifested in the fact that some right holders expect mainly to obtain property interests, some personality interests, and some privacy interests from personal data; and that some others even pursue the purpose of limiting public power of the state by claiming personal data rights. However, the realization of personal interests requires the consumption of social resources, and personal rights can be achieved only when social interests are upheld. Therefore, the realization of personal data rights usually relies heavily on the realization of social interests and in legislations concerning personal data protection, social interests should take precedence over personal data rights. However, for social interests, the priorities are also different for different social groups. Even if it is necessary to protect social interests by restricting personal data rights, such restrictions should also be appropriate and follow some basic principles (Wang Xiuxiu 2018, p. 143–172).

Data power

Transfer of power

Power is, in nature, public. It represents a kind of social relationship between people and exists in a dynamic form (Jiao Shiwen 2009, p. 21). It is always "the official representative of the whole society and the collective performance of the society in a tangible organization" (Central Compilation and Translation Bureau 1963, p. 242). Public power is also a kind of right in nature, but it is a special type of rights. State power is the manifestation of state rights. As the main symbol of the state, it is the fundamental premise of all the functions of the state. There are three basic characteristics: First, the subject of public power is the general public rather than individuals, and being for the public is the core of public power, which, in nature, is to be shared. Second, the object of public power should be public affairs, so anything that involves private rights should not be interfered by public power; otherwise it will constitute an infringement of private rights. Third, the source and foundation of public power is public interests and public power should shoulder public responsibility and serve public interests; otherwise it is likely to be privatized or become privately owned (Hao Jiming 2008).

According to a report of the United Nations, data aims to rationalize social existence and realize "rational production" of the notions and meaning systems. Therefore, data is a key strategic resource at present and in the future. More specifically, this strategic resource is data power, which dominates rationality and is dominated by it in the meantime. In the realm of politics, data power follows the logic of power which covers the two dimensions of capability and structure. It constantly produces, reshapes and dominates new political, economic and social relations. In the dimension of capability there are the roles that data power plays, the objects it governs, and the technologies on which it is based; while in the structural dimension, there are relationship, rules and patterns. These two dimensions contain positive endogenous driving forces, but also may cause risk mismatch and conflicts between the public and private spheres due to their impact on the existing social power system. Therefore, we need to forge rational and prudent consensus and governance principles for data power.

Like knowledge, data is the most democratic source of power. With the development of data power, traditional power is also undergoing transformations. First, the power center of the world is moving to a new region. Driven by digital technology, emerging countries such as China and India are rising rapidly, and their comprehensive national strength, international influence and voice are growing. In the meantime, the United States and the European Union are in relative decline, and the power center of the world is thus shifting to the East. Second, power is moving down the social ladder, and gradually spreads across the majority of people. In knowledge-intensive enterprises, managers, technical experts and workers have more power, which proves that knowledge promotes democracy. Third, the quality of power is on the rise. In the era of digital economy, data is the major source of power. It changes the world and society in a way that violence and wealth have never done and will never do. Fourth, a new power center based on data is emerging. Those who master information intelligence, the latest technological know-how and key data resources become the center of power center.[4]

Expansion of data power

Data is power and power is data. Power can be turned into data and data is a must for anyone to have power. In a sense, whoever owns data controls power. A new kind of power system – data power – is now on the rise. Data power has changed the traditional binary structure of state and society, and formed a new pattern of complex competition between public power and private rights. Public power of data and private rights of data are a dialectical unity. Under certain conditions, the public power of the state and the private rights of society form a certain coalition for governance to prevent the expansion of social private rights. Similarly, private rights tend to cooperate based on relevant claims and pursuits to jointly restrain the expansion and abuse of public power.

In the era of big data, the scope of application of power extends from the original political and legal fields to all aspects of social life, such as business, medical care, education, and culture, which undoubtedly expands the space for data power holders to exercise their power. This makes it easier to

4 In 1990, Alvin Toffler pointed out in *Powershift* that power, as a force to dominate others, has been realized through violence, wealth and knowledge since ancient times. In the third wave of civilization, knowledge will become the symbol of power. Whoever has knowledge will have power. However, knowledge is different from violence and wealth in that the latter two are exclusive. If one kind of violence or wealth is owned by one person or group, other people or groups cannot own the violence or wealth at the same time; while knowledge is not exclusive, and the same kind of knowledge can be owned by different people at the same time. Therefore, "knowledge is the most democratic source of power". Whoever has the control and dissemination right of knowledge has the initiative of power. In the era of big data, every "data center" becomes a kind of "right / power center" in a certain sense, and these "right/power centers" will have discourse rights.

abuse power in disguise, it is therefore more difficult to keep data power checked. "As the junction between rights holders in cyberspace and in the real world, accounts are where data accumulates steadily as various online activities go on. This data depicts scenario and evaluate behaviors, and such evaluation serves as an important constraint on the future activities of account holders" (Hu Ling 2018). In this process, people cannot actually participate in and have no control over other people's collection and use of their data. Basically, the use of their personal data is out of their control from the very beginning and there is nothing they can do. Even if no secret is disclosed and no one is watching, their right to data privacy is already infringed in a sense. This kind of anxiety is more worrying than the direct infringement of power.

In addition, as power is decentralized and spread at a low level, more people now have a place in the power system, and this brings new problems to power restriction. As power is transferred, the power of the government is also changing. A kind of decentralized and diversified democracy is taking shape, which has an important impact on the prevention of excessive concentration of power and corruption in the governance. In this context, one form of power may be destroyed, but another is replacing it (Lawrence Lessig 2009, p. 87), which means that the structural shift towards multi-stakeholder governance in the era of big data will lead to profound changes in legal relations, and it is necessary to strengthen legislation in fields where data power abuse is likely to occur.

Structure of data power

"Power comes from the social structure, and a specific type of power comes from a specific position on the social structure column. (Kang Xiaoguang 1999, p. 51)" Social structure is the foundation of the existence of power structure. Any social structure will have its corresponding power structure. The structural logic of data power is the product our commitment to self-development and maintenance of the modern civilization system (Lin Qifu & He Jingchao 2016). The political and social structure of data power serves as the public meaning system of the data power structure, which explains what kind of a public order data power will produce. Its functions are mainly seen in the social practices of politics on both the micro and the macro levels. It is what the state, as authorities who have data power, performs, making use of various resources for social control, mobilization, persuasion, absorption and even symbol production. In economic terms, data power evolves along the cycle of germination–formation–maturity–stagnation–recession–fission–germination, which outlines the history of economic forms and rules. The emergence of data power provides both possibilities and uncertainties for this cycle. Data power will challenge the existing market structure, exert influence on the competition for capital and induce redistribution of micro property rights in society. The conceptual structure of data power is the structure of human meaning system and cultural system, but is more diverse and complex than the two. Data is no longer the surplus of the power structure, but plays its part in the integration and reorganization of conceptual structure as a kind of power. In the future, people's identity may no longer be based on blood relationships, ethnic group, surname or place of origin; instead, they identify with those who share the same data identity, or in the same IoT community or area in cyberspace.

Types of Rights to data

The confirmation of rights to data is not only the basis of exercising and protecting the rights, but also an important way to protect relevant interests. "Parties who hold data-related interests can be individuals, enterprises, other organizations or countries. Different categories of interest subjects have different categories of rights and interests over data. (Li Xiaoyu 2019)" The development of the big data industry has given birth to new subjects of rights and interests, such as data subjects, data controllers, and data users. Based on the category of rights and interest subjects, rights to data include rights to personal data, rights to corporate data, and rights to government data. "Once the rights are confirmed, the first issue is to design its function structure, and the specific manifestation of this function structure is the claims" (Chen Zhentao 2017). Driven by interests, different interest subjects will inevitably put forward new claims for the protection of relevant rights and interests and the corresponding legal system. Therefore, it is necessary to have an in-depth study of theories on rights to data and on the establishment of the functions of rights, so as to protect data more comprehensively.

Rights to personal data

Personal data

In the era of big data, data and its derivatives have omnipresent influence on personal life. Information about all aspects of people as individuals is collected, sorted out and used in the form of data (Shi Lindong 2019). Massive personal data contains huge economic value and strategic value. On the one hand, by using personal data and constantly improving the technology and functions of data products, we will enable users to enjoy more benefits and convenience. On the other hand, everyone is a source of data, so if personal data cannot be fully protected, it is likely to result in problems such as illegal collection, sale and use of personal data, and infringement of the personality rights and property rights of individuals. When personal data is put into commercial use, its commercial value is activated indirectly because of the personality interests it carries. It can be said that the rights arrangement of personal data directly determines how data circulates and how it is shared, and this in turn has great bearing on the development of the data industry.

Personal data is also known as personal information.[5] For example, the *General Data Protection Regulation* of the European Union stipulates:

> "Personal data" means any information relating to an identified or identifiable natural person ("data subject"); an identifiable natural person is one who can be identified,

5 There are different terms referring to personal data, like "personal information" and others, but the difference mainly come from different legal traditions and use habits, and there are no essential differences. With the big data technology, information mostly exists in the form of data, so it is called "personal data" here.

> directly or indirectly, in particular by reference to an identifier such as a name, an identification number, location data, an online identifier or to one or more factors specific to the physical, physiological, genetic, mental, economic, cultural or social identity of that natural person.[6]

According to the *Act on the Protection of Personal Information* (Japan, 2003),

> The term "personal information" as used in this Act shall mean information about a living individual which can identify the specific individual by name, date of birth or other description contained in such information including such information as will allow easy reference to other information and will thereby enable the identification of the specific individual. (Wen Yu 2018)

According to the *Cybersecurity Law of the People's Republic of China*,

> "Personal information" refers to all kinds of information, recorded electronically or through other means, that taken alone or together with other information, is sufficient to identify a natural person's identity, including but not limited to natural persons' full names, birth dates, national identification numbers, personal biometric information, addresses, telephone numbers, and so forth.[7]

The mainstream in the academic community believes that the substantive standard of personal data is "identifiability". "Personal data relates to a specific person, and its processing affects or even damages the life of the natural person it is related to, which is why personal data needs to be protected" (Wen Yu 2019).

"Rights to personal data involve coordination between the protection of civil rights and interests of natural persons and the freedom of data enterprises to carry out data-related activities" (Cheng Xiao 2018). "Rights to personal data are the rights of data subjects to decide who and how to collect, process and analyze personal data, and it is a kind of rights to control personal data" (Xiang Liling & Gao Qianyun 2018). People's claims of rights to personal data are manifested in the demand that personality rights and property rights of personal data are not infringed illegally in legal

6 See Section 1 of Article 4 of the *General Data Protection Regulation*.
7 See Article 76 of the *Cybersecurity Law of the People's Republic of China*.

terms. Specifically, the new types of rights related to data are mainly manifested as follows: In addition to the right to privacy recognized by existing legislations, Internet users also claim the right of self-determination over personal data, the right to carry personal data, the right of their personal data to be forgotten, the right to transfer personal data, and the right of exclusive access to personal data. (see Table 7). It can be seen that "data rights and interests are not a single right, but a bundle of different rights" (Li Xiaoyu 2019).

Personal data rights: A new type of personality rights

Data depicts a user's habits of use, living conditions, communication privacy and other information that can identify the person. Thus, it involves individuals' right of name, right of portrait, etc., which are protection as specific types of personality rights. Based on the identification characteristics and identification benefits, rights to data undoubtedly contain personality rights (Yan Lidong 2019). However, the personal data that is anonymous or only of a low sensitivity level, such as web browsing records and that about one's personal consumption habits, is not necessarily associated with the personality and identity of data subjects and thus does not qualify as privacy and holds no risk of personality rights infringement. In addition, in terms of remedies, due to the confidentiality of data collection and use, it is impossible to prove the causal relationship between who collected and used the data and the infringement that occurs, which brings great difficulties to the identification of those who commit the infringement and to prove the infringement.

As data is a new type of social resources, it is necessary to establish a new type of personality rights to regulate and protect the collection and use of data. First of all, in terms of the inherent characteristics of different rights, the rights to personal data protect personal interests, and data subjects naturally have the right to control and dominate their data. Second, in terms of the content of its objects, the rights to personal data cover general personal information, personal privacy data and sensitive personal data, some of which have been established as separate personality rights (e.g. name, portrait, and privacy). In addition, in terms of the

Table 7. Rights to Personal Data

Right	Description
Right to privacy	Data privacy concerns not only personal identification, but also a person's behavior track, consumption tendency, habits and other related information. It has been recognized worldwide that the right to data privacy mainly means that one has the right to keep his/her private information not disclosed illegally, rather than domination or control over such information.
Right to information	The right to information, also known as the right of information self-determination, is the right to limit data processing. It emphasizes the control of personal information, including not only the update and deletion of the information, but also the understanding of the purpose, destination and use of the information.
Right to know	The right of individuals to be informed of how their data is collected and used.
Right of access	This refers to the right of access to one's personal data. The *General Data Protection Regulation* provides that data controllers should provide corresponding procedures for users to exercise this right. A data controller cannot charge for providing this service, unless the request of the data subject appears to be excessive.
Right to object	The right to object refers to the right to refuse data controller's processing of one's personal data on the basis of his/her legitimate rights and interests, and the right to refuse marketing behaviors related to his/her personal data.
Right to data portability	Users can transfer their personal data from one data controller to another without being interfered with.
Right to correct	To ensure the accuracy of data, data subjects have the right to rectify the data.
Right to be forgotten	When a user withdraws consent according to law, or the data controller no longer has the legitimate reason to continue to process the data, the user has the right to require the data to be deleted.

Source: See Sun Wei. 2018. "Data Rights, Open Mechanism and Metadata Standard in Open Data: Experiences in Global Scope." Urban Transportation Planning Academic Committee of China Urban Planning Society. *The Theories of Innovative Advancement and Intelligence Development: Proceedings of Annual Conference of China Urban Transportation Planning.*

effectiveness of protection, if rights to personal data are defined only as a kind of property rights, the protection will have limitations.

On the contrary, if rights to personal data are regarded as a new type of personality rights, relevant calculation will not differ on the basis of identity, thus upholding the general principle of equality of personality. "By establishing a new types of rights, we present the legal relations clearly, and those who use relevant legal provision can check them with the objects of the rights clearly in their minds" (Zhang Suhua & Li Yanan 2018). As Professor Wang Liming put it, "personal information should be protected by private law as an object of personality rights, and a dedicated law should be formulated for personal information protection" (Wang Liming 2013). In the era of digital civilization, rights to personal data should be established as an independent new type of personality rights, whose purpose is to protect the rights and interests of data subjects from being infringed, and to prevent the abuse and arbitrary dissemination of personal data. At present, the rights to data are widely accepted as a kind of personality rights among legal theorists as well as practitioners. Similarly, in formulating the civil code of China,[8] personality rights will constitute a separate chapter and the protection of personal information will be provided for in it. This responds to a widespread concern in society, which is the challenges brought about by the development of new technologies.

Rights to personal data as property rights

"The potential economic value of personal data makes it necessary not to ignore its nature as a kind of property, and rights to personal data cannot

8 On August 22, 2019, the 12th meeting of the Standing Committee of the 13th National People's Congress was held in Beijing. At the meeting, the third review was made about *Personality Rights of Civil Code (draft)*, and relevant provisions on the protection of personal information were improved, including the following new provisions: personality right is the civil subject's right of life, body, health, name, nomenclature, portrait, reputation, honor, and privacy, etc. And the definition of privacy is revised to "private space, private activities and private information that natural persons do not want others to know". The added provision is that no organization or individual is allowed to search, enter, peep at or photograph other people's hotel rooms and other private spaces.

be protected merely as a kind of personality rights."[9] This will inhibit the flow of data on the Internet and the development of the big data industry. In addition, with the extensive use and dissemination of personal data, more and more economic disputes have arisen highlighting the property nature of personal data. Such disputes will not be successfully settled if rights to personal data are merely treated as a kind of personality rights. Especially in the context of the digital economy, the economic value of personal data is more obvious. If data is protected only under the category of personality rights, it will be about personality and dignity only, which will inhibit data flow and the development of the data industry to some extent. Therefore, confirming the property right nature of rights to personal data can help us better regulate data transactions, provide an orderly environment with sound legal support for data market behaviors, and offer better protection for rights to personal data.

The protection of the rights to data is different from that of personality rights, trade secrets and intellectual property rights. It should be protected as an independent kind of rights, which can be called data asset right. Data asset right is a kind of incomplete ownership. The holders or controllers can neither dispose of the data they hold or control arbitrarily, nor damage the legitimate rights and interests of relevant rights holders. Therefore, it is necessary to do relevant categorization and build the relevant rights system based on the forms of existence of information (Deng Ganghong 2018). Based on this, rights to personal data refer to the independent asset rights of data subjects in the digital era. Data asset rights are the rights to directly control a specific data property and exclude interference from others. It is a new form of property right born in the era of big data. Its functions include data property owner's right to possess, use, earn from and dispose of his/her data property (Qi Aimin & Pan Jia 2015). Therefore, data asset rights are not a one-way static right, but a group of ownership-based rights.

9 Although the personality elements of personal data have the attributes of personality interests and economic interests, the personality interests can be protected by invoking personality rights, and the economic interests of data personality elements can be fully realized. For "the property orientation of data personality elements", see Wen Yuheng. 2018. "Private Law Structure of Data Property Rights." Doctoral dissertation. Xiangtan University.

Firstly, personal data, as the private property of data subjects, is in nature material property, and its value can be transformed into material benefits such as money obtained by data owner or possessor. Secondly, rights to personal data are transferable, and their owner or possessor can transfer the rights to others within the scope permitted by law, so as to make full use of the data. Thirdly, rights to personal data are remediable. When a data subject's rights are infringed, the data subject can regain control over his/her rights to personal data or claim for the loss caused by the infringement according to relevant laws and regulations. Therefore, as an independent asset right, personal data rights can ensure not only the sound operation of the data industry according to law, but also the interests of data subjects and data controllers.

Rights to corporate data

Corporate data

In the era of the digital economy, data has penetrated into all parts of our life and become an important factor of production and an important asset of enterprises. Using data, enterprises can significantly improve their decision-making, innovation and management. However, while creating huge wealth for enterprises, big data development also poses serious threats to data security and privacy protection. At the same time, data can be used without loss, so it does not seem scarce on the surface. However, because of the economic benefits that data may bring, it is collected and stored by enterprises in datasets which have been treated with special technical measures, and this makes data resources actually scarce. As a result, competition for data becomes increasingly fierce among enterprises (Wen Yuheng 2019). For example, SF Express and Cainiao compete for logistics data, Weibo and Maimai compete for microblog data, and Huawei and Tencent compete for WeChat data. All these serve to highlight the urgent need for rights to data to be confirmed in the business field. "Corporate data is a kind of derivative that can be produced by an enterprise through deep development and systematic integration after modeling the relationship between massive and complex original data by using artificial intelligence tools, mathematical and statistical analysis techniques and data mining technologies on the basis of huge input of materials, personnel, and financial resources" (Li Xiaoyu 2019). Corporate data includes not only data reflecting the basic situation of an enterprise, such as financial data, operation data (R&D, procurement, production, sales, etc.) and human resource data; but also personal data directly or indirectly collected by the enterprise through contractual authorization (Shi Dan 2018). Corporate data contains huge use value, but it cannot be used without limit. For example, when enterprises collect data, they must specify the purpose, method and scope of data collection and use, and obtain consents from their customers. When an enterprise uses the data, it should not exceed the scope of customer authorization or go beyond the purpose it stated when collecting the data. Moreover, it must not damage the freedom of data use, public security and public interests.

Power configuration of corporate data

The personal legal interests involved in corporate data can be understood from two perspectives. In terms of data collection, a considerable part of the data obtained by enterprises comes from data subjects; while in terms of data circulation and data use, enterprises do not only collect data but also process and use the data. Corporate data is taken as assets or commodity, and it is only normal for enterprises to collect, store, analyze and sell data. Large-scale data collection and processing has become part of the core competitiveness of Internet enterprises. These enterprises often take collected data as a core part of their assets. Therefore, what enterprises emphasize is the freedom of data use, and the fact that the data collected and sorted by them cannot be used by others without their consent. "As data subjects, enterprises claim absolute ownership over data relevant to their production and operation, and asset right for the data they collected and sorted."[10]

10 Enterprise data property right is the right of enterprises to control, dispose and benefit from relevant data, including right to control, right to payment, right to modification, right to integrity, and right to request judicial relief, etc. See Wang Yuan, Huang Daoli & Yang Songru. 2017. "Research on the Nature and Ownership of Data Rights." *Scientific Management Research*, 5th issue.

Some scholars believe that as data turns into assets, based on the needs of data operation and driven by interests, we should acknowledge data enterprises' right to data operation and data asset rights. In particular, the right to data operation is in a sense exclusive. It is for specific matters and has its excludability, which is established by way of legal authorization or administrative licensing. Data asset rights are an absolute kind of rights endowed by law on the interest from data operators' data asset management (Long Weiqiu 2017). However, "enterprises' data interests are essentially a kind of right to control and dominate data, which, with excludability, is a kind of control right weaker than ownership but stronger than relative rights" (Li Xiaoyu 2019). Enterprises' right to control data has positive and negative functions. The positive part allows enterprises to directly process, collect, use and trade their data without intervention from other parties; while the negative part enables enterprises to exclude other parties and guard against improper intervention, which constitutes *erga omnes* effects.

In cases of disputes related to data rights, there are court verdicts that distinguish between rights and interests. For example, in *Taobao v. Meijing* concerning some big data products,[11] Taobao claimed that it held the data asset right over "the derivative data formed with certain algorithms, anonymous desensitization, filtering and refining and that the Gugu Mutual Aid Platform developed by Meijing using some technologies obtained the derivative data of Taobao and used it for commercial purposes. Taobao believed that Meijing's conducts constituted unfair competition and infringed on its data asset rights. On the one hand, the court acknowledged that Taobao had competitive property rights and interests over the derivative data formed by collecting, desensitizing, refining and integrating original data; while on the other hand, it denied Taobao's property rights over the original data and derivative data. However, the court did not give a direct response as to what the competitive property rights and interests over corporate derivative data were.

11 See Hangzhou Railway Transportation Court (2017) Zhe 8601 Civil Judgment No. 4034.

New ways to protect rights to corporate data

Existing judicial decisions mainly deal with the protection of corporate data according to the *Law of the People's Republic of China against Unfair Competition*. However, corporate data protection is emerging as a new issue with significance beyond that, and new laws are needed to tackle this issue in a timely manner. "From the perspective of private law, it is inevitable that we shift from applying traditional laws to making new ones for corporate data protection" (Long Weiqiu 2018). However, some scholars believe that "in terms of their legal nature, the rights and interests over corporate data are neither real rights, nor merely intellectual property rights or property rights. It is a bundle of rights, including statutory rights and interests protected by law" (Li Yang & Li Xiaoyu 2019). With new technologies of the era of big data, laws on corporate data and information must shift their focus from the controllability of data to a balance between controllability reasonable flow and use of data and the prevention of abuse. It is obvious that the traditional criminal law, which is made from the perspective of secrets (including state secrets and trade secrets) or intellectual property rights, needs to be expanded (Tang Jiyao 2019). Therefore, it is advisable to explore the legal protection of corporate data from the perspective of law-based interests protection, that is, from the perspective of new types of rights, before existing corporate data can be protected by statutory rights. Some scholar also proposes that "corporate data interests should be protected by taking the right to control corporate data as a new type of rights" (Li Xiaoyu 2019). Corporate data cannot rely on possession in physical forms for protection, and rights to corporate data should be justified by endowing exclusive rights over data on the enterprise concerned by law. In terms of the effectiveness of possession, due to the constraints from rights to personal data, enterprises do not have complete control over the data they collect and possess, and individuals have the right to delete, correct and withdraw their data. In terms of legal system and norms, it is necessary to restrict and regulate rights to corporate data, especially in regard to data collection, processing and use by relevant enterprises. In practice, both the application of data technologies and the means of competition in cyberspace are constantly changing, and the corresponding interest distribution among data operators, Internet users and the general public is also in a dynamic process of balance and rebalancing.

Rights to government data

Government data

Data is an important kind of asset of the government, an important means of government administration, and a representation of what government administration has achieved. The agglomeration of data on the block can form internal correlations and reveal a wide range of public needs and public concerns. This contains great value and potential. These data profoundly change the notion, paradigm, content and means of government administration, transforms the traditional governance model where authority is maintained by information control and monopoly, and truly establishes a new model that is based fully on data, promoting the development of digital government.

Generally speaking, government data includes all kinds of data resources that are made, obtained, recorded and preserved in a certain form by the government and administrative institutions affiliated to them in the process of performing their duties according to law (Shi Dan 2018). Specifically, each department of the government holds a large number of raw data that constitutes the foundation of our society, including meteorological data, road traffic data, power data, judicial data, customs data, entry and exit data, and more. Government data is only part of the massive big data resources. It refers in particular to the big data accumulated by government departments in the process of data collection, IT system building and handling all kinds of affairs over the years. Government data is closely related to the national economy and people's life. If this part of data is put into effective use, users are likely to develop innovative applications, provide better services, create more value, promote economic growth and facilitate the shift of economic growth model on the whole.

At the Fourth Plenary Session of the 19th CPC Central Committee, it was proposed that it is necessary to establish and improve systems and rules of administration by making good use of the Internet, big data, artificial intelligence and other technologies; promote the building of a digital government, strengthen the orderly sharing of data, and protect personal information in accordance with the law. Different from personal data and corporate data, government data should remain public goods, since the government is the holder of public power, rather than a market player. It should be said that except the data that should be kept confidential according to relevant laws and regulations, government data should all be shared with the general public and treated as open data available to data professionals. At present, the State Council of the People's Republic of China is building a national integrated big data center, promoting technological integration, business integration and data integration, and realizing cross-level, cross-region, cross-system, cross-department and cross-business management and service delivery. Local governments are also working to pool and share government data, and many of them have explicitly expressed support for data purchase from society.

System of rights to government data

The government is the one who manages government data, or even the first to obtain this data to some extent. Here, the government is the most important subject of government data. Government data can not only provide basis for administrative institutions to make well-informed decisions, but also be used as a kind of resources that can be repeatedly copied and disseminated. Unlike the abstract concept of "data" which is difficult to define, government data at least has a reduced scope since there is a specific data subject, and the nature of rights to government data can be inferred according to the different occasions where such data is shared. Open access to and sharing of government data is an important basis for the development of big data, and is becoming a general trend of our times. However, open access to and sharing of government data should be carried out according to law.

If administrative institutions are the providers of government data, at least one thing is for sure: These institutions have a certain degree of control over the data they provide. Here comes the right to possess and the right to use. On the one hand, as the users of government data, administrative institutions have the right to fully develop and use the data they possess; and on the other hand, they have the right to use the government data provided by other government departments with additional restrictions, which mainly refer to restrictions on the processing, use, transfer and sharing of government data that does not belong to the department that do these. First, this data can be used only for the performance of administrative duties, and data transaction and data exchange for commercial interests should be prohibited. Second, it can happen only within the scope of departments who share data with one another, and departments that do not participate in such data sharing should not be included (Zhang Yanan 2019). According to the special features of government data sharing, the right to possess and the right to use that are derived from the existing theoretical basis of real rights can reduce the constraints imposed by ownership on government data sharing to a certain extent.

However, as a new type of data rights, rights to government data not only include the right to possess and the right to use government data, there are many other rights to be developed within this category. Some scholar has proposed that "the government exercises the right to manage big data on behalf of the state, which is manifested in the right of access to data, the right to control data, and the right to plan data development and grant permission to use data" (Lv Tingjun 2017). For the purpose of state security and social public interests, the government has the right to obtain political, economic, cultural, social and ecological data through certain technical means. The power to obtain data resources for free or with compensations paid is part of the government's administration power which is governed by administrative law.[12] Therefore, in the face of legal system reform in response to the development of big data resources and technology, we should

12 Data control power is the normalization power of data management power, which refers to the government's control and daily management of the acquired big data, including the management and control behaviors such as classification, sorting, storage and protection of big data according to the procedures. Data development planning power is the government's overall arrangement for the development of big data, including the formulation of big data policies, future stage development plans and coordination of big data development subjects. The licensing power of data is one of the core powers of government data management. The licensing power of big data is not only related to state security and public interests, but also related to the rights of enterprises, social organizations and citizens. Therefore, the licensing power of big

establish as soon as possible a new legal system that encompasses multiple power and right systems with the rights to data at the core.

Open government data and its governance

Although there is not yet any consensus on the rights to data in the world, the value of data as a kind of resource can never be denied. Because government data is shared by and among administrative institutions only for performing duties according to law, and what administrative institutions can do with their data is no more than offer it for sharing or using what is shared, the sharing of government data that flows among government departments is practically feasible (Zhang Yanan 2019). Government data is the most massive, important and core component of our data resources, and has high potential for added value. However, due to the government's unwillingness or difficulty to offer access to its data to society, a large amount of high-value data cannot be effectively used. "From the perspective of the relationship between public rights and private rights, the rights to data are fundamental rights of citizens. Citizens have the right to know the data controlled by the government and the government has the obligation to share government data with citizens" (Lv Tingjun 2017).

Open government data is part of the open data efforts. It means that the government grants access to the data it generates, collects and possesses, which has clear ownership, after permission is secured for knowledge sharing, and allows such data to be shared, disseminated and modified, or even used commercially (Chen Shanglong 2019). In recent years, many countries have made active efforts to formulate open government data policies, gradually establish and improve relevant legal systems, and guide and regulate activities related to open government data. Open government data is an objective requirement as the public's demand for government data resources upgrades from the demand to know to the demand to use in the era of big data. However, to facilitate data use for value creation, it is necessary that we reshape the relationship between the government

data has become the focus of social attention and the core content of legal system creation. See Lv Tingjun. 2017. "Data Rights System and Its Legal Significance." *Journal of the Party School of the CPC Central Committee*, 5th issue.

and the general public, fully consider the ownership and distribution of benefits from government data assets, constantly improve the mechanisms related to the right to possess, the right to use and the right to earn from government data; strengthen the cost control for government data governance, and give full consideration to the sustainability of data governance.

As we are making progress in the implementation of the national big data strategy, a sound policy and regulation system should be established concerning open government data and government data sharing. Specifically, the policy system should comprise the infrastructure layer, the data management layer, and the governance layer" (Huang Ruhua, Wen Fangfang & Huang Wen 2018). Specifically, it is necessary to further consider how to curb the power inequality in data development and use among different stakeholders such as the government, enterprises, society and hackers, and clearly define the functions and duties, activities, tasks of different parties, so as to achieve a balance between the economic and social value of government data and the maximization of the value of personal data (Xia Yikun 2018). At the same time, we need to promote the overall development and strengthen top-level design of government data governance from a global perspective, establish a cross-regional, cross-departmental and cross-system open data system, and form a new pattern of data governance with interactions between multiple parties including the government and society. It is not enough to merely emphasize that government data is assets. We also need to reshape or build a value system of government data, and explore ways towards good data governance from the perspectives of theory, system and methodology.

Confrontation within the Scope of the Rights to Data

In the era of big data, the connotation and denotation of right and power have both changed dramatically. Private rights and public power over data are usually in a state of confrontation, competition and check-balance in cyberspace. According to the overall structure of data related rights, individuals and enterprises have different pursuits out of their respective interests and what lie behind this are competitions between personal interests and data use by enterprises. Moreover, it is also a game between individuals and the government, and between different enterprises for control over data. The transfer of data rights and the decline of data power are the trend of the development of rights to data as is required by both the differences between individuals and by sharing in and between groups. Therefore, it will be possible for us to make the most out of big data only when the existing stable rights structure is adjusted, and the data rights and interests of individuals, enterprises and the government are balanced and coordinated after the list of data-related rights is expanded and refined.

Transfer of private data rights

Data rights and private rights

Personal data comes from personal behaviors, so rights to this data belongs to the individual who provides and possesses it. Personal possession is the precondition and ground of legitimacy of the private rights system. Private rights are a kind of personal rights, possessed by individuals and related to private interests. Some data is exclusively possessed by some individual and that means it contains private rights. The characteristics of data determine that data-related rights are private rights in multiple dimensions, especially personality and property. Rights to data are a combination of personality rights and property rights. These two kinds of rights coexist and are inseparable, breaking through the boundary of traditional civil rights and establishing the rights to data as a new kind of civil rights. Civil law in the traditional sense, thus, cannot be used to regulate rights to data, and it is necessary to establish a new rights protection system. Both data personality rights and data asset rights hold economic value, so our analysis here aims to find out whether it is better to protect rights to data as personality rights or as asset rights.

Diffusion of data rights

Although data rights have not been an established concept until quite recently in the era of big data, the notion behind this concept has actually existed for a long time. Data in traditional sense, such as personal information, personal privacy, knowledge patterns, and trade secrets, have been incorporated in the scope of civil rights in many countries. We propose data rights as both an extension from this and a new kind of rights. This is because the scope of objects of data rights now is much larger. It covers not only specific personal information and knowledge patterns but also countless other kinds of data. To make use of and explore such data with relevant technologies is the core of the big data era, and the rights that arise therefrom have gone beyond the scope of the traditional civil rights. As people grow more aware of and concerned about data protection, data rights are more and more widely accepted. However, unlike the development of private rights in the past, the development of data rights clearly takes the form of diffusion. First, such diffusion is seen in the expanded scope of objects. The objects of data rights included previously only several items such as knowledge, secrets and privacy, but now the coverage is all kinds of data. Moreover, data itself is also going beyond the traditional forms of electronic data to all forms of records, which makes data rights ubiquitous. Second, this diffusion also happens to the subjects of data rights in both quantity and types. The types of subjects of data rights have expanded from natural persons to legal persons and non-legal person organizations. In terms of quantity, all owners of data have their claims. With further progress made in the field of big data, more and more subjects will voice their claims. Third, diffusion occurs to the way people exercise their data rights. With the rapid growth of the total volume of data and clarification of its status as a kind of resource, the space for people to exercise their data rights will grow, and data rights will be used much more frequently.

Sharing of data rights

Individuals are the producers of data, the government owns the largest amount of data, and enterprises are the main force that promotes the development and application of data. Driven by data interests, enterprises put in large quantities of capital and human resources to develop and improve data technology, create new methods for data production, collection and analysis, seek improvements in various data activities, and straighten out various data relationships, so as to achieve prosperity and economic efficiency in relation to data. From traditional information protection to what is provided for in the *General Data Protection Regulation*, the protection of private rights to data has become much stronger, However, such protection, weak or strong, is not conducive to the development of big data and will likely lead to imbalance in the distribution of data rights. In order to achieve balance, in addition to keeping public data power checked, ensuring appropriate transfer of private rights to data is particularly important. If personal data is protected strictly without differentiation, there may be two adverse results: First, the development of big data depends heavily on a good overall data environment, in which smooth and active data flow is a central element. However, excessively strict protection of personal data will seriously impede data flow, hampering big data development to a large extent. For example, the *General Data Protection Regulation*, as the most stringent data protection law ever, may cause huge GDP loss.[13] Second, big data contains great value. Faced with huge interests, too strict protection will increase the risk of data-related crimes, which makes personal data protection fall into a dilemma where more stringent protection brings more risks while looser control brings chaos.

Data shows the characteristics of non-excludability, non-expendability, and replicability. It should not be turned into a scare resource because of protection. Instead, it should remain universally available, common, convenient, and renewable in use.[14] The essence of the transfer of private rights to data is to eliminate barriers to data flow as much as possible, promote

13 The *General Data Protection Regulation* is very stringent in the protection of personal data. For technology and finance industry, the implementation of the regulation will further aggravate the difficulty in personal access to credit. According to the estimation of Deloitte Touche Tohmatsu Limited, the regulation will reduce the consumption credit in the EU by 19 percent and lead to an annual loss of 83 billion euros in the GDP and unemployment of 1.4 million people.

14 Renewable resources in use refer to those resources that will not be consumed when used. Example include data, technology, and knowledge.

smooth data circulation, and thus maximize the value of data. Sharing lies between free transfer and restriction. Data sharing represents a basic value in the era of big data. The sharing of data rights is not only what is required for data development, but also an important way to achieve balance in relation to data rights.

If we regard data as a kind of resource, maximizing the use of data as a typical kind of renewable resource is the essential requirement, and sharing is the best way to achieve this. From the perspective of rights, sharing and possession are the essential difference between data rights and real rights. When the right to use a property is transferred, the existence of the right to possess protects the interests of the property owner, ensuring that he/she still has control over the property. By contrast, once the right to use data is transferred, the party who obtains the right to use will possess the data completely, and the data will get out of the control of the one who has transferred it out. At this time, the right to possess the data itself will be meaningless. Data rights break through the limitations of one ownership for one object and the principle that things must be tangible. This is often manifested in the multi-ownership of data. To emphasize the rights to share in the realm of data rights is just like emphasizing the right to possess in the realm of real rights. It is an essential requirement as we are moving from making the best use of property to making the best use of data (Key Laboratory of Big Data Strategy 2019, p. 266).

Restrictions on public data power

Data rights as public data power

Data power is in nature a kind of public power. In terms of the consequences that may arise from data power, though the virtual world, as a mirror world of the real world, serves as a new space and new ways of realization for public power, public power, while enjoying the convenience brought by the cyberspace and relevant technologies, must face the threats of malicious attacks, dark power, and other factors in the cyber world. Fear abounds. Highly integrated, the cyberspace and the physical world have formed a pattern of mutual independence and mutual influence between them. The exercise of data power will affect the public interests protected by law. From an economic perspective, big data constitutes a kind of "quasi-public goods" with both public and private natures in legal terms. It is a kind of private right in the first place, but since the exercise of such rights will affect public interests, so it has the characteristics of pubic power too. As a kind of private rights, data rights need to be governed by law. Individuals cannot monopolize data or sacrifice public interests in order to protect personal data. If there is no balance between private and public interests, private interests will be the only pursuit of society, and data rights system will become an obstacle to the development of the big data industry. In China's socialist legal system, both public and private rights are governed and protected by law. Protecting the rights to personal data is only one of our purposes, and what is more important is the protection of public interests and the maximization of the value of data.[15] "The proposition of the rights to data is in line with deontonic principles, that is, citizens shall claim their data rights as a kind of remedy, precaution or guard against possible infringements on their private rights from public power and other enormous data controllers" (Liu Jiangang 2016).

Expansion of data power

Public power is naturally compulsory and expansive, so it is necessary to keep it checked. In the era of big data, the lack of a data rights system and the expansion of public power may lead to the abuse of data public power, which can cause infringement on private data rights to varying degrees. It is mainly reflected in the following two aspects:

15 When analyzing the phased achievements of *Internet Economic Governance Manual*, Professor Xue Zhaofeng, an economist, holds that the governance rules will move towards a balance point, which is the maximization of the value of data assets. Whoever can use the data well is more likely to own it. The governance rules that can maximize the potential value of data assets and the property rights defining principle that can give full play to data assets are good and stable rules that can be abided by everyone and survive well.

First, public power may be exercised for private interests. The vague boundary between the rights and power of the multiple parties engaged in governance makes it possible for public power and private rights to interfere each other to a certain extent. Technically, citizens can enjoy the freedom to exercise their private data rights only when they are subject to the regulation of data public power. However, in reality, public power tends to be exercised for private interests in some cases, which affects the security of private data rights. There are two forms of this: One is the abuse of data public power, which means data use in violation of set rules and procedures, resulting in infringements on citizens' freedom to exercise their private rights. The other is rent-seeking and rent-setting on some platforms, which also infringes on the private data rights of citizens.

Second, the focus of power is tilted. In the physical world, public power is always superior to private rights. Public power, which is naturally expansive, tends to erode the space of private rights. The same is true in cyberspace. Holders of data power tend to enjoy comparative advantages in resources, most of which are big data or big data-related resources. Thus, data reshapes the modern power structure in capital use, and the exercise of data power changes the position of power subjects in the market. Weak entities in the big data market tend to be deprived of their power, and new capital power holders come into being. At the same time, the enhancement of data power will boost the ability of power holders to control and monopolize the market (Tong Linjie & Guo Chengcheng 2019). The development of modern information technology has increased the information asymmetry between the government, enterprises and the general public, seriously tilting the balance towards those who hold public power in their hands (Zheng Ge 2016).

The boundary between public power and private rights is being redefined, and the space of private rights against public power is being reduced. Data power is absolutely insulated and virtual in nature, and there are data risks and blind spots in the exercise of power, which is likely to cause social anomie and political disorder in dealing with the interest relationship between different parties (Lin Qifu & He Jingchao 2016). The appropriate expansion of data power is an important condition for the rapid development of big data in the early stage, but its unrestricted expansion will inevitably lead to the shrinking of or infringement on data rights. Only by striking and maintaining a general balance between data rights and data power, can we build more trust for the rapid development of big data (He Dingding 2018).

Decline of data power

Data power and data rights are twins. In the traditional legal framework of rights against power, self-control over personal information is used to prevent the abuse of government power and infringement on personal privacy (Wang Xiuzhe 2018). Along with the rapid growth of data rights, the formation of data power is also accelerating: On the one hand, the growing demands for data rights brought by the development of big data require the development of data power which serves as the legal basis and practical guarantee of data rights since data rights can never exist without state power. On the other hand, it is a priority for the government to ensure the development of big data within its control and to keep the use of data rights within a reasonable range and in appropriate ways.

In the process of the development of big data, if data power is not regulated, there will be inaction, inappropriate actions and excessive intervention. Thus, the effective implementation of data power will be seriously hampered and undermined, and the protection of data rights will be impossible, which is harmful to both the development of big data and social stability on the whole. Only by regulating public power in relation to data and preventing the abuse of such public power, will we be able to effectively protect private data rights. However, regulating data public power does not mean undermining the authority of it. This should be done on the basis of sound relevant rules and procedures.

In the long run, the expansion of data power is inevitable, so is the decline of data power. The value of data does not lie in being large in quantity but in being in wide use. Today, as data activities are growing rapidly, although data power is on the rise, it will inevitably turn and decline at a certain point. This is because in the early stage of big data development, strong data power is needed as administrative support and legal support to provide sufficient driving force for the development in a short time.

However, with the maturity of the big data industry, the existence of some kind of data power has become an obstacle to further development and data rights claims also require the retreat of data power to make more room for further development. This will bring about the decline of data power. Yet a retreat or decline is not extinction. It is the transfer of power with the ultimate goal of ensuring data security, including state security and privacy protection. This transfer of power is determined by the fact that data is naturally inclined to flow freely. It is the basis of making the most out of data, and plays an extremely important role in the future development of our society.

Public power in the realm of private data rights

Public power in the realm of private data rights

It was jurists in ancient Rome who first divided law into public law and private law. Domitius Ulpianus,[16] according to the purpose of law, regards the law for protecting national interests and public interests as public law and the law for protecting private interests as private law. At present, most jurists in civil law countries agree with the theory of relations adjustment, which holds that "private law is the law regulating the relationships between equal subjects in civil life, while public law is the law regulating relationship between state organs and between the state and its citizens in political life. In this vein, the law regulating the civil relations between the state and its citizens also falls into the category of private law. In China, the most typical public law is the criminal law and the administrative law, while the civil law falls into the category of private law. In the theory of relations adjustment, there is a clear boundary between the public law and the private law" (Chen Hongzhi 2018).

16 He created the system of "public law" and "private law" in jurisprudence and advocated the system of protecting slave owners' private property, which has a significant impact on the later capitalist jurisprudence. His representative works include *Ad Edictum*, *Libri ad Sabinum* and *De omnibus tribunalibus*.

When elements of the public law appear in the realm of private rights, it means public power is involved, for some reason, in fields of private rights which govern relations between equal subjects, and public power, thus, intervenes in the autonomous behaviors of exercising private rights to a certain extent (Wang Chunye 2008).

With the advancement of digitalization, conflicts related to personal data rights occur more frequently, and the frequency of public power intervention is also increasing. Firstly, due to the existence of data gap and data monopoly, when extreme unfairness results from the unequal status of private rights holders and their autonomy, in order to protect the rights of vulnerable groups and curb the abuse of monopoly power by the very few powerful parties, public law incorporates some elements that originally belong to the field of private rights, so that public power can step in according to law when necessary. This is how public power gets into the realm of private rights. Secondly, because private data rights can be regarded as a kind of property rights in nature, when the infringement on private data rights obviously damages public interests, it can be put in the category of civil private rights. Private rights are civil rights, and in the realm of civil rights, parties are equal even if state organs become one party in it, and the will of civil subjects shall be fully respected in dealing with anything related to civil rights, private data rights included.

As a new type of civil rights, personal data rights have more to do with the protection of interests, defending against infringement on data rights, and allowing data rights to directly play their legal roles. The recognition of data rights in the field of private law should be closely related to remedies in case of infringement and data rights need to be jointly protected by both private law and public law (Lv Zhixiang & Zhang Qiang 2019). When public power is involved in the protection of private data rights, the principle of autonomy in private law is undermined to some extent, but it has no influence on the essence of civil law and private rights. This is because in such cases, the emphasis is on both the state's intervention in the data rights system and the establishment of a balancing mechanism between personal interests and public interests of society. It will never change the nature of data rights.

Tendency of public power intervention

Today, as the intervention of public power in the protection of data rights is increasing, various kinds of infringements not only hamper the rights of data rights holders and dampen the vitality of enterprises, but also seriously damage public interests. The protection of data rights should focus on individuals so as to safeguard citizens' rights to personal data and their processing activities. However, stipulations on personal data rights are not enough because stipulation may not be fully enforced in reality. In addition, the big gap in the data processing capacity between different parties related to personal data will produce imbalance with one party enjoying huge advantages, making it easy for this party to grab interests that should belong to another party. Therefore, the government, with its public power, becomes the one to balance between personal data protection and the development of the big data industry. It needs to ensure data security on the one hand, and invigorate data development and promote the healthy development of the data economy on the other. This is the only way towards use of data by the people and for the people.

"Faced with threats from the state to personal information rights, civil law alone cannot provide sufficient protection. It is necessary to regulate public power based on the principles of legal reservation, due process and proportion" (Zhang Xinbao 2018). For example, both the *Passport Law of the People's Republic of China* and *Law of the People's Republic of China on Resident Identity Cards* stipulate the protection of collected personal information. Up to now, there is no dedicated personal data protection law in China. Although there are more than 70 laws and regulations concerning the protection of personal data, they all give relief through *ex post* punishment, without *ex ante* protection. Personal data is generally protected indirectly through the protection of personal privacy, human dignity and other things related to personal data.

In this context, the mutual penetration and integration of public law and private law has become an important trend in the development of data rights protection. On the one hand, "the field of private rights is constantly invaded by public law to make up for the insufficiency of the traditional regulation of private law, which leads public law into the field of private rights" (Wang Chunye 2018). On the other hand, the state adopts the traditional approach of public law and introduces a large number of private law systems and notions, so as to better realize the purpose of public law, which also pushes public law into the field of private rights. Generally speaking, personal data should be regulated as public goods. The use of personal data should be governed by dedicated government agencies. Governance, in itself, should fall in the realm of public law rather than private law. The purpose of governance is to promote the free sharing of personal data for the sake of public interests and public security (Wu Weiguang 2016).

Value of public power intervention in our times

From the perspective of civil law, any right that is protected should be personal right or property right in nature. As marks of personal behaviors, data is undoubtedly something personal in nature and data rights are traditionally regarded as a kind of right to privacy which is to be protected strictly.[17] In the big data era, the property nature of personal data is getting more conspicuous. In the face of a crisis where data rights are more likely to be infringed on, protection can be effective only if we can put in place sound relief mechanisms. If a data subject believes that his/her legitimate rights and interests have been infringed on, or that the administrative acts of an administrative institution are in violation of the law, he/she has the right to file a request for review or lodge an administrative lawsuit with relevant organs. The illegal or improper acts of administrative institutions should be revoked or confirmed to be in violation of the law, and as to those acts that result in infringement on the legitimate rights and interests of citizens, compensation should be made. As an important way to settle administrative disputes, administrative litigation will play a more important role in the future. In the judicial practice in China, infringements on personal data rights of citizens does not fall in the scope of administrative law. In view of the practical needs, it is therefore necessary to

17 *The Tort Law of the People's Republic of China* incorporates the right to privacy in its protected civil rights and interests. *The Decision of the Standing Committee of the National People's Congress on Strengthening Cyber Information Protection* states that no organization or individual shall steal or obtain citizens' personal digital information by any unlawful means, or sell or provide citizens' personal digital information to others unlawfully.

expand the scope to cover such cases so that administrative disputes related to data rights can be settled in this way, and the legitimate rights and interests of citizens can be better protected. It should be noted that although public power intervention in the field of private data rights helps to protect vulnerable groups and safeguard public interests, it is also an important cause of abuse of public power. Therefore, in order to reduce the negative impact, it is necessary to restrict public power and prevent the abuse of public power.

Protection of Rights to Data

The allocation of data resources and the social problems thus caused should be dealt with first with technology, but existing technologies seem to be unable to provide effective solutions. At this time, it is necessary to seek solutions through legislation (Wen Yuheng 2019). However, the lack of the specificity and independence of data objects and the diversity and scattered distribution of data subjects make the rights to data difficult to justify. In addition, the high cost of defining data rights and the many difficulties that may materialize once the rights to data are established all make it difficult for us to erect rights to data as an independent kind of rights. In practice, the complicated disputes over data rights desperately need to be settled by law, and data rights and interests urgently need to be protected by legislation Therefore, a perfect solution here is technological governance plus efforts to improve ethics and legislation.

Technology-based governance of rights to data

Technology-based governance of rights to data

Technology offers effective protection to data security. On the one hand, it is necessary for the state and enterprises to put funds into the R&D

and innovation efforts so as to constantly improve cybersecurity systems and equipment and ensure data security with advanced technology. On the other hand, it is also necessary to borrow methods and models from various other fields and transform smoothly from the traditional model of technology-based data security protection to the modern model. Of course, data is governed by codes or technical rules, and it exists in and is transferred across computer terminals or storage media. Therefore, technologies are needed to prevent stealing data.[18] Some scholars even believe that "data is not an object of civil rights, so there is no such thing as rights to data, and data can only be governed by code rules. The protection of data should be realized by technological rather than legal means" (Mei Xiaying 2016).

The security of mass data storage is the premise of realizing the use value of big data. When data is stored in a user terminal, protection should change from traditional passive protection to active counterattack. Traditionally, ownership is confirmed by requiring the submission of ownership certificate for expert review, but it lacks technical credibility, and there are potential uncontrollable factors such as tampering. In order to solve these problems, there is an urgent need for an ownership confirmation scheme that is highly operable. To guard against risks such as data leakage and abuse we may draw reference from anti-missile systems. We may conduct timely security analysis to detect suspicious events and stop anything that is identified as dangerous, so as to realize progressive protection of data. Technology-based governance is different from state-centered law-based governance, and it can even impose some constraints on law-based governance on some occasions.

18 For example, in the case of unfair competition disputes concerning Beijing Baidu Netcom Science & Technology Co., Ltd. and Shanghai Jietu Software Technology Co., Ltd., the defendant Beijing Baidu Netcom Science & Technology Co., Ltd. obtained the data of online users' comments in public comment network operated by the plaintiff Shanghai Hantao Information Consulting Co., Ltd. through crawler technology, and used it on its web services such as Baidu Map and Baidu Know (<https://zhidao.baidu.com/>). See Shanghai Intellectual Property Rights Court (2016) Hu 73 Minzhong Civil Judgment No. 242.

Blockchain technology provides a new option for data rights protection. Blockchain technology, also known as distributed ledger technology, is a series of data blocks generated in encrypted ways. It is a new application of computer technology such as distributed data storage, point-to-point transmission, consensus mechanism, and encryption algorithm (He Pu, Yu Ge, Zhang Yanfeng & BaoYubin 2017). Firstly, the audit center and watermark center are introduced to separate the responsibility of big data integrity audit and watermark generation. Secondly, lightweight audit of big data integrity is realized based on data holding proof technology and sampling technology. Thirdly, the digital watermark technology is used to confirm the origin of big data. Lastly, in view of the integrity and consistency of the evidence involved in the whole process of right confirmation, the strong consistency between right confirmation result and the relevant evidence can be achieved by using the original characteristics of blockchain. Therefore, blockchain technology can be used to meet data security requirements such as integrity, restrictability and auditability of data and solve the most basic trust problem of data sharing.

Regulation by code technology

In the era of big data, law-based regulation should depart from the traditional way of forced intervention, and take more technology-based strategies and measures, so that law-based regulation can be transformed into law–technology regulation. With the integration, substantiation and intelligent development of the Internet, the software and hardware that create the cyberspace control and regulate the cyberspace more and more. "Code is law" (Lawrence Lessig 2009, p. 6). As far as intellectual property rights, privacy and freedom of speech are concerned, standard setting and code writing are new forms of regulation and control. The generation, translation, transmission and storage of data all depend on codes. Data is naturally controlled by codes and is not subject to any human intervention independent of codes. Codes can create a set of technological rules, and people can use codes to control human behaviors (Zheng Zhihang 2018). Therefore, the design of rights structure or benefit distribution related to data order can be realized through appropriate coding.

In cyberspace, the law cannot directly interfere with data operation, and the explicit agreement in contracts is far less effective than the automatic adjustment of the code framework. "As data and algorithms become important factors of production, a large number of production and life relationships will be created and maintained by code" (Ma Changshan 2018). In particular, we should respect emerging rights and legal interest claims in the process of legal reform, as they are reflections of the code of conduct and new legal relations in an era when both the virtual and the real worlds are dominated by algorithms and when man and machine are coming together. We should incorporate technological elements in our legal concepts and mechanisms, and explore ways to shift our institutional arrangements from a binary system to an integrated, so as to shape a new legal order in the era of digital civilization. Of course, this is not to abandon existing legislations or to replace them with anything else, but to inherit and develop them. In fact, code is not completely uncontrollable. Instead, codes are written and modified by people, and people's actions are subject to laws. Thus, there is a bridge between codes and laws, that is, they influence each other indirectly through the chain of law – human behavior – code – data (Zhang Yang 2016). Therefore, in the face of disputes caused by data (such as differences in data transmission routes, poor data confidentiality, and difficulties in translating data codes), first of all, it is necessary to respect the technological rules and use code to maintain data order. When the problem lies with the codes, data rights disputes can be solved through regulating the human behavior of coding in accordance with laws.

Regulation of algorithm power

Data carries information and social interests. Because the computing power required to process the massive data we now have access to goes far beyond what man can do manually, when it comes to allocation of social resources manual work has to give way to algorithms. Our traditional legal system tends to pay more attention to data protection but ignore the regulation of algorithms. Now, in the era of artificial intelligence, data production and circulation occur in ways vastly different from before, and data use brings about huge risks in addition to huge value. Power is an important concept in sociology and philosophy. Anyone who possesses enough resources to dominate or exert influence on others can be deemed as having power (Jurgen Habermas 1999, p. 76). As a force to conquer and transform the nature, technology has no value orientation or power in itself (Liu Yongmou 2012).

However, "if technology can directly affect and control human interests, it will lose its purity and have power in it" (Mei Xiaying & Yang Xiaona 2017). Therefore, the force of resource allocation that algorithm holds forms a kind of technology-based power in fact, which can be called algorithm power.[19] Algorithm power can mobilize data, affect human behaviors and allocate public power resources, and this makes it totally different from any other forms of power.

"Both commercial platforms and the public sector seek to expand the scope of their power by making use of algorithm power, and this results in new models of knowledge production and governance. Because of this, the traditional data protection approach does not work anymore, the principle of informed consent in personal data protection has been basically ineffective, and the standard about what qualifies as sensitive personal data is rendered almost meaningless by algorithms" (Zhang Linghan 2019). Therefore, algorithm plus data produces knowledge, generates profits and controls human behaviors, but it also brings the risk of the alienation of algorithm power.

Algorithm power is embedded into the operation of public power at different levels, and it even becomes an independent decision maker in some cases. "From the perspective of power control, the right to interpret algorithm basically follows the logic of power control – restricting power by rights" (Zhang Endian 2019). The *General Data Protection Regulation* of the European Union approaches algorithm power regulation by improving the transparency of algorithm and enhancing the accountability of algorithm-based decision-making by granting interpretation rights. Algorithm power, as it crosses various different fields and is highly isolated, can exert great influence on our economy and politics, free from the constraints of the

19 Algorithm power refers to a new kind of power obtained by some commercial organizations and public sector organization with big data algorithms.

existing legal systems thanks to the "veil" of technology. This further enhances algorithm power indirectly. Therefore, it is necessary to adjust our approach of regulation in the traditional legal systems in a timely manner to keep algorithm power checked, limit the application scope of algorithms, establish due processes and accountability mechanisms, and grant personal data rights and right relief measures to resist infringement from algorithm power.

Ethical regulation of rights to data

Ethical culture and privacy protection

Generally speaking, privacy refers to the private field that has nothing to do with public interests and in which the interference of others is unwelcome or unacceptable.[20] As Confucius put it, "Look not at what is contrary to propriety; listen not to what is contrary to propriety; speak not what is contrary to propriety; make no movement to what is contrary to propriety." Propriety here means etiquettes and rites. One should refrain from doing what is contrary to propriety and from deliberately inquiring about other people's secrets. One should do

20 According to the World Privacy Organization, the concept of privacy is combined with data protection, that is, with the management of personal information. Of all categories of human rights, privacy may be the most difficult to define. The definition of privacy has changed a lot because of different backgrounds and environments. The right to privacy can be divided into four independent but interrelated categories: information privacy, physical privacy, correspondence privacy, and regional privacy. Among them, information privacy covers the relevant systems regulating the collection and disposal of personal data, such as credit information and medical information. As the manager and service provider for society, the government is the biggest consumer of citizens' personal information. There is no doubt that citizens have an absolute right to their personal information. Government agencies cannot enjoy the right to control citizens' personal information simply because they possess the information. They should be restricted and supervised by citizens. Personal information and the right to privacy ultimately reflect the protection of human rights, which has the legitimacy and inevitability of legislative protection in legal theory, and the legal status of which cannot be shaken.

things in line with propriety, and respect others' privacy. This is the traditional doctrine on privacy in Confucianism. It can be said that propriety is a central concept in traditional Chinese culture and runs through the whole ancient Chinese society. The mutual penetration and integration of propriety and law have endowed the traditional Chinese legal culture with clear ethical features. Confucian principles and norms in ancient China are the theoretical basis for the development of China's legal system, and "ethics thus form close combination with law and morality," which shows clear Chinese characteristics (Zhang Jinfan 2009, p. 113–129). In other words, the basis of ancient Chinese law is Confucian ethics. In fact, any country must consider its own values, the history of its legal system, and the development of its legal thoughts when making its own laws, including those on privacy protection. In the twentieth century, with the rapid development of science and technology, human society entered the information age, and people changed the way they communicate. This has made issues such as information security and privacy protection a focus of social attention. "One of the ethical bases of personal data protection is the protection of human dignity and the prevention of objectifying individuals through personal data informatization" (Guo Yu 2012, p. 83–84). The emergence and evolution of personality rights are closely related to the ethical culture. Everyone has dignity and purpose of the right to privacy is to safeguard human dignity, freedom and independence of personality. Ethical culture not only has an important impact on the system of data rights protection, but also plays a significant role in the judicial field in China. In the specific judicial practice, ethical standards are usually used to interpret laws when there is ambiguity or conflict, so as to make the judgments more in line with social moral standards. In the current era of big data, the government should establish and improve the legal system of personal privacy protection, so that there are laws to abide by in relevant cases. As the collectors of data, enterprises should use data according to law on the one hand, and improve their data security capability on the other hand. In addition, citizens should establish a correct view on privacy.

Moral self-regulation of industries

"Moral character is a habitual, stable, permanent and overall psychological state of a person in a long-term and a series of behaviors" (Wang Haiming 2009, p. 373). Good moral character is of great benefit to the development of human society, and bad moral character is harmful to society. The cultivation of good moral character is a long process. It is urgent to strengthen the cultivation of good morality of data stakeholders in the era of big data. In cyberspace where ethical regulation is relatively weak, big data technology is more likely to be widely applied. If moral self-regulation of data stakeholders is not strengthened, technology may be alienated and get out of control, and the consequences can be disastrous and beyond our imagination. It may even lead to the illusion that bad moral character has become what is normal in the era of big data, that is, once data stakeholders form stable bad moral character, good moral character will become abnormal and then there will be a huge risk of alienation of big data technology.

American scholar Richard A. Spinello proposed three principles of cyber ethical norms[21] and pointed out that "technology tends to develop faster than ethics, and the lag effect in this aspect will bring us considerable harm". "Compared with the legal provisions, self-regulation norms can establish an 'endogenous mechanism' to effectively reduce the cost of state regulation" (Lu Li 2003, p. 190–193). The *General Data Protection Regulation* of the European Union regards the industry to play a leading

21 The first is the principle of autonomy. Autonomy means that individuals have the ability to decide their own way of life. When this idea is combined with personal data, it means that data owners have the right to decide what their personal data can be applied to and what value can be achieved. The second is the principle of harmlessness. When using modern technology to process personal data and obtain corresponding value, it can not cause any damage to data owners, which is one of the approaches to protect personal data. The third is the principle of informed consent. "Consent" is the expression of people's subjective will, which requires data subjects to clearly understand the way and purpose of data processing, that is, based on the premise of being informed. See Richard A. Spinello. 1998. *Ethics of the Century: the Ethical Aspects of Information Technology*. Trans. Liu Gang. Beijing: Central Compilation and Translation Press.

role and the government needs only to impose moderate restriction. Or, to put in another way, at the macro level, the government regulates and formulates the basic framework and principles of personal data protection, while the market plays the basic role of self-management at the micro level. Different from the comprehensive legislation adopted by the European Union, the United States relies on industrial self-regulation to protect personal data in the private sphere. In the United States, in addition to specific federal legislations, state legislations and common laws in some fields, the industrial rules issued by non-governmental institutions and articles of association of companies constitute an important part of the norms for personal data protection (Qi Aimin 2015, p. 89).

At present, there is no special law on personal data protection in China. Personal data is protected by department legislation in different fields. Now industry self-regulation is only in the initial stage, and industrial rules related to personal data protection are rare (Zhang Jihong 2018). Therefore, we need to give better play to self-regulation of industrial associations based on relevant legislations and encourage industrial associations to actively participate in the formulation and implementation of data protection rule and form a self-regulation mechanism to meet the objective needs of the industries. Furthermore, government guidance is needed to form synergy between appropriate government supervision and industrial self-regulation and gradually improve the effectiveness of data protection.

Regulation of ethical system

"Justice is the primary value of social system" (John Rawls 1988, p. 11). However, our current ethical system is not entirely just, because an ethical system suitable for the past may not be suitable for the era of big data today. This requires us to pay attention to meta ethics of justice and its realization in the ethical system of modern society. Therefore, on the one hand, we must improve the relevant ethical systems, so that they can help eliminate the negative consequences caused by the alienation of big data technology, and strive to ensure the justice of relevant ethical systems themselves, that is when designing the relevant ethical systems, we must focus on how to eliminate dehumanization, non-humanism and non-liberalization in the era of big data. On the other hand, we must formulate specific ethical norms for data stakeholders so as to ensure that the relevant ethical systems themselves are just. Ethical norms need to be formulated for different groups of data stakeholders, so that big data technology can run in a healthy manner in society (Chen Shiwei 2016).

Data security is not only a technical issue, but also a trade-off of interests, values and ethics. According to *The Plan to Establish the National Science and Technology Ethics Committee*, which was reviewed and adopted by the Central Committee for Comprehensively Deepening Reform, it is necessary to improve institutional norms, improve governance mechanisms, strengthen ethical supervision, refine relevant laws, regulations and ethical review rules, and regulate various kinds of research activities. It was proposed at the Fourth Plenary Session of the 19th CPC Central Committee that it was necessary to improve the governance system of science and technology ethics" and "privacy can't be understood as just keeping a secret, but as a set of rules about the ethics of personal information collection and disclosure (Wu Weiguang 2016). From the perspective of institutional ethics, the ethical governance of data protection in the era of digital civilization is to adhere to ethical norms. Therefore, in the social governance with private rights and public power in synergy, public power is to keep control in order to shape a new order and ethics for competition, and focus should be put on cultivating and training employees in terms of data-related ethical standards and moral responsibilities.

It is generally believed that relevant ethical principles should be established for the ethical problems caused by big data technology: The first principle is doing no harm. That is, in the development of big data technology, we should always be people-oriented so as to serve the healthy development of human society and improve people's life. The second is the unity of rights and responsibilities. Those who collect and use data should be held responsible for what they do. The third is the principle of respect for autonomy, which means that the right to store data, the right to delete data, the right to use data and the right to know should be fully granted to data producers (Yang Weidong 2018). For historical reasons, enterprise conglomerates with strong self-regulation and ethical norms have not been fully formed in China, so we cannot rely on industrial self-regulation as much as in the United States. This means that our government must act to shape such regulatory systems and mechanisms.

Legal protection of rights to data

Necessity of legal protection of rights to data

"Law is not abstract mechanical rules. It carries certain social values and reflects people's code of conduct and life experiences" (Ma Changshan 2018). Therefore, the development of law cannot ignore social reality and adjustments to laws need to be based on the actual needs of society. In this vein, we need to put in place legal norms for the protection of rights to data and establish a protection system that meets the needs of social development. In today's society, data subjects tend to pursue more and diverse interests, and they are keen to define new interests claims as new types of rights. There are even calls for legislation to protect their rights and interests. Individuals (users) and enterprises have different claims based on their own interests. Deep down, it is the competition between rights to personal data and data use by enterprises, and competition between enterprises for the right to control data. It is also a breakthrough and revision of the existing rights system after the list of data-related rights is expanded and refined. Due to the different social backgrounds of data subjects, their data interest claims are significantly different, showing an obvious trend of differentiation. Therefore, balancing and coordinating between the data rights and interests of individuals, enterprises and the general public is not only a new task of our judicial system, but also a test of the wisdom of legislators (Li Xiaoyu 2019). Since the twenty-first century, work towards legislation on data has been in full swing in many countries, and China is also speeding up its progress in the aspect.[22] There seems not to be any specific legal provisions on rights to corporate data so far, and such rights can only be protected and regulated through the *Law*

22 In the *Legislative Plan of the Standing Committee of the 13th National People's Congress* released in September 2018, personal information protection law is the 61st item on the agenda.

of the People's Republic of China Against Unfair Competition. At the same time, the management and disclosure of government data require a sound system, especially technical standards and regulations. We should have a deep understanding of the international legislative trend related to data protection, take effective measures to protect rights to data, and build a reasonable legal system for this purpose.

Predicament of legalization on rights to data

Whether the rights to data can be established through legislation or not requires careful reasoning. In fact, there are many obstacles on our way to legalization on the rights to data either with forward deduction or reverse hypothesis (Zhang Yang 2016). Internet enterprises may infringe on data rights in the whole process of collecting and using customers' data, but it is very difficult to regulate it with the tort law, because data collection and analysis are conducted in a way invisible to outsiders. Even if people suspect that their rights have been infringed on, they may not know who to sue, or lack necessary evidence to hold anyone liable or support their claims. In addition, the data property right system is the product of government regulation of data flow, but practical adjustments need to be made according to the overall efficiency so as to ensure the balance of interests between data users, data processors and the general public. The ultimate goal is to build a balanced and well-coordinated mechanism for the distribution of data rights and interests that will bring benefits to all parties and provide support for all parties to use data in an orderly manner. However, there are still many deficiencies in the legal protection of the rights to data in China. First of all, there is a lack of jurisprudential research. *The General Provisions of the Civil Law* and other relevant laws mention the measures for data protection, but in essence, there are no specific provisions laying out the definition, nature and structure of data rights, which cannot meet the current needs of citizens for the protection of their rights to personal data. Secondly, there is a lack of constitutional support. *The Constitution of the People's Republic of China* does not explicitly regard rights to personal data as a kind of rights to protect like many other kinds of rights. Moreover, there is no dedicated personal data protection law in China, and the protection of rights to personal data is scattered and fuzzy. In addition, some civil law scholars emphasize the rights of data subjects, such as the right to know, the right of access, the right to correct, the right to data portability and the right of data to be forgotten. Even with explicit personal consent, enterprises cannot fully enjoy the right to control personal data and must guarantee the fundamental rights of data subjects while collecting and processing their personal data (Shi Dan 2019). At the same time, enterprises and governments should improve the transparency of big data application, encourage open access to and sharing of corporate data and government data, and promote the development and use of data products. The key to balance between the rights to data and the development of the data industry is to clarify the authority of enterprises to use and process data. However, the provisions on the protection of rights to data are not specific and such rights are even being established as an independent category of rights.

System building for the protection of the rights to data

In protecting the rights to data, we cannot focus solely on the protection of the rights and interests of any certain type of data subjects. We need to adjust the data relations between different subjects of rights such as individuals, enterprises and governments. Law sets part of the rules to adjust social relations. A system to protect the rights to data can play a role in settling disputes in a society with complex data relations. Therefore, in the building of system to protect the rights to data, it is necessary to clarify the status of the government, enterprises and individuals, define the connotation and boundary of rights to data, reasonably set the rights and obligations of data rights holders and data users, carry out classified protection based on the types of data, and finally formulate law for the confirmation of rights to data and corresponding protection system that are in line with both our national conditions and international practices (Zhu Lei 2019).

Firstly, the rights to personal data should be protected as a fundamental right. Article 8 of *Charter of* Fundamental *Rights of the European Union*[23]

23 *Charter of Fundamental Rights of the European Union* is different from the traditional legal documents of human rights, such as *The European Convention on Human Rights* in that it is not a universal and independent human rights law: it is only applied

stipulates that "Everyone has the right to the protection of personal data concerning him or her. Such data must be processed fairly for specified purposes and on the basis of the consent of the person concerned or some other legitimate basis laid down by law." It can be seen that the European Union promotes the protection of personal data by establishing the rights to personal data as fundamental rights which are the category of rights best protected in the European Union's legal system. China should speed up the legislation on the protection of the rights to data to offer direct protection to the rights to personal data which is recognized as a kind of independent and fundamental civil right.

Secondly, the protection system for fundamental data rights and interests should be established drawing reference from the protection of other rights. The rights to data are property rights, intellectual property rights and personality rights in nature and interests from data are open for sharing. These characteristics together make it impossible to build the system for the protection of the rights to data while focusing on any one dimension of them like what we do in our existing systems (Deng Ganghong 2018). Provisions for defining data ownership need to be aligned with right protection systems defined in the current legal system, and reference should be drawn from other similar systems.

Lastly, it is necessary to properly handle all kinds of new complex relationships in the era of big data. For one thing, it is necessary to clarify the relationship between data collection by government departments and personal data protection. In view of state security and interests, rights to personal data need to be partially transferred. However, the government should strictly abide by legal procedures when collecting personal data, and clarify the purpose. For another thing, it is necessary to draw a clear boundary between rights to corporate data and rights to personal data. The

---

when the EU institutions and Member States implement the EU laws. The laws of the EU and EU Member States shall be in line with *Charter of Fundamental Rights of the European Unio*n and take it as the minimum requirement. The provisions of the laws of the EU and EU Member States that conflict with *Charter of Fundamental Rights of the European Union* shall not be applied. See Menno Mostert, Annelien L, Bredenoord, Bartvander Sloot, Johannes J. M. van Delden. 2017. "From Privacy to Data Protection in the European Union: Implications for Big Data Health Research." *European Journal of Health Law*, 25th issue.

big data possessed by enterprises are basically derived from personal data. On the one hand, personality interests such as personal privacy should be protected, while on the other, enterprises' data rights should also be sufficiently protected, especially the big data formed after anonymization and desensitization (Song Jianbao 2019). Also, governments, enterprises and individuals may infringe on citizens' rights to personal data, but no matter what kind of infringement occurs, corresponding relief measures must be available.

Bibliography

Bei, Ke, Deng Zhenglai and Shen Guolin. 2010. "Risk Society and China: A Dialogue with Ulrich Beck." *Sociological Research*, 5th issue.

Brocks, Hans, and Wolff Dietrich Walker. 2019. *General Theory of German Civil Law (41st Edition).* Trans. Zhang Yan. Beijing: China Renmin University Press.

Chen, Hongzhi. 2018. "Preliminary Exploration into Private Law Orientation of Public Law." *Legal System and Society*, 2nd issue.

Chen, Shanglong. 2019. "Research on Legislation of Government Data Openness in the Era of Big Data." *Local Legislation Research*, 2nd issue.

Chen, Shiwei. 2016. "Ethical Governance of the Alienation of Big Data Technology." *Studies on Dialectics of Nature*, 1st issue.

Chen, Zhentao. 2017. "Powers and Functions Structure and Power Item Analysis of Personal Information Rights." *Fujian Jurisprudence*, 1st issue.

Cheng, Xiao. 2018. "Personal Data Rights in the Era of Big Data." *China Social Sciences*, 3rd issue.

Compilation and Translation Bureau of the CPC Central Committee. 1963. *Complete Works of Marx and Engels (Volume 19).* Beijing: People's Publishing House.

Deloitte and Ali Research. "The Approach of Data Assets: Data Assets Valuation and Industry Practice." October 29, 2019. <https://www2.deloitte.com/cn/zh/pages/finance/articles/data-asset-report.html>.

Deng, Ganghong. 2018. "Legal Logic Analysis of the Attributes of Big Data Rights: The Protection Approach of Personal Data Rights." *Jianghai Academic Journal*, 6th issue.

Dong, Zhiwei. 2001. *Legal Power and Constitutionalism.* Jinan: Shandong People's Publishing House.

Gao, Jianping, and Qi Zhiyuan. 2019. "Big Data and Reconstruction of Contemporary Social Order." *Natural Dialectics Research*, 5th issue.

Guo, Yu. 2012. *Research on Personal Data Protection Law*, Beijing: Peking University Press.

Habermas, J. 1999. *Technology and Science as "Ideology"*. Trans. Li Li and Guo Guan. Shanghai: Academic Press.

Hao, Jiming. 2008. "Alienation and Control of Public Power." *Social Sciences Review*, 7th issue.

He, Dingding. 2018. "How Does Data Power Respect Users' Rights." *People's Daily*, March 23, 8th edition.

He, Pu, Yu Ge, Zhang Yanfeng and BaoYubin. 2017. "Overview of Blockchain Technology and Application Prospect." *Computer Science*, 4th issue.

Hu, Ling. 2018. "Beyond Code: Control/Production Mechanism from Cyberspace to the Physical World." *Journal of East China University of Political Science and Law*, 1st issue.

Huang, Ruhua, Wen Fangfang, and Huang Wen. 2018. "The construction of China's Open and Sharing Policy System of Government Data." *Books and Intelligence Work*, 9th issue.

Jiao, Shiwen. 2009. "Philosophical Research on the Transformation of China's Power Structure." Dissertation. Party School of the CPC Central Committee.

Kang, Xiaoguang. 1999. *The Shift of Power: the Change of Power Pattern in China during the Transformation Period.* Hangzhou: Zhejiang People's Publishing House.

Kelly, K. 2012. *Technical Elements.* Trans. Zhang Xingzhou, et al. Beijing: Electronic Industry Press.

Key Laboratory of Big Data Strategy. 2019. *Block Data 5.0: Theory and Method of Data Sociology*, Beijing: CITIC Press.

Lessig, L. 2009. *Code Version 2.0.* Trans. Li Xu and Shen Weiwei. Beijing: Tsinghua University Press.

Li, Xiaoyu. 2019. "Type-oriented Protection of Data Rights and Interests from the Perspective of the Distinction between Rights and Interests." *Intellectual Property Rights*, 3rd issue.

Li, Yang, and Li Xiaoyu. 2019. "Definition of the Nature of Enterprise Data Rights and Interests in the Era of Big Data and Construction of Its Protection Mode." *Xuehai*, 4th issue.

Lin, Qifu, and He Jingchao. 2016. "Big Data Power: a Modern Power Logic and Its Experience Reflection." *Journal of Northeast University (Social Sciences Edition)*, 5th issue.

Liu, Hong and Hu Xinhe. 2013. "Data Revolution: a Historical Perspective from Numbers to Big Data." *Natural Dialectics Communication*, 6th issue.

Liu, Jiangang. 2016. "The Justification of Data Rights." *Journal of Beijing Vocational College of Political Science and Law*, 4th issue.

Liu, Yongmou. 2012. "Machine and Rule: the Power Dimension of Karl Marx's Theory of Science and Technology." *Studies in Philosophy of Science and Technology*, 1st issue.

Long, Weiqiu. 2017. "Research on the Construction and System of New Data Property Rights." *Political and Legal Forum*, 4th issue.

Long, Weiqiu. 2018. "Reconsidering the Approach of Property Rights of Enterprise Data Protection." *Oriental Jurisprudence*, 3rd issue.

Lu, Li. 2003. *Study on Economic Autonomy of Industry Associations*, Beijing: Law Press China.

Lv, Tingjun. 2017. "Data Rights System and Its Legal Significance." *Journal of the Party School of the CPC Central Committee*, 5th issue.

Lv, Zhixiang, and Zhang Qiang. 2019. "Jurisprudential Analysis of Data Rights in the Context of Big Data." *Journal of Kunming University of Science and Technology (Social Sciences Edition)*, 1st issue.

Ma, Changshan. 2018. "Legal Reform in the Era of Intelligent Internet." *Chinese Journal of Law*, 4th issue.

Mei, Xiaying. 2016. "The Legal Attribute of Data and Its Civil Law Orientation." *China Social Sciences*, 9th issue.

Mei, Xiaying, and Yang Xiaona. 2017. "The Formation and Regulating Approach of Network Power on We Media Platforms: Based on the Analysis of the Impact on the Freedom of Online Speech." *Hebei Law Science*, 1st issue.

Mostert, L., Annelien L. Bredenoord, Bartvander Sloot, and Johannes J. M. van Delden. 2017. "From Privacy to Data Protection in the EU:Implications for Big Data Health Research." *European Journal of Health Law*, 25th issue.

Qi, Aimin. 2015. *International Comparative Study of Personal Information Protection Law in the Era of Big Data*, Beijing: Law Press China.

Qi, Aimin, and Pan Jia. 2015. "The Establishment of Data Rights and Data Sovereignty and the Basic Principles of Big Data Protection." *Journal of Suzhou University (Philosophy and Social Sciences Edition)*, 1st issue.

Rawls, J. 1988. *A Theory of Justice*. Trans. He Huaihong, et al. Beijing: China Social Sciences Press.

Ru, Xin. 2005. *History of Western Aesthetics*. Beijing: China Social Sciences Press.

Russell, B. 1982. *Introduction to Mathematical Philosophy*. Trans. Yan Chengshu. Beijing: The Commercial Press.

Shi, Dan. 2018. "Research on Data Ownership and Protection Approach in the Era of Big Data." *Journal of Xi'an Jiaotong University (Social Sciences Edition)*, 3rd issue.

Shi, Dan. 2019. "Legal Protection and Institutional Construction of Enterprise Data Property Rights." *Electronic Intellectual Property Rights*, 6th issue.

Shi, Lindong. 2019. "Analysis of the Protection of Personal Data Rights." *Journal of Fuzhou Party School*, 2nd issue.

Shi, Pengpeng. 2013. "The Pedigree of Fundamental Rights and the New Development of French Criminal Justice: Focusing on the Influence of the European Convention on Human Rights and the Precedents of the European Court of Human Rights on French Criminal Justice." *Journal of Jinan University (Philosophy and Social Sciences Edition)*, 7th issue.

Song, Jianbao. 2019. "Strengthening Judicial Protection of Big Data to Ensure the Implementation of National Big Data Strategy." *People's Court Daily*, July 22, 2nd edition.

Spinello, R. A. 1998. *Ethics of the Century: the Ethical Aspects of Information Technology*. Trans. Liu Gang. Beijing: Central Compilation and Translation Press.

State Council of the People's Republic of China. *Action Plan for Promoting the Development of Big Data*. August 31, 2015.

Tang, Jiyao. 2019. "An Outline of the Protection and Regulation of Enterprise Data Rights by the Criminal Law of China in the Era of Big Data." *Journal of Shandong Police Academy*, 3rd issue.

Tong, Linjie, and Guo Chengcheng. 2019. "Expansion, Alienation and Regulatory Approach of Big Data Power." *Journal of Commercial Economics*, 4th issue.

Wang, Chunye. 2008. "Orientation of Public Law, Public Law Orientation of Private Law and the Improvement of Administrative Law." *Inner Mongolia Social Sciences (Chinese Version)*, 1st issue.

Wang, Haiming. 2009. *Principles of Ethics*, Beijing: Peking University Press.

Wang, Liming. 2013. "Legal Protection of Personal Information Rights: Centering on the Boundary between Personal Information Right and Privacy Right." *Modern Jurisprudence*, 4th issue.

Wang, Xiuzhe. 2018. "Reconstruction of the Legal Protection System of Personal Information in the Era of Big Data." *Legal Forum*, 6th issue.

Wang, Xiuxiu. 2018. *Legislative Theory of Personal Data Protection in the Context of Big Data*. Hangzhou: Zhejiang University Press.

Wang, Yuan, Huang Daoli, and Yang Songru. 2017. "Research on the Nature and Ownership of Data Rights." *Scientific Management Research*, 5th issue.

Wen, Yu. 2018. "Legal Attribute and Classification Significance of Big Data." *Gansu Social Sciences*, 6th issue.

Wen, Yu. 2019. "An Outline of Personal Data Rights System: Concurrent Discussion." *Journal of Gansu University of Political Science and Law*, 2nd issue.

Wen, Yuheng. 2018. "Private Law Structure of Data Property Rights." diss. Xiangtan University.

Wen, Yuheng. 2019. "Paradigm Evolution, Concept Selection and Subject of Ownership of Data Confirmation." *Journal of Northeast Normal University (Philosophy and Social Sciences Edition)*, 5th issue.
Wu, Weiguang. 2016. "Criticism on the Protection Theory of Private Rights of Personal Data under Big Data Technology." *Politics and Law*, 7th issue.
Xi, Po. 2018. "Silent Data Rights Are Awakening." *CPPCC News*, April 25, 12th edition.
Xia, Yikun. 2018. "The Connotation, Generation Background and Main Problems of Government Data Governance." *Books and Intelligence Work*, 9th issue.
Xiang, Liling, and Gao Qianyun. 2018. "Analysis of the Characteristics, Basic Attributes and Contents of Personal Data Rights in the Era of Big Data." *Intelligence Theory and Exploration*, 9th issue.
Yan, Lidong. 2019. "Exploring Data Rights from the Perspective of 'Bundle of Rights.'" *Oriental Jurisprudence*, 2nd issue.
Yang, Weidong. 2018. "Effectively Dealing with the Ethical Issues of Big Data Technology." *People's Daily*, March 23, 7th edition.
Zhang, Endian. 2019. "Algorithm Interpretation Right in the Era of Big Data: Background, Logic and Structure." *Legal Forum*, 4th issue.
Zhang, Jihong. 2018. "Dilemma and Solution of Industry Self-regulation of Personal Information Protection in the Era of Big Data." *Law and Economy*, 6th issue.
Zhang, Jinfan. 2009. *The tradition and Modern Transformation of Chinese Law*, Bejing: Law Press China.
Zhang, Linghan. 2019. "The Rise, Alienation and Legal Regulation of algorithm power." *Studies in Law and Business*, 4th issue.
Zhang, Xinbao. 2015. "From Privacy to Personal Information: Theoretical and Institutional Arrangements for Measuring Interests." *China Legal Science*, 3rd issue.
Zhang, Xinbao. 2018. "The Contradictions in the Legislation of Personal Information Protection Law in China." *Jilin University Journal Social Sciences Edition*, 5th issue.
Zhang, Suhua, and Li Yanan. 2018. "Approach Selection of Data Protection." *Academics*, 7th issue.
Zhang, Yanan. 2019. "Government Data Sharing: Internal Essentials, Legal Barriers and the Approach to Break Them." *Theoretical Exploration*, 5th issue.
Zhang, Yang. 2016. "The Dilemma of Right Orientation and Contractual Regulation of Data." *Science-Technology and Law*, 6th issue.
Zheng, Ge. 2016. "Between Encouraging Innovation and Protecting Human Rights: How Should Law Respond to the Challenges of Technological Innovation of Big Data." *Exploration and Free Views*, 7th issue.

Zheng, Zhihang. 2018. "Dual Governance of Legal Governance and Technological Governance in Network Society." *China Legal Science*, 2nd issue.

Zhu, Lei. 2019. "Clarifying Data Rights Ownership through Legislation." *Economic Daily*, May 21, 12th edition.

CHAPTER 3

Rights to Share

Data has become a kind of basic national strategic resource. Like all resources on the earth, data has the characteristic of scarcity. However, data multiplies when it is shared, with its value increasing. Sharing, so to speak, serves as an important way for people to deal with the issue of data scarcity and to increase data value. It is also an inevitable trend and requirement of our time that human civilization develops. In order to promote the orderly development and sharing of data, we propose the concept of "rights to share" to raise the shared value of data to a right. The rights to share, which are based on altruism, is the essence of data rights. Its birth will surely reshape the legal principles, social order and economic foundation of the human world.

Justification of the Rights to Share

The rise of the sharing economy makes people reconsider sharing. In human history, the idea of sharing has long been present as a basic and normal way to use materials and data. Credit, exchange, sharing and open access are all common types of sharing. The sharing value has taken root in people's minds and become part of the basic values of mankind long ago. To protect the sharing value, we propose the concept of "rights to share" so that the sharing value can be upheld as part of the basic value of data. Like the right to freedom and right to equality, it is one of the basic rights of human beings.

From sharing things to sharing data

Sharing has been an integral part of production and life since ancient times. Things are borrowed, rented, and traded, people communicate with one another, and companies cooperate for shared benefits. All these can be deemed activities of sharing. With the arrival of the era of big data and the rise of the sharing economy, public data becomes open, business data is traded and personal data shared. Sharing gradually plays an increasingly important role in economic and social activities and become the most important means to explore the data value.

Development of the awareness of sharing

Sharing is one of the hallmarks of the human civilization. In modern language, sharing means to make things public and available to others. In Chinese, the word first appeared in *Chronicles of the Eastern Zhou Kingdoms*: "Duke Jing of Qi does not enjoy happiness alone and is willing to share." This demonstrates people's preference to sharing. In *The Conveyance of Rites* of *The Book of Rites*, there was the early concepts of "the whole world as one community" and "society of great harmony" which also have much in common with the awareness of sharing. In the meantime, the awareness of sharing can also be found in ancient Greece. For example, there was the concept of a political community which had common goals, interests and values like those shared by citizens of the same city state. However, with the rise of large-scale industrial production and modern rationality, the paradigm of sharing gradually changed from simple moral ideas such as universal love, harmony and fairness to a kind of social contract and rationality-based value. Thus sharing has become a rational norm for resolving problems in personal and social relationships (Liu Ling 2019). Before the rise of the sharing economy, however, the sharing value had long been ignored. The sharing economy emerged from "collaborative consumption" which was first proposed in 1978 by Marcus Felson and Joel Spaeth, American professors of sociology, as "those events in which one or more persons consume economic goods or services in the process of engaging in joint activities with one or more others." Then, in 1984, Martin L. Weitzman raised the concept of "sharing economy" in *The Sharing Economy: Conquering Stagflation*, which was mainly about how to share enterprise revenue between workers and capitalists. The author placed emphasis on profit distribution on the micro level and suggested establishing new profit sharing system and fiscal and taxation policies to tackle the problem of stagflation in economic development of the West. In 2010, Rachel Botsman and Roo Rogers defined and explained the sharing economy for the first time in *What's Mine is Yours: The Rise of Collaborative Consumption*. According to them, "it is a new pattern of consumption and life". As sharing-oriented companies like Uber, Airbnb and DiDi grow rapidly and penetrate every aspect of production and life, people has begun to reconsider the shared value. Thus, sharing has broken the boundary of a single enterprise to cover the society as a whole and it then freed itself from the constraint of ownership so that resources can all be shared.

Types of sharing

The early awareness of sharing gave rise to several types of sharing: division of labor and cooperation, verbal communication, written records, commodity trade, data sharing, and more. These common types of sharing are an important force promoting the development of human civilization. The things that are shared are either tangible articles of things or data. The sharing of tangible things belongs to the physical world, while the sharing of data, which is intangible, belongs the virtual world. The sharing of languages, writing systems, data and information can all be covered in the category of the sharing of data.

In ancient times, in order to cope with the challenges of nature, people had to stand together and share their abilities. Some were responsible for potting and knitting, some for gathering wild fruits and some for hunting. This greatly improved their productivity and life. This was how human survival was secured. In various primitive tribes that gradually emerged, people thrived and made their first step towards being the master of the earth. It is therefore fair to say that division of labor and cooperation, as an important part of sharing that people practiced, was both a choice of the nature and what was needed for human development. Language is a tool of communication while communication is another type of sharing. There are still disputes concerning the origin of language in the academic world. We hold that language is a product of the human struggle against nature. During the process of collaborative labor, people needed communication and gestures were far from enough in the face of harsh natural conditions. Spoken language thus was badly needed to improve the efficiency of collaboration and communication. With language, people can share their thoughts and ideas with others, communicate in a different way, and greatly improve their productivity. Today, language still remains a major means of expression for people to communicate and nothing is likely to replace it. Writing, born out of ancient murals, is another tool of sharing that is unique to human beings. Ancient people carved patterns into cave walls to keep records of their heroes, but this multifarious method later became insufficient for meeting the need of human development. Eventually, the pattern on cave walls evolved into image-like writing systems, such as hieroglyphics and cuneiforms, which then transform into the writing systems today. The emergence of writing systems is a big event in the history of human civilization. It carries the experience of survival, achievements in development and accumulated knowledge of mankind forward so that they can be shared with others and descendants and drive human civilization forward. Language and writing are both ways of sharing, but they greatly differ from each other. Language focuses on information sharing while writing shares information and knowledge. Transmission of information and passing of knowledge were early sharing activities in human history. The contribution of language and writing to human beings is fundamental and revolutionary, helping mankind to stand out from all species amid evolution and competition and finally become the master of the earth (Key Laboratory of Big Data Strategy 2019, p. 188).

Commodity transaction is one of the most important features of modern society and is also an important type of sharing. From barter to the emergence of money, and to the formation of economic theories, commodity transaction grows and expands all the time and has become an indispensable social and economic activity in the human society. Sharing can be divided into paid sharing and free sharing and commodity transaction generally belongs to the former. Through commodity transaction, one shares what he/she owns with others and get paid for it. This enhances the motivation for sharing, achieves win-win results for both sides of the transaction, and solves the problem of commodity scarcity. With the arrival of the era of big data, data, and an important means of production, has also become part of what people share. However, due to historical inertia and the lack of top-level planning, lots of "data islands" have formed and data resources are not effectively used. Since data is relational by nature, only when "data islands" are eliminated and data become better connected, can the value of data be brought into full play. Sharing serves as an important means for eliminating "data islands". There are mainly two methods for data sharing: open access to data and data transaction. Both are still in the early stage of development and have many problems to be solved. However, as the most important engine of big data development, data sharing has large room for further development.

Value implication of sharing

In human history, every leap in productive forces pushed human civilization forward in a large stride. Sharing maximizes public interest, drives profound changes in the way of production and life, promotes greatly the productivity and living standard of mankind, and gives birth to new paradigms that push the human civilization forward. As we can see, sharing has different implications for those who share, those who receive what is shared, and the things that are shared. Thus, sharing plays unique roles in responding to the needs of economic and social development. For those who share, the coverage of sharing is broad and sharing can bridge differences of forms and mindset and eliminate discrimination on that basis. Everyone can take the initiative to share. For those who receive what is shared, all achievements of human civilization can be shared. In terms of the content of sharing, progress in all aspects of human civilization can be included. With these characteristics, sharing provides a realistic path for economic and social development and proves itself to be in line with the essential requirements of the economic and social development of the human society, offering positive expectations to those who pursue a better life and progress in civilization. Sharing is an important driving force for the survival and development of mankind as it enhances the collective strength of people to make effective use of and transform nature, promotes communication to make cooperation more efficient; passes wisdom to future generations to facilitate human progress, promotes commercial activities to solve the problem of resource scarcity, and creates the digital space to bring mankind into a new era of digital civilization. Sharing was, is, and will continue to be of immeasurable significance the life that every persons shares.

From surplus value to shared value

In Marxism, the contradictory interactions between productive forces and relations of production and between economic base and superstructure serve as the fundamental driving force that pushes the human society from a low level to a high level. The capitalist world, since its inauguration, has created greater social productive forces than ever before and promoted the progress of the human society. However, according to the logic of capital, technical revolution, industrial transformation, political revolution and philosophical revolution all work for the increase of the value of capital. As a result, capitalists try harder and harder to exploit surplus value and people go further and further on the road of alienation (Hu Shouyong 2018). The theory of surplus value then gradually loses its explanatory power and the theory of shared value emerges.

Development of theories of value

As an important category of theories in economics, theories of value date back to the time when commodity came into being. A good becomes a commodity because it has value. A good that has no value can hardly become a commodity. Based on the thoughts of his predecessors, especially Socrates and Plato, Aristotle created a relatively complete set of thoughts on value which is the origin of various theories of value. For 2,000 years or so after that, however, Aristotle's thoughts on value didn't get much chance to be proved and developed in practice and thus no theory of value really took shape.

In *An Inquiry into the Nature and Causes of the Wealth of Nations*, Adam Smith created a complete system of political economics. According to him, the quantity of labor it costs to produce a commodity determines the value of the commodity; or in other words, the value of any commodity is equal to the quantity of labor which it enables him to purchase. Labor, therefore, is the only real measure of exchangeable value and value. Smith also broke price down into three types of revenue, wages, profits and rents (Guan Dehua & Kong Xiaohong 2013, p. 8). These lay solid foundation for future studies on value. However, Smith's theory has its flaws: It lacks elaboration on labor force and production price and confuses value creation with value distribution. Based on this, three major schools came into being with different theories of value.

The school of labor theory of value, represented by David Ricardo and Karl Marx, analyzes value from the perspective of the supply side. David Ricardo made correction on Adam Smith's argument that a commodity with no use value also possesses exchange value, holding that value is determined by the labor consumed other than the labor purchased. This made Ricardo the one who completed the labor theory of value. However, as productivity increases, a relative surplus of commodities emerged and the value of many commodities could not be realized in the market, rendering Ricardo's value theory inadequate. Based on Ricardo's theory, Karl Marx proposed the duality of commodity and the duality of labor, dividing labor into concrete labor which creates use value and abstract labor which creates value. Then, he proceeded to propose the theory of surplus value and completed the conversion from value to production price (Meng Kui 2013). The value theory of Marx reflects the profound social relationships behind commodity exchange and nails it down as relationships between people. This is the fundamental difference between his and Ricardo's labor theory of value.

The school of marginal utility theory, represented by Carl Menger, William Jevons, Leon Walras and John Bates Clark, advocates demand determinism and defines value as the marginal utility based on subjective evaluation.[1] This school deems that the utility change caused by the change of consumption is marginal utility and value is determined by the marginal utility of a commodity. It proposes the theory of marginal productivity which subverts the objectivity of the substance of value and thoroughly denies the labor theory of value. Since the marginal utility theory focuses on consumption and distribution in the field of consumption, it systematically illustrates consumer equilibrium (equilibrium of exchange) and producer equilibrium (equilibrium of inputs of labor and capital), and pushes consumption to center stage in microeconomic research, laying foundation for microeconomics and giving birth to modern Western economics (Guan Dehua & Kong Xiaohong 2013, pp. 99–102).

The school of equilibrium theory of value, represented by Alfred Marshall and Paul Samuelson. This school shares the belief that neither supply nor demand can be neglected in determining the value of a commodity. Value is determined by market forces, that is, equilibrium of supply and demand, not production or consumption alone. It can be seen that the equilibrium theory of value is a combination of the above two schools. It reflects the relationship between people and things, namely, the relationship between certain goods and the need of the whole society, or more broadly, the relationship between human and nature. By the benefit measure,[2] it reflects the relationship between how much people need and how scarce a commodity is or how difficult is it to obtain a certain good. This has strong explanatory power for many economic phenomena today (Meng Kui 2013). Therefore, the equilibrium theory of value has been dominant in Western economics since it was proposed by Marshall.

1 Marginal utility refers to the increased satisfaction degree by consuming an additional unit of certain material. The meaning of margin is increment, which refers to the increment of dependent variable caused by the increase of independent variable. In marginal utility, independent variable is the consumption of material while dependent variable is the satisfaction degree or utility.

2 The benefits here mainly refer to the difference between the utility brought about by meeting social demands and the cost it takes to meet the social demands.

Since the establishment of the equilibrium theory of value by Marshall no real breakthrough has been achieved so far in the field of value theory. Especially since the birth of the Internet, globalization, networking, informatization and virtualization are the growing trends today, but none of the three major theories of value can give a convincing explanation to ongoing economic phenomena or offer guidance to modern economic operations. Many emerging economic schools, such as information economics, public economics, game theory, new institutional economics and psychological economics, propose new theories of value but they are merely development from and supplement to the three major theories explained here, neither systematic, nor universally applicable. Therefore, we are now in need of new theories of value.

From surplus value to shared value

From the perspective of economic and social forms, there are capitalism and socialism in today's world. The theory of surplus value proposed by Marx and Engels is a theory that analyzes the capitalist production process. According to this theory, surplus value refers to the balance of the commodity value less the value of expended product-forming elements, that is, means of production and labor (Central Compilation and Translation Bureau 1972, p. 235), and the capitalist production process as a whole is the production process of surplus value. In terms of production, surplus value is produced in the form of commodity, while in terms of circulation, surplus value is realized when commodity is sold. Hence, a sharp contradiction is formed between the production and realization of surplus value: the producer would appropriate as much surplus value as possible in the process of commodity production in order to make more profits, while in the meantime, a high rate of surplus value would inevitably hinder the realization of surplus value in circulation, which is why an economic crisis hits (Meng Kui 2013).

The theory of surplus value of Max and Engels reveals the fundamental pattern of the capitalist economy, the economic root of the antagonism between capitalists and the proletariat, and the fundamental reason why capitalism is bound to die. However, the theory of surplus value cannot reflect the nature of a socialist economy and no value theory is available at present to do this. Under such a circumstance, with the rise of the sharing economy, the shared value has begun to draw renewed attention and the theory of the shared value stand out to give a new explanation of a socialist society and even all societies.

The theory of the shared value centers around the value created by sharing. Scarce as resources are on the earth, every bit of them are useful and must be made full use of. Meanwhile, we have only this one earth that we all share and everyone has equal right to use its resources (Key Laboratory of Big Data Strategy 2019, p. 194). This requires us to improve the efficiency of resource use through sharing. This is why we must share and how sharing creates value. During the process of value formation, providers of the three factors of production, namely, labor, capital and land, all play their roles. They share what they have directly or indirectly and naturally should participate in value distribution. Therefore, sharing creates value. Like the theory of surplus value, the theory of the value of sharing is also based on the labor theory of value. The theory of the value of sharing, whether in a capitalist or socialist society, advocates that workers should be able to enjoy the value they create. This combines distribution according to labor and distribution according to factors of production, lays the theoretical basis for income distribution, brings the all members of society into a community of shared interests, unleashes the enthusiasms of all parties for production, and further emancipates and develops productive forces.

Creation of shared value

With time, the influence of sharing grows around the world and shared value increases with it. Firstly, the rise of new-generation of information technology such as the Internet, big data and artificial intelligence reduces the cost of sharing and platforms for sharing make it much easier to match supply and demand, reducing the marginal costs of sharing to almost zero and expanding the scale of sharing. Secondly, sharing finds solid ground as material and cultural resources grow in quantity on the whole: On one hand, taking things into one's ownership is no longer the ultimate goal and people are more willing to share what they have, laying foundation for the creation of shared value; on the other hand, differences in consumption power between different strata of society provide conditions for the vertical flow of resources. Thirdly, people now understand production and life in a vastly different way and have better and deeper understanding of the sharing economy on the whole. They are willing to reallocate resources that lay idle through sharing and this greatly improves the efficiency of resource use, reduces overproduction, and lowers external dependence. This is how shared value created (Liu Genrong 2017).

Sharing is both an economic model and a social model whose value is mainly reflected in the following three aspects: First, it provides more room for consumers to make choices on their own and ensures safety and transparency. In the traditional economic model, the market lacks transparency. Uncertainties abound in terms of the quality of goods and services and consumers did not have much room to make their choices. Sharing economy provides consumers with better access to information so that they know more about the goods and services and are better positioned to choose. This, in turn, ensures safe consumption. Second, it settles the crisis of trust between different parties involved in sharing. For both commodity transaction and information exchange, information asymmetry creates a natural distrust between the two parties involved and both commodity transaction and information exchange can be hindered. In contrast, sharing builds trust between relevant as it is highly visible throughout the whole process. Third, sharing improves the well-being of both parties. Those who offer what they have for sharing gains profits by providing products or services, while those who consume what is shared get the products and services they need at a lower price. Thus the well-being of both parties is improved.

Examining how shared value is created, we find that there must at least be the following factors: First, there must be active sharing activities. The behavior of sharing is the source of the shared value. In the model of sharing, one can share as long as he/she has resources. Any person or organization can share what he/she has with others, any commodity or service, whether tangible or intangible, can be shared as long as it has value and is needed. Second, there must be a platform for sharing. Sharing is only possible when there is a platform for it. This is the foundation for value creation through sharing. During this process, the platform mainly functions as an intermediary to provide information of supply and demand as well as matching services. Since the resources to be shared are scattered in society, it is necessary to have a platform to bring them together, put them on display, make connections, and nail deals, Supply and demand are thus brought together so that resources can be shared in spite of distances in time and space. Third, what is shared is the right to use. This is the top motivation for value creation through sharing. In the traditional model, one must first obtain ownership if he/she wants to use something. Thus a lot of resources are wasted. Sharing sets apart ownership and the right to use, forms a model where people do not seek to own things but only seek to use them. Here, what is shared is the right to use. Fourth, there must be a sound trust mechanism to serve as the bond. Sharing mainly happens between strangers so a sound and reliable trust system is needed. It is an important guarantee for sharing to happen. Fifth, there must be an open system for sharing so that all parties involved can remain active in creating value through sharing. This open system of sharing must have a low threshold so that more people can join it. Otherwise, the scale of sharing will shrink as people are shut out and resources to be shared exhaust. In this case, sharing will lose its momentum. Only openness can ensure that sharing can rapidly expand its scale at low cost and create more shared value (Liu Genrong 2017).

Right to freedom, right to equality and rights to share

Can sharing be a right? This is a question worth discussing. The theory of the rights to share, which first came into being in Germany, has evolved into a comparatively mature system after radical changes along the way.

Rights to share as a replacement of right to freedom

The rights to share, as a replacement of the right to freedom, aim to take the central position of the right to freedom in the existing right portfolio.

This is what Ernst Forsthoff, a German administrative jurist proposed in his famous work of 1938, *Administration as a Service Provider.*[3] This article is actually regarded as the origin of the rights to share and has had far-reaching influence. In Part III of this article, Forsthoff stated that the rights to share, as a replacement of the right to freedom, originated from changes in people's lifestyle and represented a departure from the idea of *liberaler Rechtsstaat* [literally "liberal rule of law"]. In the age of *liberaler Rechtsstaat,* administrative jurisprudence aimed to protect the right to freedom of individuals. However, as *Daseinsvorsorge* [literally "general interest"] took priority over other tasks of the state, the importance of individuals' right to freedom gradually declined. Therefore, a fair social order must be established and it should be ensured that individuals can share this order. this is the primary reason why Forsthoff updated the principles of administrative jurisprudence. To establish a fair social order, we must cast aside the right to freedom and turn to the rights to share. The traditional right to freedom is not necessarily economical, while the rights to share, which are to take its place, is economical, fair and public in nature. By introducing the concepts of *Daseinsvorsorge* and the rights to share, Forsthoff greatly expanded the coverage of administrative law and administrative jurisprudence and was honored as the father of *Leistungsverwaltung* (theory of benefiting administration). Forsthoff's research on the rights to share as a replacement of the right to freedom had far-reaching influence. It removed the right to freedom from the sole central position in the entire right portfolio and gave rise to discussions on the rights to share which has lasted till today. Moreover, he also built organic connections between service administration and the rights to share and excluded the right to participate in public affairs and the right to social remedy from the coverage of the rights to share. These viewpoints are still accepted by many today. However, by proposing the rights

3 Chen Xinmin, a scholar from Taiwan China, published his translation of the main part of this article in the third section "*The Original Appearance of the Concepts of 'Leistungsverwaltung' and 'Daseinsvorsorge' – Discussion on Administration as a Service Provider by Forsthoff* in his work *Essays on Public Law.* For more information on Forsthoff's theory of the rights to share, see Chen Xinmin. 2010. *Essays on Public Law,* Law Press China, p. 39–80.

to share as a replacement of the right to freedom, Forsthoff exaggerated the drawbacks of the right to freedom and *liberaler Rechtsstaat* after the Industrial Revolution, overlooked what was fundamental and ensures stability, overstated the positive aspects of the rights to share, and underestimated its negative side. This determined that the concept of the rights to share as a replacement of the right to freedom would not last long. As may be expected, the *Basic Law for the Federal Republic of Germany* after World War II emphasized the right to freedom, which was a clear sign of rejection to Forsthoff's preference of the rights to share over the right to freedom.

Rights to share in juxtaposition with right to freedom

In his *Legal Issues of Service Administration* published in 1959, Forsthoff gives up the proposal of the rights to share as a replacement of the right to freedom, and instead, he differentiates the two by taking the right to freedom as the guiding principle of intervening administration and the rights to share as the guiding principle of benefiting administration. Henceforth, as Forsthoff's viewpoint on the rights to share changed drastically, the rights to share is now in juxtaposition with the right to freedom. Also in this book, he proposed the supplementary theory of *Daseinsvorsorge*, arguing that the basic living needs of social members should be attended to by society and the state should only play its "supplementary function" when society fails to meet such needs. Thus, *Daseinsvorsorge* becomes passive, no longer indicating anything to be done proactively. The power of individuals and society, previously understated by Forsthoff, now regain recognition and individuals are less dependent on the state and the rights to share (Luo Ying 2014). If Forsthoff's viewpoint of the rights to share as a replacement of the right to freedom reflects contempt of the right to freedom and a "revolutionary" way of thinking, then putting the rights to share in juxtaposition with the right to freedom shows respect for the right to freedom and a "reformist" way of thinking. With the development of society, people's living standards, lifestyles and needs have all changed, and the interests they pursue diversify. Our legislation on human rights must respond to such changes. Human rights are not a rigid or closed portfolio, and the right to freedom is not everything. The rights to share, which emerged after the Industrial Revolution, should have its foothold in the system. Seeing and accepting the emergence and development of service administration, Forsthoff proposed the rights to share in juxtaposition with the right to freedom, taking them respectively as the guiding principles of service administration and intervening administration. This helped improve the theory of service administration and had great influence on modern administrative jurisprudence. However, such influence is more about concept than practice, and more on the macroscopic level than the microcosmic level. Therefore, Forsthoff's rights to share in juxtaposition with the right to freedom is not a concept that can stand on its own with self-consistency, clear connotation and definite extension (Luo Ying 2014).

Rights to share as a derivative of right to equality

Whether the rights to share are taken as a replacement of or in juxtaposition with the right to freedom, Forsthoff's analysis is from the perspective of administrative jurisprudence in his own words and from that of public administration in nature. It is not from the perspective of human rights or constitution. Also, Forsthoff's research on the rights to share revolves around the concept of *Daseinsvorsorge* which is only part of the theory of service administration. In contrast, the mainstream theory of the rights to share in contemporary Germany is based on the *Basic Law for the Federal Republic of Germany* and stresses that the rights to share are a derivative of the right to equality. Here, the rights to share mean that when the state has provided some services for some people but the distribution is unfair, those who do not have access could demand what is provided to shared based on the right to equality. Therefore, the rights to share are also known as a derived right to request service provision. It is the right to request service provision derived from a combination of the principles of *Sozialstaat* [social state] as specified in the *Basic Law for the Federal Republic of Germany* and the right to equality. The principles of

Sozialstaat emphasize social responsibilities that should be shouldered by the state, providing some room for the existence of the rights to share. Yet in the meantime, the *Basic Law* is cautious when it comes to the issue of fundamental rights, so the space for the rights to share to exist is limited. Based on a combination of the principles of *Sozialstaat* and the right to equality, the rights to share comes into being as a derivative of the right to equality, and gains wide acceptance in the academic circle as well as among practitioners. Here, the rights to share are premised on the existence of service provision and its boundary is therefore clearly defined. Moreover, according to the conditions and scope of the rights to share as specified by the Federal Court of Germany, having no access to certain services provided by the state to some people but not others does not constitute a sufficient condition for those who do not receive the services to claim the rights to share. The rights to share only apply when the state's failure to provide services for some people is arbitrary or violates the specific discriminative prohibition according to constitution (Zhao Hong 2010).

Basis of legitimacy of the rights to share

The traditional legal system for property rights is established on the basis of private ownership and pursues exclusivity of things. The private ownership or exclusivity of things forms an effective incentive mechanism which unleashes the creativity of people and promotes the efficient use of things. However, "making the most of things", as one of the goals of legislation on property rights, has not been achieved even today. The open access movement and the sharing economy, on the contrary, have changed the way people use things and prompted them to reflect on how to make better use of things. In the traditional legal system for property rights, due to the excludability of property rights and the principle of one ownership for one object, sharing did not receive sufficient attention. However, with a careful review of the history and current status of property rights laws, we can see clearly that the idea of sharing has already infiltrated into the way we use things and become a basic and routine pattern (Key Laboratory of Big Data Strategy 2019, p. 223).

With the continuous development of society, we see two changes in regard to the means of production: Some means of production has become abundant while others have become scarce. For the latter category, sharing is highly necessary because it enables us to make more efficient use of what we have to bring benefits to more people and curb the growing appetite for what is scarce. For the former part, the cost goes continuously down and will eventually approach zero, making exclusivity pointless and sharing the ultimate outcome. Data is a kind of scarce means of production, but it can become abundant through sharing and generate infinite benefits without any damage to the content. Meanwhile, the costs of replication and sharing is extremely low and may as well be ignored (Key Laboratory of Big Data Strategy 2019, p. 223). Therefore, for data, the central concern is efficient use while sharing is the most important approach.

Technological development has changed the original picture where machinery and chemistry play the central role, breaking the current balance in interest distribution and dealing a heavy blow on the existing rights system. On the one hand, the existing rights system is not adequate to effectively deal with existing data security problems and data infringement and other similar hazards have been perplexing for a long time. On the other hand, the existing rights system hampers the well-regulated transmission of data, which undermines data acquisition and free expression and lowers the efficiency of data use. The value of data thus cannot be effectively realized. People have raised doubts about the applicability and justifiability of the existing rights system and have solved some problems through technological means. However, for problems concerning data rights and interests, technology is only the outer layer while the internal problem lies in conflicts between different kinds of rights. The traditional rights system, as it has possession at the core, can no longer meet the needs as the digital civilization progresses. It is urgent that a new rights system focusing on sharing is established in order to achieve data circulation featuring freedom, security, and equality. The key to this is the rights to share.

From the perspective of value, data has the shared value and sharing is in fact where the greatest value of data lies. However, currently, the distribution of the shared value is unreasonable and data exploitation is serious hampering progress in data liberalization and equality. Technological means have limited effect in making improvements in this regard and a fundamental solution can be found only when we define sharing as a kind of right. Actually, the rights to share have already gained wide acceptance as a fundamental right of people in the academic circle and is turning into a consensus of all mankind. Therefore, it is reasonable and well-grounded for us to propose the concept of "the rights to share" so as to protect the shared value as part of the basic value of data and to make access to the shared value of data a legitimate right.

As data, as a means of production, restructures traditional production relations and social relationships, market transactions will no longer be needed for the realization of the division of labor and the sharing of scarce resources and labor contributions. By then, the right to possess data will lose its value and human society would enter into a new social order built on the basis of the rights to share. The rights to share make it possible to separate ownership and the right to use, and forms a sharing-based development pattern where people seek not to own but to use. In the meantime, since one piece of data can be owned by multiple parties, and data is intangible and can involve multiple right holder by nature, sharing is bound to be the premise for effective data use. Hence, the rights to share are a necessary condition of a digital civilization.

Claims of the Rights to Share

Data rights are in essence the rights to share, which is the basis for establishing a complete and independent set of data rights for one piece of data and for data to be controlled and used by multiple parties, adding to its value. Traditionally, rights are established on the basis of egoism and are meant for self-protection. In contrast to this, the rights to share rest on altruism and sets out to protect of the shared value of data. Thanks to the extremely low cost of reproduction, data sharing creates infinite value which is far more than the value of data without being shared. Hence, it is much more important to protect the value created by data sharing than the original value of data. However, since there are intense conflicts between the rights to share and the right to privacy, balance between the two must be achieved in order to fully exploit the value of data resources.

Rights to share: Essence of data rights

Law protects rights while rights protect value. The purpose for establishing data rights is to protect the value of data. Data has its original value plus the value created by sharing it. The latter is infinite and much higher than the former, so data rights are mainly used to protect the latter. Apart from protection, data rights are also needed in promoting the continuous and healthy development of the data industry which requires the increase in the value of data. Increase in the original value of data lies in expanding production while the increase in the shared value of data depends on sharing more. Comparing the two, the cost of sharing is far lower than that of expanding production. Hence, the key to increasing the total value of data rests with sharing. The rights to share thus become the top engine that drives up the shared value of data, and the essence of data rights.

Rights to share vs. right to possess

Sharing and possession represent the essential difference between data rights and real rights. Property rights include the right to possess, the right to use, the right to earnings, and the right to disposition. The right to possess is the right to control and control is the foundation of ownership. Without the right to possess, all of the other three rights would be hampered. Only when a person really has the right to possess can he/she better enjoy the right to use, the right to earnings and the right to disposition. Private ownership and personal ownership both have possession as the final goal. With the rise of the sharing economy, however, people realize that what is important is not the right to possess but whether things can truly be used. The essence of sharing is to share the right to use and the right to earnings so as to obtain benefits (He Zhe 2017). The transfer of the right to use helps us make the most out of idle resources, but its premise is that those who hold the right to possess has the willingness to transfer the right to use, and the key lies in having the right to possess. Since the essence of property rights is possession and the root lies in the exclusivity of things, it determines that an object cannot have multiple right owners at the same time. Possession thus becomes the only way to master property rights.

In the process of the transfer of property rights, the existence of the right to possess prevents impairment of the interests of the right holder because he/she still holds control over what is in his/her possession. Different from that, data can have multiple right holders at the same time since it can be infinitely reproduced at extremely low cost and with no loss. Under such a circumstance, one can control and use data regardless of whether he/she has the right to possess it. Without the right to possess it, people can exercise the right to use, the right to earnings and the right to disposition over data all the same. Once the right to use data is transferred, the party who receives it takes complete possession of the data concerned and the data is out of the control of its original owner and possession over data would become meaningless. It is necessary to share data with others if people want to maximize the value of data, but there will inevitably be conflict with possession. Therefore, the rights to share data and the right to possess property are equally important. They are the inevitable result of making the best use of data. In addition, the real value of data lies in infinite reproduction at low cost, which is the foundation of digital civilization and determines that sharing becomes a basic and central demand in the era of big data and the rights to share become the essential part of data rights. Once we depart from this basis and impose the right to possess in the realm of data rights as we do in the field of property rights, the application and development of data will be severely hampered, and we will betray the original intention of establishing data rights, which is to protect data and promote development in relevant fields (Key Laboratory of Big Data Strategy 2018, p. 159).

One ownership for one object vs. multi-ownership of data

"One ownership for one object" is the core representation of the dominance of property rights. With the development of technology, more types of property rights gradually came into being and the power-function distinction of ownership becomes increasingly complicated. People are also changing the way they use things. In judicial practice, "one ownership for one object" collides more and more with "multiple ownership for one object" and "one ownership for multiple objects". All of them have, to a certain extent, obtained indirect or vague consent in law, which deviates from the original meaning of "one ownership for one object". In contrast, data, intangible and replicable as it is, can contain interest in multiple forms. The rights to share enable data to have multiple right owners, who share not one same data right but separate and complete data rights that they each can own. This forms the pattern of sharing where people seek not to own but to use.

Since data is replicable and inconsumable and has special commonality, multi-ownership of data is at least possible. This means that endowing absolute right to dominate data on any right holder runs counter to the development purpose of sharing. With the development of the times and the advances of technology, when the cost of an object approaches zero, possession will no longer be unnecessary. This is especially true for data resources as they are abundant and with zero marginal cost. Thus, sharing of multi-ownership of data will inevitably become the general trend. In the long term, many scarce resources will become abundant as sharing will ease scarcity to a large extent. "The point is this: When seen through the lens of technology, few resources are truly scarce; they're mainly inaccessible" (Peter H. Diamandis & Steven Kotler 2014, p. 8).

Connotation of the rights to share

The rights to share provide an approach to data rights that balances between public interest and private interests and helps unleash people's creativity so that they can contribute to the development of the digital civilization. The core of the rights to share is a balance in the distribution of data interest. Whether the public interest of data outweigh its private interest or the other way round, it will be against the basic spirit of freedom and equality. Any imbalance here will dampen people's enthusiasm and initiative to create wealth with data. One of the objectives of the rights to share is to modify the traditional approach to rights and data which values private interest more than public interests, and advocates an approach to data rights that balances between public and private interest. The premise for data use is the right to share data which is both the fundamental requirement of the digital civilization and the key to a new social order (Long Rongyuan & Yang Guanhua 2018).

The rights to share, taking altruism as the fundamental basis, are an important component of the basic system of the digital civilization. From the perspective of equity, balance between public and private data interests is a central topic in the digital civilization. Firstly, in order to ensure sound relationship between the public and private spheres in terms of data interests, the rights to share must function to maintain fair distribution and balance between public and private interest of data, upholding equity. Secondly, the distribution of public interests and private interests of data is absolute, objective and universal. Nobody can impose subjective will on this through agreements of any form. Any subjective, relative or excessive interpretation will hamper equity. Therefore, the rights to share have extremely important practical significance in the building of a new order for the digital civilization (Key Laboratory of Big Data Strategy 2018, p. 225).

The rights to share help resolve conflicts among different data right holders and provides a value basis for the settlement of strife concerning data interests. The rights to share set out to uphold balance between public interests and private interests of data and provides the basic value orientation for the development of the digital civilization, giving high priority to equity. Based on the principle of balance between public interests and private interests of data, legislation can be put in place to resolve conflicts between data right holders and coordination mechanism for a balance of interest among these rights holders can be improved so as to open up channels for data right holders to express their demand for data and defuse social crises caused by conflict of data interests. This will allow data right holders to do everything they can and get what they should. In the meantime, the rights to share can also help resolve problems such as unfair allocation of resources, inequality of opportunities and social injustice brought about by data monopoly, ensure social equity and justice, achieve optimal data resource allocation and zero marginal cost, increase data wealth, and promote economic growth and social harmony in the age of digital civilization.

Logical starting point of the rights to share

The rights to share are a type of rights that is opposite to the right to possess. The right to possess data is based on egoism and protects the interests of data right holders. To a certain extent, it serves as a basic driving force for expanding data production. However, human beings cannot produce data resources without limitation and the possession of data will inevitably result in huge waste of resources. This determines that the right to possess data cannot meet the needs of data development. Scarcity, which is a fact, further highlights the altruism of development. Due to the extremely low cost of data reproduction, there is a natural bond between data and sharing. The rights to share will eventually replace the right to possess and become the core driving force for the development of the digital civilization. The rights to share stem from altruism and with altruism as the conceptual foundation, the rights to share shape people's way of thinking in regard to data, have data shared, and explores the shared value of data. In this sense, altruism is the logical starting point of the rights to share.

Altruism of data rights. Altruism is traditionally regarded as a typical characteristic of moral behaviors. In the field of law, however, it is merely manifested in a small number of actions which aim to help those in need. Generally, altruism is more of a moral pursuit while egoism tend to prevail in law. However, the essential characteristics of a data man do not offer sufficient support for egoism. The reason is that people work and live better when they act as data men, and the instrumental value of a data man determines that egoism is natural. The altruism of a data man has brought huge benefits to mankind, and in pursuit of interests, people choose to interact with data men so that there can be more altruistic behaviors. If a data man finds the necessary legal basis for its rights, altruistic behaviors will have profound influence on the nature of data rights. Some scholars believe that species with altruistic tendency is at a disadvantaged position in competition in the ecosystem with low adaptability (Li Jianhui & Gong Xiaole 2009). However, interdisciplinary studies on the game theory and biological evolutionism show that compared with selfish species, species with an altruistic spirit have more evolutionary advantages in competition the ecosystem (Liu Heling 2005). By this token, the altruistic nature of data does not necessarily constitute a disadvantage in competition for rights. In contrast, it promotes human development. Besides, the altruism of data rights is also helpful to interactions between a natural and a data man. By doing something altruistic, a data man sends out a signal for interaction so that it secures more space for action and more cooperation opportunities. This will benefit only a small number of people at first, who can make money from it. As more people get involved, altruism will turn from what is embodied in occasional interactions into something legalized and long term interests will thus be ensured. Therefore, to improve data well-being of society and promote human progress, the state must establish mechanisms to protect altruistic behaviors, that is, establish the right of altruism. This is a kind of right given to a data man with an aim to meet the development needs of mankind as well as a legal representation of the altruistic function of a data man (Zhang Yujie 2017).

Altruism and the sharing of data rights. In the era of big data, data sharing, as a typical extra-role behavior, significantly promotes the development of teams and organizations. However, when there is competition among individuals within an organization, data sharing may cause damage to personal interest. For self-interest, therefore, people tend not to take the initiative to share data. Under such a circumstance, data sharing by individuals stems mainly from altruism manifested in the following four aspects: First, the tendency of individuals to helping others, or more specifically, the willingness of individuals to share data with others with no strings. Second, reciprocal altruism, a typical example of which is the prosocial cooperation and mutual help that individual shows in a relational society; third, reputation-oriented altruism, which is represented by the inclination in people's value structure towards being a "good person" which leads people towards altruistic behaviors with the purpose of maintaining their reputation or upholding the value the expect; and fourth, imperative sharing which can be seen, for example, in sharing data according to instruction from a superior. It can be seen that altruism significantly promotes prosocial behaviors (e.g. cooperation, actions of mutual benefits, helping others, etc.) (Zheng Jianjun & Fu Xiaojie 2019). In terms of its nature, the rights to share is clearly prosocial and actions to share data are extra-role behaviors which are helpful to the development of an organization. The rights to share constitute an important dimension of the behavior of a corporate citizen. In sum, the rights to share have the same characteristics as prosocial helping, cooperative, and selfless behaviors. Hence, altruism produces significant positive influence on people's willingness and actions to share data. Altruism is the essence of sharing and provides necessary basis for the realization of the rights to share. Altruism, as an internalized spiritual need as well as an externalized conscious action, tends to bring benefits to others. In the age of big data, the ultimate significance of altruism lies in promoting the integration between data rights and the use, protection and value of data. Altruism improves people's willingness to transfer and share data rights, facilitates the establishment of the rights to share, and helps turn the transfer and sharing of data into an action with highly positive significance.

Data man's rights to share. Traditionally, basic rights are considered as a fundamental and core component of civil rights and the basis for their existence is the basic values and universality of rights. In this sense, the rights to share, as a basic right of a data man, provide necessary support for the data man hypothesis. The rights to share are the primary basic right of a data man, but for the moment, there are clearly some conflicts between the rights to share and other rights. On the one hand, since data resources have commercial value and may contain privacy and even state security information, the general public and business organizations tend to claim their data rights and seek protection for them (such as the right to be forgotten and data asset rights). This will reduce the scope of data sharing and hamper the realization of the functions of the rights to share. On the other hand, a data man relies heavily on data analysis. and without the rights to share, it may face risks of rights infringement. Hence, should the law protect civil rights or the request of a data to share? Whichever is the choice, the side that is left unprotected will probably fight back hard. At present, though personal privacy can be protected to a certain extent, social changes brought by the rights to share go far beyond what can be measured by the value of data protection. Meanwhile, data rights protection, which flourished in the sphere of private rights has seen only minimal success in the sphere of public rights. Nothing but the rights to share represent the general development trend in the future digital civilization. Therefore, from the perspective of laws, efforts should be made in the following two aspects: First, data should be classified for both security protection and disclosure so as to protect the data privacy rights and trade secrets of citizens and business organizations. Second, efforts should be made to promote the sharing of data resources in all forms, affirm data man's rights to share, and reduce conflicts of rights.

Balance between the rights to share and the right to privacy

Data circulation and data sharing is the inevitable choice for industrial upgrading, scientific and technological innovation and the building of governance capacity in the age of digital civilization. However, there are natural conflicts of interest between data sharing and privacy protection, and the tension has been growing. This stems from the game between public interests and personal interests of data and the divergence between property interests and personality interests of data. Therefore, the balance between the rights to share and the right to privacy must be achieved in order to fully explore the value of data resources.

Public interests vs. personal interests. The conflicts between the rights to share and the right to privacy, to some extent, go down to the game between public interests and personal interests of data. On the one hand, the rights to share are clearly inclined towards public interests in terms of its purposes and functions. The purpose of the rights to share is to promote data resource sharing, put data resources to better use and realize free circulation and sharing of data among governments, enterprises and the public.

From the perspective of function, data possesses huge economic and social value. Free data circulation and sharing contributes to the transformation of government functions, the growth of the government's governance capacity and the quality of public services. In the meantime, data sharing lays solid foundation for industrial development, enables customers to enjoy more timely and better-targeted services, saves time and energy for people, improves the allocation of social resources and enhances the efficiency of data resource use. On the other hand, from its very first day, the right to privacy has always focused on non-interference from others, emphasizing the protection of individuals' right to enjoy private space without interference from others. This shows distinct features of the autonomy of private law. With social development and scientific and technological progress, the coverage of the right to privacy gradually extended to such fields as self-determination privacy, space privacy and information privacy. However, "any privacy which an individual is unwilling to disclose should be protected on the basis of the right to privacy as long as that data does not belong to the public sphere and the right holder is unwilling to share it, regardless of whether the disclosure of such information will have a positive or negative impact on the right holder (Zhang Xinbao 1998, p. 21)." The right to privacy always puts the personal dignity and autonomy in the first place so that individuals may keep some information to themselves, which may help them withstand external pressure and protect their own interest. As Professor Wang Liming once said, the right to privacy is naturally "anti-social" to some extent. It separates the private sphere from the public sphere so that individuals can enjoy their life alone with no interference. To some extent, this goes against what society prefers (Wang Liming 2005, p. 604). Therefore, conflicts between the rights to share, which is conducive to industrial and social development, and the right to privacy, which upholds the legal rights and interest of individuals, in essence, rise from the game between public interest and personal interests in the circulation and sharing process consisted of data collection, data use, and data transfer.

Property interest vs. personality interest. Another reason for the conflicts between the rights to share and the right to privacy lies in the discrepancies between property interest and personality interests of data. On the one hand, as the property interest contained in data become more prominent and business data activities increase, it is not realistic to treat data as having only personality value. Data holds both property value and personality value, and has already become a kind of intangible property that generates profit. We should be fully aware that data can be regarded as property and give better play to its role of driving economic growth. On the other hand, the traditional right to privacy stresses the protection of data based on the personality value it contains. The personality value of data is as important as the property value. Data is generated all the time, gathered through sharing to form a detailed profile of daily life and even our future. Such description tends to be more accurate than the description we can give about our own life. Hence, data sharing helps us have a better look at people's life and even their mental state, keeping everyone monitored at all time in a panopticon. People's freedom to choose their lifestyle, free will for daily affairs, secrets and peace in their private space and control over their own data may all be infringed when all data are shared. People may even feel unsure about whether the choice is made by themselves or by data. Therefore, data brings two-fold interests: Data sharing focuses on the protection of the property interests in data, while the protection of privacy pays more attention to the personality interests of data. The discrepancies between the two in terms of the protection of interests lead to conflicts between the rights to share and the right to privacy (Wang Yan & Ye Ming 2019).

Path towards balance between the rights to share and the right to privacy. Settlement of disputes is one of the basic functions of law. To realize this, laws must seek balance between multiple types of interests. To be more specific, the rights to share stress the free circulation and sharing of data and represents public interests and property interests; while on the contrary, the right to privacy represents private interests and personality interests. Conflicts between these two sides are inevitable. Nevertheless, these two are not completely opposite. To a certain extent, the pursuit of public interests and that of private interests have common grounds: Public interest is the sum of private interest that is universal. In the meantime, protecting the property interests of right holders does not exclude the protection of personality interests. Hence, when dealing with conflicts between the two, simply giving priority to either side will not do, and what we need to do is to find a balance between public interests and private interests as well as between property interests and personality interests. In other words, data rights law not only protects the personality and dignity of individuals but also gives due consideration to the rights to share by imposing some restrictions on the right to privacy. Meanwhile, the rights to share and the right to privacy are like the two sides of one coin. In order to ensure public interests and promote economic development, it is necessary to realize the free circulation and sharing of data among governments, enterprises and the public. Here, some restrictions should be made on the right to privacy to transfer some non-core interests and ensure the basic conditions for the rights to share to help realize core interests. At the same time, the rights to share should not be allowed to grow unrestrained either. Restrictions should also be imposed on it so that the right to privacy can be ensured appropriately. However, examining the existing laws of many countries, we can see that legislation on data now lags far behind the practical needs of the development of the data industry. Therefore, to meet the needs of practice and theoretical development and achieve win-win results for data use and data protection, it is necessary to formulate a data rights law as soon as possible to balance between the rights to share and the right to privacy, deal with basic issues concerning the rights to share and the right to privacy, define the scope and boundary of rights, set strictly rules for the realization of the rights to share, enhance supervision over the exercise of the rights to share and improve the liability and remedy mechanisms regarding privacy infringement by the rights to share.

Content of the Rights to Share

Based on their nature, we may divide the rights to share into three types, the right to share public data, the right to share business data, and the right to share personal data. By managing the rights to share based on this classification, we will realize the free and orderly development of data sharing and increase the shared value of data. In the meantime, based on the functions of property rights, we divide data rights into four parts: the right to access shared data, the right to use shared data, the *jus fruendi* of shared data, and the right to disposition of shared data which provide a basis for the exercise of the rights to share. However, data can also be divided into public data and non-public data. Therefore, in order to make the best use of these two types of data, we separate the functions of the rights to share and establish data rights of public interests and usufructuary data rights, which are the basic ways to realize the rights to share.

Types of the rights to share

The establishment of the right to share public data, on the one hand, breaks the data island of the public sector through data sharing and, on the other hand, releases public data dividends by offering open access to data openness. Business data accounts for a relatively low share in the total quantity of data compared with the other two types, but both public data and personal data can transform into business data under certain conditions. Therefore, business data, based on economic activities in the market, has the biggest development potential. The establishment of the right to share public data can promote the transformation into business data, increase data transaction, and add to the use value of data. Personal data contains tremendous value. The establishment of the right to share personal data ensures the gains that people can get from sharing data and this motivate people to produce and share more data.

The right to share public data

The right to share public data is the right to have public data shared. Public data in jurisprudence refers to data resources that are closely related to public interests. Data related to government affairs is the most important and largest part of public data since the government collects massive data resources while performing public functions. According to statistics, the government has 80 percent of all data resources. However, since public data is scattered extensively among different government departments, a large number of data islands are formed. In addition, people sometimes lack the motivation to share their data due to the involvement of departmental interests. As a result, government monopoly is likely to occur but poor data integration will cause serious waste. In the meantime, data movement under the influence of the Matthew effect tends to create a data divide and the public, usually marginalized, may not enjoy the dividend of data to the full. This may give the public a relative sense of being deprived of their data rights which may intensify with time. In essence, however, public data is public property that belongs to all. Under the premise of guaranteeing personal privacy, trade secrets and state security, the state should return these data to the people. In this sense, the establishment of the right to share public data represent a movement towards sharing where the people claim their public data rights from government authorities. At the same time, as the public grows more and more aware of their data rights, it is imperative to establish the right to share public data.

The right to share public data is a basic civil right which allows the general public to control and use public data resources. This right, on the one hand, stems from the obligation of people to accept and support data collection, and on the other hand, it comes from the fact that public data, in nature, belongs to the whole people. Under normal circumstances, people have the right to know about, use and share all public data except for sensitive data like personal privacy, trade secrets and state security information. Hence, the right to share public data can be divided into two parts. One is the right to share data within the public sector, or the right to sector-wide data sharing. It promotes the free circulation of public data within the public sector, helps reduce barriers between higher and lower levels and between different departments of the public sector, so that more data resources can be shared. The other one is the right to make data public to the whole society, or the right to offer open access to public data. Compared with the former part, this part of data has a relatively small scale because some public data must be kept confidential, not open to the public.

The right to share public data pursues to uphold the value that people should be allowed to know about public data, but it is not simply a copy or upgraded version of the citizens' right to know in the field of public data.

The citizens' right to know means that citizens have the right to demand the disclosure of some information by state organs. It allows the public to acquire government information and aims at helping build an open government. In contrast, the right to share public data emphasizes the sharing and use of public data: On the one hand, the purpose of people's demand for public data has long been beyond better transparency of government operations. It is now more about the creation of social and economic value through the use and mining of public data. On the other hand, the right to share public data requires the public sector to take the initiative to share data without delay and it represents the upgrading of public service approach from passive disclosure at requests to sharing without being asked. In legal theory, though there has been no direct or explicit expression of the right to share public data, it does not prevent the right to share public data from becoming a basic civil right. In terms of its coverage, the right to share public data is actually a bundle of rights and interests therein stem from the added value generated from the sharing of public data. From this perspective, the right to share public data, as a civil right aiming to share the results of public data exploration, is a mixture of rights in nature. It can be the right to development based on jus fruendi, or the right of supervision in the circumstance of data-powered administration, or the right of participation aimed at reducing information asymmetry (Cheng Tongshun & Shi Meng 2018).

The right to share business data

During their production and operation processes, enterprises gather vast amounts of business data which can be divided into two parts. One is business data related to identity and behavioral characteristics of consumers, which is owned by the relevant individuals and cannot sold or transferred by the enterprises. The other is consumption data obtained by enterprises. This part of data, after masking and decryption, can be regarded business data of the relevant enterprises and be controlled and traded as such by the enterprises. This categorization makes it possible for enterprises to trade business data continuously and orderly, while the right to share business data helps unleash the potential value of business data.

The value of data lies in being constantly used, analyzed, and mined. The non-expendability of data use ensures that the more data is used, the more interests it brings, yet at the same time risk of trade secret leakage will also rise. As more potential value is being discovered from data, data, as a resource or property, is gaining more and more attention. Many enterprises purchase business data in pursuit of profits. However, enterprises that have business data tend to take it for granted that they possess and own the data they aggregate, that the data has already got away from its provider, and become data assets of the recipient. Thus, a series of disputes arise over business data (Du Zhenhua & Cha Hongwang 2016).

Enterprises that rely on business data tend to possess or have the ability to amass large amounts of data, but they may not have the ability to get value or innovations out of business data. Therefore, it is necessary and important to allow for smooth flow of business data so that such resources can be mined and used repeatedly from multiple angles and on different levels. To achieve this, we must ensure good order on the data market by clearly defining the property rights related to data and make data ownership clear. Therefore, in order to realize the highest data value, the right to share business data must be established to balance the interests of the various parties involved, protect their interests, and enable business data to be put into wide use.

The right to share business data is a right to have business data shared. In a sense, the sharing of business data is another way to refer to business data transaction, so the right to share business data is also known as the right to trade business data. At present, the scale of business data is relatively small but it can be enlarged by transforming public data with open access and shared private data into business data. Only when put into commercial use can data release its value to the greatest extent. Therefore, transformation into business data represents the general trend and the right to share business data is the most promising part of the right to share data. The right to share business data facilitates the free circulation of business data within the whole society, to give more people the opportunity to use data and thus increase data value through sharing.

The right to share personal data

People are the primary source of data and research on data should return to the people-oriented analysis paradigm. To some extent, all data can be considered as personal data and the personal information contained in data can be related to a certain natural person and may even involve sensitive personal information and core privacy. If such data is not fully desensitized, other people may get the personal information and privacy, which can result in infringement on the data rights of individuals. Meanwhile, with the development of modern science and technology, the collection and transmission of data become easier and more efficient. To some extent, data sharing is a way to collect and transmit personal data as well as to reuse it. Since shared data may contain a good deal of personal information, the right to share personal data should be based on the premise of lawful processing of personal data.

Data sharing involves personal data but there is a lack of sound protection for personal data in the chain of sharing: On the one hand, the protection of personal data can be undermined during data collection, which is the initial part of the chain, mainly because of the abuse of authorization. Personal data owners tend to lose control over their personal data after they give the authorization the first time, and it is therefore difficult to ensure that the personal data is used as they intended it to be. On the other hand, the lack of an effective authorization mechanism brings into question the lawfulness of the transferee's use of personal data, which hampers the efficiency of personal data sharing. Based on the above, the establishment of the right to share personal data can help us protect and distribute the rights and interests related to the sharing of personal data in an effective and reasonable way. The right to share personal data encourages people to cooperate with data collectors and produce more data. It motivates people to produce data and thus provide constant data supply for society. In that sense, the rights to share personal data is the most important part of the rights to share.

In essence, sharing personal data means that other people can collect and use personal data. Hence, the right to share personal data has two dimensions: Firstly, for those who collect personal data, the right to share personal data allows them to transfer the personal data they collect and the recipient can either be specified or not. Secondly, for those who receive the shared personal data, the sharing not only lets them reuse the data, but also makes it possible for them to process and exploit the personal data and even to share it further. Therefore, data holders should not be allowed to share data arbitrarily, while those who receive shared data should neither be allowed to share at will or allow others to use the data they acquire (Wang Liming 2019). The right to share personal data should maintain individual's dominance over data, autonomy in private law and personal dignity. Or, plainly put, it should promote personal data openness and sharing under the premise that individuals' basic rights over personal data are effectively protected.

Functions of the rights to share

There is the narrow sense and the broad sense of the rights to share. In the narrow sense, the rights to share refer to the right to share data with others; while in the broad sense, they refer to the rights that arise from the full life cycle of data sharing behaviors. Here, we mainly use the term in the broad sense and the rights to share, therefore, has four functions: the right to access shared data, the right to use shared data, *jus fruendi* of shared data, and the right to disposition of shared data. The right to access shared data allows people to acquire data that is shared; the right to use shared data allows people to use data that is shared; *jus fruendi* of shared data allows people to obtain earnings generated from shared data; and the right to disposition of shared data means people have the right to share the disposition of data. Data here include both shared data and original data.

The right to access shared data

To get access to shared data is a basic data activity. Only when one has access to some data can he/she take control over it and truly share it. The right to access shared data should be established in order to ensure the legitimacy and fairness to access shared data. The right to access shared data means that people have the right to acquire shared data according to laws and regulations. The exercise of the right to access shared data must be put under restrictions. It must be premised on the will of people who offer data for sharing. No one can get access to data without that. Otherwise, severe data security breaches would arise.

Holders of the right to access shared data can be anyone who needs shared data, including natural persons, legal persons and public institutions. The right to access shared data, in the broad sense, is a basic right of citizens in the sphere of public law, as well as an important civil right in the sphere of private law. From the perspective of public law, free access to data is a precondition for citizens' political participation; therefore, without the right to access shared data, the basic rights of citizens will not be guaranteed. The state, as a holder of public rights, also enjoys the right to access shared data. If the state cannot get full access to data, the political, economic and cultural development of the country will lack sound basis. From the perspective of private law, the right to access shared data is a basic right, with which civil subjects accomplish civil activities. Only when consumers can have sufficient access to business data, can commodity transaction be fair and just. Interests of civil subjects will only be a fantasy if the right to access shared data is not at the back. The right to access shared data is a type of absolute right and every organization and individual should support its realization (Zhou Shuyun 2014).

The objects of the right to access shared data are the data shared and that is where the interests of data holders lie. Shared data fall into various types, each with distinctive characteristics. From the perspective of access to shared data, the shared data can be categorized into several types according to different classification criteria. Broadly, the objects covered by the right to access shared data may include data resources, data technologies, data channels and data services that are shared. Or, in the narrow sense, there is only data shared, which is public, renewable, time-sensitive, valuable and scarce in nature. These characteristics are the premise of the establishment of the right to access shared data. Only when this right is established and protected can the demand of citizens for access to shared data be satisfied and the shared value of data be maximized (Zhou Shuyun & Wang Haoyun 2015).

The process to access shared data is complicated. The content of the right to access shared data, that is, what can be truly acquired by citizens, is the interests attached to core elements such as data resources, data technologies, data channels and data services. Therefore, the right to access shared data contains four basic items: the right to select the content of shared data, the right to know technologies of shared data, the right to approach communication channels of shared data, and the right to guaranteed service quality of the shared data. The right to select the content of shared data means that a right holder has the freedom to select the content of shared data; the right to know technologies of shared data means that a right holder, in order to acquire the content of the share data, has the right to learn about relevant data acquisition technologies; the right to approach communication channels of shared data means that a right holder, in order to acquire the content of the share data, has the right to approach media for data sharing; and the right to guaranteed service quality of shared data means that in the process of using shared data, the user have the right to request relevant service providers to provide high-quality, efficient and fair data sharing services and to ensure relatively high quality of the products of shared data content (Zhou Shuyun & Luo Xueying 2014).

Right to use shared data

Shared data is to be used and to use it is how we explore the shared value of data. The right to use shared data means that people have the right to make use of data that is shared. The purpose of the rights to share is not for people to have access to shared data but instead for them to use it. Through data sharing, data holders help others have their needs met and thus obtain due interests. It is necessary to establish the right to use shared data and this is determined by the use shared value of data. In the meantime, the right to use shared data can be separate from the rights to share so as to become an independent function and serve as an important foundation for establishing usufructuary rights of data and usufructuary rights of public data. Different from the right to use in its traditional sense, the right to use shared data must be exercised in accordance with those who offer the data for sharing. Hence, the right to use shared data is actually a restricted version of the right to use. It is the right to pursue the use value of data and to obtain corresponding interests through data use. It mainly covers the right to process shared data and the right to reproduce shared data. Processing is a basic method to use shared data, and data processing explores and builds the shared value of data. Therefore, the right to process shared data is an important part of the right to use shared data. The right to process shared data can also be shared yet those who receive this right because of the sharing may only process the data in manners agreed upon. In order to build the shared value of data, it is necessary to enlarge the scale of data sharing so that more people can use the data. Data reproduction, as its cost is extremely low, is the most important to achieve this, and the right to reproduce shared data thus, has a significant position in the right to use shared data. It is an important condition for the use of shared data and ensures complete reproduction of the information that data contains (Key Laboratory of Big Data Strategy 2018, p. 195).

Jus fruendi of shared data

The *jus fruendi* of shared data refers to the right for people to obtain earnings with shared data. After the getting access to shared data, in addition to using it, people can also obtain some earnings from it. Since these earnings are derived from the shared data, the *jus fruendi* of shared data is also called the right to obtain natural fruits and *fructus civiles* of shared data. In modern society, a significant tendency in the development of rights is the shift from abstract domination to concrete utilization. The establishment of the *jus fruendi* of shared data conforms to this tendency and makes it possible to divide the rights to share. However, the *jus fruendi* of shared data is subject to restrictions that stem from the objects of the right, that is, the data that is shared. While the purpose of data transaction is to obtain earnings, the *jus fruendi* of shared data plays an important role in enlarging the scale of and establishing order for data transaction. The capitalization of shared data is, in fact, the process of obtaining *jus fruendi*, as well as a way to realize the *jus fruendi* of shared data in economic terms.

Shared data can only realize its value when *jus fruendi* is obtained, and this proves the externality and long cycle of returns of the *jus fruendi* of shared data, as well as the diversity of the parties it involves. Externality comes from the ratio of the earnings obtained from using and sharing the data to the costs paid. It determines that shared data is nothing absolute. Hence, necessary restrictions should be placed on the *jus fruendi* of shared data in order to balance between private interests and public interests. The earnings from shared data has a long cycle since the shared value of data cannot be sufficiently explored by using or consuming the data only once. When new data resources are added and connected to what is already there, the shared value of data will increase and new earnings will come. In the meantime, shared data does not wear out. It can be shared more extensively and used again and again, bringing returns over a long period of time. The shared value of data will never reach its peak. Instead, it accumulates and grows all the time. The earnings of shared data show a kind of diversity because, as data cannot be delivered in an absolute sense, it is impossible to complete transfer the control over completely and entirely, there can be multiple parties who gain *jus fruendi* over the same body of shared data (Key Laboratory of Big Data Strategy 2018, p. 196).

The right to disposition of shared data

Disposition represent ultimate domination over data. The right to disposition of shared data is the right for people to have shared data disposed of. From a different perspective, disposition can be regarded as the end use of data. Therefore, the right to disposition of shared data is the right to consume and share the shared data which is the ultimate manifestation of the rights to share. The right to disposition of shared data does not cause those who offer the data for sharing to lose control over the data. Rather, it is an independent part of the rights to share formed through data reproduction which enables several holders of the rights to share to get access to and use the same data simultaneously. The right to disposition of shared data does not eliminate the original value of the shared data. On the contrary, it increases the shared value. For *res corporales*, disposition leads to the absolute or relative extinction of its ownership and the right to disposition of them determines their ownership (Lu Xiaohua 2009, p. 373). For data, in contrast, the traditional right to dispose is no longer applicable. It goes against the development trend of data to seek to possess data. Since the value of data lies it being shared, control over data is not the purpose of the rights to share. To solve the problem of data scarcity and give full play to the value of data, it is necessary to enlarge the scale of data and let more people to have opportunities to use data. The right to disposition of shared data is more about the use of shared data which is the way for people to pursue the value of data. Therefore, the right to disposition of shared data is as important as the ownership of shared data.

Usufructuary right of and usufructuary right of public data

The establishment of the rights to share enables data to be shared among different parties and also inevitably causes conflicts between data ownership and data use. In order to solve the conflicts, we propose the usufructuary right of data and the usufructuary right of public data, both are restricted forms of and realistic choices for the realization of the rights to share. These two rights make it possible to separate data ownership from the right to use data. The usufructuary right of data refers to the right to use and obtain earnings from other people's data under certain conditions. It is an important way to realize the rights to share and adds to the value of the rights to share. The usufructuary right of public data is a kind of transferred usufructuary right of data. It refers to the right of administrative institutions represented by the government, as well as public institutions and public interest organizations to access, manage, use and share public data for public interests.

Usufructuary right of data

The usufructuary right of data refers to the right to use shared data as well as to obtain earnings from it. It means that a right holder authorizes others to use and benefit from data. The usufructuary right of data is established to settle the conflict between the ownership and the right to use shared data and it allows people to use shared data and obtain earnings under certain conditions. The usufructuary right of data represents the shift of data rights from domination to use which helps realize the value of the rights to share. It is a realization form of the rights to share. The emergence of the usufructuary right of data enables us to distinguish the different functions of the rights to share. It is a kind of data right formed on the basis that a right holder separates some functions of the rights to share and share them with others, so that people can enjoy some kind of right over other people's data. Hence, the usufructuary right of data has the rights to share as its foundation, and its existence in itself constitutes a restriction on the rights to share. The establishment of the usufructuary right of data is often out of the will of a data right holder who, under the circumstance that he/she is not able to actually use or put into full play the value of data, act to share his/her data with others so that they can use and obtain earnings from the data and fully realize the value of the data. As the age of digital civilization is dawning, the scale of data resources expands and the usufructuary right of data becomes more and more prominent.

Since the basis of the usufructuary right of data is shared data, which is similar to rights over the property of others, the usufructuary right of data can be referred to as rights over the data of others. Since the usufructuary right of data allows dominance over the data involved only within an agreed scope, it is also known as restricted data right. Holders of the usufructuary right of data cannot be owners of the same data. Since the usufructuary right of data is established on shared data, the subject can be natural persons, legal persons or other organizations who have rights over shared data, while the object is the shared data which possesses such characteristics as incorporeity, replicability and non-absolute delivery. With the diversification of ways people use data, especially advances in science and technology and innovations in systems and mechanisms, the shared value of data continually improves. Therefore, in order to use shared data more efficiently, it is necessary to establish the usufructuary right over shared data, and this is an irresistible trend in the development of data rights.

The usufructuary right of data is the right to dominate the use shared value of data. Legally, the main content of the usufructuary right of data is to use and earn from shared data. Hence, the content of the usufructuary right of data includes the right to get access to shared data, the right to use shared data and *jus fruendi* of shared data. On the one hand, in order to use and earn from data, it is necessary to get access to shared data. Without the right to do so, right holders cannot possibly make actual use of shared data. Since the usufructuary right of data is the right to use and earn from shared data, as a way to get the use value out of data, it is necessary that the right holder gets access to the target data. The right to access shared data is usually the focus of conflicts over the usufructuary right of data since access is the prerequisite of the usufructuary right of data. On the other hand, the usufructuary right of data takes the use and earnings of shared data as its purpose. The right to use shared data means to use according to the nature and purpose of shared data based on laws or relevant agreements. The purpose for the establishment of the usufructuary right of data is to put shared data into better use and get more use value out of it. To earn from shared data means to gain natural fruits and legal fruits by using shared data. The rights to use and to gain earnings are usually closely related since people can only gain earnings after using the shared data. Hence, the usufructuary right of data should include both the right to use shared data and the *jus fruendi* of shared data. This is because, in the legal field, the direct denotation of the usufructuary right of data is the right to use. It is a type of data right which takes advantage of shared data for the purpose of utilization. In the meantime, the usufructuary right of data allows right holders to make use of the use value of data to meet their various interests needs. In this sense, the usufructuary right of data also includes *jus fruendi* of shared data (Key Laboratory of Big Data Strategy 2018, p. 203).

Usufructuary right of public data

The usufructuary right of data mainly emphasizes the use of and earnings from data from the perspective of private rights. As the opposite of the usufructuary right of data, the usufructuary right of public data refers to the right for administrative institutions represented by the government, as well as public institutions and public interest organizations to access, manage, use and dispose of public interest data for the public good. In terms of its legal nature, the usufructuary right of public data is a kind of transferred usufructuary right of data and a basic data right of citizens. It is a new claim of data rights which is non-profit and used for public utilities, public services and public administration. The usufructuary right of public data belongs to the whole people. Administrative institutions represented by the government, public institutions and public interest organizations are only entrusted by the people to dominate such right for the public good. Safeguarding public interest is the fundamental purpose of the usufructuary right of public data and an effective restriction on private rights (Key Laboratory of Big Data Strategy 2018, p. 212).

For the ultimate goal of safeguarding public interest, the usufructuary right of public data should include the following functions: the right to access, the right to manage, the right to use and the right to disposition. Though the public can obtain earnings by using public interest data, the usufructuary right of public data itself does not include the *jus freudi*. This is because when the uses public interest data, they are, in nature, exercising the usufructuary right of data over public interest data rather than the usufructuary right of public data. Only administrative institutions represented by the government, public institutions and public interest organizations are eligible for exercising the usufructuary right of public data. During the process of exercising the usufructuary right of public data, they are not allowed to make earnings from public data. Therefore, the usufructuary right of public data do not include the function of earnings.

The right to access public interest data refers to the right of administrative institutions represented by the government, public institutions and public interest organizations to, according to the relevant legal provisions, timely, accurately and integrally access all kinds of public interest data needed through certain means. Of course, the exercise of the right to access public interest data must be put under restrictions, otherwise, public data rights will expand without limits. The right to manage public interest data refers to the administrative right exercised by administrative institutions represented by the government, public institutions and public interest organizations over public interest data, in order to achieve the purposes of public use of public interest data. In terms of its legal nature, the right to manage public interest data is a legal obligation because it is the administrative power exercised by administrative institutions represented by the government, public institutions and public interest organizations to guarantee and enhance public interests and perform administrative obligations. Hence, the usufructuary right of public data is a kind of administrative power which possesses binding force in public law. In the meantime, the right to manage public interest data can help guarantee the right of citizens to use public interest data and check arbitrary behaviors of administrative organs. The right to use public interest data is the core part of the usufructuary right of public data and its purpose is to make public use of public interest data and to ensure and increase public interest. Therefore, the right to use public interest data refers to the right of administrative institutions represented by the government, public institutions and public interest organizations to use public interest data. The right to disposition of public interest data refers to the right for management organizations of public interest data to share the public interest data in their charge with others. There are two types. One is the right to disposition of public interest data in the narrow sense, which refers to the sharing of public interest data among different administrative organs. The data remains public interest data after it is shared. The administrative organs who receive shared public interest data enjoy part of the functions of the usufructuary right of public data and can use and manage these data. The other type is the right to provide access to public interest data, which refers to the right of management organizations of public interest data to offer open access to the data in their charge towards enterprises and individual citizens. After enterprises and individual citizens obtain control over public interest data, such data transforms into usufructuary data and thus can be used to make earnings.

Value of the Rights to Share

From the perspective of justice, the rights to share are public rights established on the basis of altruism which will inevitably come into conflict with existing individual rights based on egoism and thus promote the continuous improvement of the rights system. From the perspective of order, the rights to share will surely reshape the rules of data sharing and openness, promote the free and orderly circulation of data resources, and contribute to the new order of a society of sharing. From an economic perspective, the theory of the shared value is a major theoretical discovery in the field of economics and will inevitably rebuild the current basis of economic value. The proposal of the rights to share will surely add new momentum for economic development and serve as a cornerstone for the rule of the digital economy.

Justice value of the rights to share

The relationship between private rights and public rights is contradictory: The former claims the supremacy of private rights holding that no one can be taken as a means for obtaining interests for others and that individual rights are superior to the general interests of society. The latter, in contrast, advocates taking individuals as the means for certain purposes and evaluating any behavior, law and policy against the criterion of maximal public interest. Since the Enlightenment age, emphasis on personal rights has always been the mainstream in Western society. In the West, a widespread view is that society and government serves to protect private rights and that the pursuit of public interests of society cannot be achieved at the expense of private rights. However, the viewpoint that gives priority to public rights also has considerable influence. It pursues the interests of the majority rather than the minority. A just society should enable the majority to obtain larger interests and increase the maximal net balance even at the expense of the interests of the minority who may be put at a disadvantaged position. Hence, there are natural conflicts between private rights and public rights and the major divergence lies in whether rights are taken as an independent consideration. Those who prioritize public rights regards rights as a function rather than a variable for realizing social utility. Conversely, the viewpoint that prioritize private rights take individuals as the center, believing that everyone individual is the best judge of his/her own interests and how to promote them, and that social utility and the various ways to control individuals cannot replace or suppress private rights (Dong Yurong 2010).

The theory of private rights and the theory of public rights respectively explain their basic concepts from the perspectives of egoism and altruism. Both choose one value over the other. In the complicated real world, such a unitary way of thinking tends to be too simple to make generalization and this is the main reason why both theories have their limitations. Private rights implicate the principle of state neutrality[4] which ignores the positive function of the state. Some scholars believe that only individuals have the right to pursue self-value and self-good, and the state only protects individuals' pursuit of self-good in the weakest sense (Dong Yurong 2010). It only sees the "personal good", not the "basic social good" which the state should uphold and thus ignores the positive function of the state. In addition, private rights cut up the connections between society and individuals and contribute little to the realization of self-value. Private rights emphasize the priority of individuals in ontology, deeming that society or the state serves only as an instrument for realizing the personal goal of rational self-interest. Therefore, liberalism endows individuals with supreme rights from the perspective of private rights and takes private rights as superior to public interests of society.

The biggest problem in the sphere of public rights is the neglect of basic rights. The purpose of public rights is to maximize public interests. It requires the transfer of the personal interests of some people so that other people can obtain comparatively more interests and the total interests of society can increase. The viewpoint that emphasizes public rights deems that such an transfer is worthwhile and the resulted injustice is justifiable. This approach concerns about the increase of the total public interests of society, rather than the distribution of the such interests among people. For a long time, people have always doubted

4 State neutrality means that the state has nothing to do with goodness and values. The British scholar Joseph Raz wrote in *The Morality of Freedom*: "governments must be neutral regarding different people's conceptions of the good. That is, that governments must so conduct themselves that their actions will neither improve nor hinder the chances individuals have of living in accord with their conception of the good."

whether public rights can quantize public interests. Public rights usually measure public interests with intuition and have never been able to avoid the problem that different people may have different perceptions. Therefore, it is difficult to objectively calculate public interests (Dong Yurong 2010).

The conflicts between private rights and public rights are the inevitable results of the development of society and they could be settled with the rights to share. Firstly, the rights to share push private rights out of the private sphere and into the public sphere. The existence of individuals does not exist in isolation but as part of the social cooperation system. The rights to share enables people to benefit from one another through cooperation and justice is thus guaranteed. Therefore, the logical result of the rights to share is heightened attention to the value of equality and to private rights in public life, which is surely just. Secondly, the rights to share make adjustments to the totality of public rights. As public rights pursue interest for society as a whole, they may lead to the loss of interests for some people. In response to this, the rights to share can make unfair arrangement well suited to reciprocity. By avoiding accidental factors in the natural and social environment in the structure of equality and freedom, people can show the justice of mutual respect in the social structure. It requires people to regard one another as ends rather than means. Hence, the rights to share guarantee the effectiveness and harmony of cooperation between people based on self-esteem and mutual benefit and prevents infringements on the rights of some people resulted from the totality of public rights. Lastly, the rights to share prevent the injustice caused by public rights. The rights to share emphasize that the distribution of social wealth is good for everyone in society, especially the disadvantaged groups, and thus corrects the problem that public rights restrict personal choices to those that maximize public interests. Furthermore, the rights to share also solve the problem of contingency in utilitarianism. While people are made innately unequal by differences in natural endowments and aptitudes, the rights to share can make up for such differences with institutional arrangements, and thus it helps achieve justice of equality in its real sense.

Order value of the rights to share

The order of sharing refers to the kind of social order that takes sharing as its basic pursuit. The order of sharing, in the broad sense, has been in existence since the birth of human civilization. Languages, in their oral and written forms, are the channels for sharing, while division of labor, cooperation, and commodity transaction are the means of sharing. These have always been part of the human civilization. Sharing serves as the goal and direction of the development of the human society. As the rights to share gradually take root, the order of sharing has come back to the center stage of human development.

The rights to share change the institutional arrangements of society. From the perspective of social justice, substantial justice and institutional justice of sharing demonstrate a mutually reinforcing relationship. On the one hand, substantial justice of sharing is the basis of its institutional justice. The criteria for deciding whether an institution of sharing is just must be whether it promotes the development of productive forces and whether it is consistent with our mode of production. On the other hand, institutional justice of sharing is the guarantee of substantial justice, the concretization and materialization of the value of justice, and the institutional guarantee for realizing substantial justice (Miao Ruidan & Dai Junyuan 2017). Hence, it is necessary to guarantee the exercise of the rights to share by building sound sharing systems. This system must maintain a good between the economy and society since the economy pursues efficiency in order to bring more material wealth, while society pursues fairness so that more people can benefit from the material wealth. To a certain extent, the sharing economy and sharing society is contradictory, and a sound system of sharing is what enables them both to better play their roles. The rights to share are the result of institutional arrangements for sharing which represents balance between efficiency and justice.

The rights to share optimize the data hierarchy. The data hierarchy refers to the stratification structure resulted from differences in status in regard to data. In this hierarchy, strata are formed on the basis of not only occupations, but also such factors as data capacity and the volume of data resources one possesses. There tend to be clear lines between different data strata and the trends of stratification, hierarchy and solidification are clear in the data structure. The liquidity of such factors as data technologies, data capital and data resources is low, and factors all tend to concentrate in the higher strata while those in the lower strata have little sense of gain. This leads to imbalance in the distribution of data resources among different strata. However, no matter how much data policies incline towards the lower strata, it is difficult to change the situation that those in the middle and lower strata have low data income or to move them into higher strata. Through the rights to share, idle data resources privately or publicly possessed can be fully used to create more data products for sharing, more opportunities and more services to satisfy the data needs of the various strata, especially the underclass. Thus, resources and opportunities are shared, barriers between data strata are removed, and it becomes possible for the lower and middle strata to improve their situation. The establishment of thc rights to share enables all to enjoy the right and have the ability to use data resources, changes the pattern where data sharing interests are distributed strictly according to specific factors such as chain, ability and resources, and extends the benefits of sharing to all (Zhang Guoqing 2018).

The rights to share enhance the governance capacity of the government. The government plays a crucial role in data resource allocation and influences the distribution of data interests. In the traditional order, it is difficult to strike a balance between efficiency and fairness. However, with the rights to share, the government, based on its strong data capability, can achieve institutional innovation, transform government functions, enhance the governance capacity, realize a dynamic balance between the functions of the government and the market, and strike a balance between efficiency and fairness which is also the greatest common divisor of the government and the market. On the one hand, the rights to share move personnel, capital and resources to the greatest extent, revitalize various factors for the development of the data industry, build the wealth of public data, and extend data welfare to more groups of people. Enterprises become active in pursuing data efficiency and in undertaking social responsibilities through the exercise of the rights to share which maximize the economic and social interests brought about by data. On the other hand, in order to satisfy the public's demand for data, the government provides high-quality data products and services through sharing, and unleashes the enthusiasm, initiative and creativity of all parties to pool wisdom and strength and ensure the interests of all participants. This helps solve the problems of the ownership of public data resources and the distribution of incremental data value, and enhance people's sense of gain (Tian Xinqiao & Zhang Guoqing 2018).

The rights to share ensure fairness and justice in the realm of data. Data sharing, as a new kind of resource allocation, makes up for the unbalanced distribution of data resources between the government and the market, reduces unfairness in data resource allocation and secondary allocation, and overcomes inequality in data transactions and waste of data resources resulted from information asymmetry in the traditional pattern. The rights to share make up for the neglect of the market for social justice in the realm of data, makes all members of society able to equally enjoy all types of data resources and obtain data rights and economic interests on an equal footing and enables the public to enjoy basic data value. Data sharing works as a coordinator between the government and the market which endows people with equal opportunities in respect to the access to, use of, and earnings from data resources. The rights to share provide huge space for all members of society to have equal rights over data resources, and realizes the shift of focus from the redistribution of individual wealth and public wealth to the equal sharing of data resources. Under the circumstance of a growing data wealth gap, it is necessary to regulate and make improvements through the rights to share. Therefore, the rights to share need to work for both the protection of private data ownership and the equal rights over basic data resources so as to achieve data justice (Zhang Guoqing 2018).

Economic value of the rights to share

The digital economy has brought profound changes to the driving force and pattern of economic development. The proposal of the rights to share motivate people to produce and share data and this which provides endless data resources for the development of the digital economy. To develop a data-centered digital economy and a sharing-based interest distribution mechanism will surely promote the deep integration between digital economy and the sharing economy.

The rights to share promote the reform of the property rights system. The property rights system is an important component of modern economic systems. In existing theories, property rights are the legal manifestations of relationships in economic ownership, which include such rights as ownership, possession, domination, the right to use, *jus fruendi,* the right to disposition and so on. Current economic systems stress the completeness, inalienability and inviolability of property rights, and property rights systems are thus competitive and exclusive. In the meantime, due to the huge gap in resources and wealth, the exclusiveness of the property rights systems continuously pushes resources and wealth in the market towards a small number of parties in the system, hampers the transaction and transfer of property rights, and hinders economic development. Therefore, excessive stress on the completeness, inalienability and inviolability of property rights is averse to the free flow of talents, capital and resources as well as the healthy and free economic development (Zhang Guoqing 2018). The rights to share offer a new approach towards the drawbacks of the property rights system. It has the right to use the data shared while reserving data ownership, thus forming a new point of view regarding property rights. This new point of view presents a two-leveled structure: On the upper level is the ownership which decides to whom the data belongs; while on the lower level, there are the rights to share which shares the right to use and *jus fruendi* of data. As data is shared with others so that more people can use it, data resources are likely to be revitalized and put into better use. The basic philosophy of the rights to share is that we seek not to own but to use. This, in essence, is to shift focus away from data ownership and towards the right to use data and the *jus fruendi* of data, thus promoting the transformation from the private ownership of data property rights to data rights sharing, realizing the free and orderly circulation of data resources, and raise the efficiency of data resources allocation. Hence, while reducing the waste of resources, the rights to share also expand channels for people's demand for data to be better met and enhances data freedom. In other words, the rights to share offer people a path to get what they desire and achieve data freedom without taking data resources into their possession (Han Jing & Pei Wen 2017).

The rights to share increase consumer surplus. Consumer surplus refers to the difference between the peak price a consumer is willing to pay for a certain quantity of a commodity and the actual price he/she pays for it. It comes from Alfred Marshall's marginal utility theory and is used to measure the extra earnings of consumers. On the one hand, the rights to share provide more data channels for consumers to choose from, which weakens the monopoly of data producers, spreads the forces on the data market, and reduces the passivity of data consumers on the market. Through a game over data prices, it is easier to satisfy the demands of data consumers. Thus, the actual price of data products is reduced and data consumer surplus is increased. On the other hand, the rights to share open the market of the usufructuary right of data, lowers the costs of data transaction, improves the use rate of data resources and creates more data wealth. Consequently, the rights to share fill the gap between the supply and the demand of data and has data resources in society better used. As the demand and supply are matched in a more accurate, free and orderly manner, opportunity cost as well as the actual data price paid by consumers are lowered, creating higher data value for participants on the micro level and thus increasing the consumer surplus of data (Zhang Yuming 2017).

The rights to share change competition paradigm. The rights to share change the traditional competition logic of a zero-sum game and achieves the transformation towards a new competition paradigm based on the shared value. From the perspective of business practice, the rights to share shift the focus of data enterprises from the economic value of data to the shared value of data, and pushes them to pursue of comprehensive rather than solely economic benefits. Consequently, in order to fully tap the potential of enterprises in creating data wealth and obtaining comprehensive data benefits, the most realistic choice is to conduct competition and cooperation on the basis of the rights to share. In other words, data competition and cooperation are the two sides of one single thing for relevant enterprises. They work together, have influence on each other, and can transform into each other under certain conditions. On the one hand, the exercise of the rights to share by enterprises enlarges the scale of data exchange, accelerates the spread of all kinds of data, promotes the use efficiency of factors such as data resources, technologies and services, gives better play to data resources and capital, stimulates data innovations, pushes the boundary of the possibilities of data production, forms synergy and the coupling effect, and creates more development opportunities and business opportunities so that enterprises can generate more value from data sharing and expand their value network. On the other hand, the rights to share help enterprises break through the boundaries of data, obtain more data products including more data resources, technologies and services, enhance the driving force and capability for data innovation, get more benefits out of their data value surplus, and better satisfy the data demands of their own and of society on the whole (Xiao Hongjun 2015).

The rights to share make up for market failures. The rights to share reduce information asymmetry and negative externality of the market, break monopoly, and make up for market failures. In terms of information asymmetry, consumers lose their advantaged position when making a purchase since they lack access to all relevant data and information, leading to a situation where "bad money drives out good money". With the rights to share, information transparency and market efficiency are greatly improved. In terms of negative externality, by the rights to share, people can use and earn from data without increasing their private data property. It reduces the possession of means of data production, avoids the influence of negative externality to the maximum extent, and relieves the pressure from data scarcity. Therefore, the rights to share can reduce the asymmetry of information on the market, reduce negative externality, promote the accurate match between supply and demand, put resources in to full use, and make up for market failures (Zhang Yuming 2017).

Bibliography

Cheng, Tongshun, and Shi, Meng. 2018. "Usufructuary Right of Public Data and Political Democracy." *Jianghai Academic Journal*, 4th issue.

Compilation and Translation Bureau of the CPC Central Committee. *The Complete Works of Marx and Engels (Volume 23)*. Beijing: People's Publishing House.

Diamandis, P. H., and S. Kotler. 2014. *Abundance: The Future Is Better Than You Think*. Trans. Jia Yongmin. Hangzhou: Zhejiang People's Publishing House.

Dong, Yurong. 2010. "'Sharing Concept of Justice' and Balance of Interests: Way for Realizing the Integration of Private Rights and Social Utility." *Social Sciences in Guangxi*, 10th issue.

Du, Zhenhua, and Cha, Hongwang. 2016. "Analysis on the Reality of Data Property System." *Chongqing Social Sciences*, 8th issue.

Guan Dehua, et al. 2013. *The Evolution of Western Value Theory*. Beijing: China Economic Publishing House.

Han, Jing, and Pei, Wen. 2017. "Sharing Idea, Sharing Economy Development and Creative Innovation of Economic Structure." *Shanghai Journal of Economics*, 8th issue.

He, Zhe. 2017. "Forms and Orders of Human Society in Network Civilization." *Nanjing Journal of Social Sciences*, 4th issue.

Hu, Shouyong. 2018. "Global Historical Significance of Philosophy of Sharing Development." *Studies on Marxism*, 4th issue.

Key Laboratory of Big Data Strategy. 2018. *Block Data 1.0: The Theoretical Foundation for Data Rights*. Beijing: Social Science Academic Press.

Key Laboratory of Big Data Strategy. 2019. *Block Data 5.0: The Theory and Method of Data Sociology*. Beijing: China CITIC Press.

Li, Jianhui, and Gong, Xiaole. 2009. "Beyond Self-Interest: Darwin's Altruism Puzzle and Its Solution." *Studies in Dialectics of Nature*, 9th issue.

Liu, Genrong. 2017. "Sharing Economy: A Subverter of Traditional Economic Model." *The Economists*, 5th issue.

Liu, Heling. 2005. "From Competitive Evolution to Cooperative Evolution: New Development of Darwin's Theory of Natural Selection." *Science, Technology and Dialectics*, 1st issue.

Liu, Ling. 2019. "Historical Origins and a Unified Governance Pattern for Fairness and Justice, and Shared Development." *Humanities & Social Sciences Journal of Hainan University*, 4th issue.

Long, Rongyuan, and Yang, Guanhua. 2018. "Researches on Data Rights, Data Rights System and Data Rights Law." *Journal of Science Technology and Law*, 5th issue.

Lu, Xiaohua. 2009. *Information Property Rights: A New Wealth Protection Model from the Perspective of Civil Law*. Beijing: Law Press China.

Luo, Ying. 2014. "The Position of the rights to share Under the Circumstance of Comprehensively Deepening the Reform." *Search*, 6th issue.

Meng, Kui. 2013. "Comparison of Three Major Value Theories in Economics." *Economic Review*, 7th issue.

Miao, Ruidan, and Dai, Junyuan. 2017. "Research on the Theoretical Connotation and Practice Path of Sharing Development." *Studies in Ideological Education*, 3rd issue.

Tian, Xinqiao, and Zhang, Guoqing. 2018. "The Road to Sharing – Why Socialism Is Right." *Zhejiang Social Sciences*, 2nd issue.

Wang, Liming. 2005. *Researches on Personal Rights Law*. Beijing: China Renmin University Press.

Wang, Liming. 2019. "Data Sharing and Protection of Personal Information." *Modern Law Science*, 1st issue.

Wang, Yan, and Ye, Ming. 2019. "Conflicts and Balance Between Individual Data Sharing and Privacy Protection in the Age of Artificial Intelligence." *Journal of Socialist Theory Guide*, 1st issue.

Xiao, Hongjun. 2015. "Sharing Value, Business Ecosystem and Transformation of Competition Paradigm of Enterprises." *Reform*, 7th issue.

Zhang, Guoqing. 2018. "Justice as Sharing: On the Imbalance in China's Social Development." *Zhejiang Academic Journal*, 1st issue.

Zhang, Xinbao. 1998. *Legal Protection of the Right to Privacy*. Beijing: Masses Publishing House.

Zhang, Yujie. 2017. "The Rights of Robots and Its Risk Regulation in the Age of Artificial Intelligence." *Oriental Law*, 6th issue.

Zhang, Yuming. *Sharing Economics*. Beijing: Science Press. 2017.

Zhao, Hong. 2010. "Social State and Fundamental Social Rights of Citizens: Extension and Limitation of Fundamental Rights in Social State." *Journal of Comparative Law*, 5th issue.

Zheng, Jianjun, and Fu, Xiaojie. 2019. "The Influence of Altruistic Motivation on Knowledge Sharing of Primary and Secondary School Teachers: The Moderating Roles of Organizational Identification and Perceived Organizational Support." *Psychological Development and Education*, 4th issue.

Zhou, Shuyun. 2014. "Analysis on Subjects of the Right to Access Information." *Library*, 5th issue.

Zhou, Shuyun, and Luo, Xueying. 2014. "Analysis on Content of the Right to Access Information." *Information studies: Theory and Application*, 5th issue.

Zhou, Shuyun, and Wang, Haoyun. 2015. "Analysis on Objects of the Right to Access Information." *Library*, 1st issue.

CHAPTER 4

Data Sovereignty

Data sovereignty is an important component of state sovereignty and a manifestation and natural extension of state sovereignty in the data space. Data sovereignty refers to the power enjoyed by the state to generate, disseminate, manage, control, use and protect data within its jurisdiction. It is an inevitable requirement for all countries to safeguard state sovereignty and independence, and to combat data monopoly and hegemonism in the era of big data. Data sovereignty includes the following rights: data jurisdiction, right to independence over data, right to equality over data, and right to self-defense over data. In practice, the competition between different countries for data sovereignty has given rise to a state of disorder featuring conflict between multiple jurisdictions and state security dilemmas. At the same time, data sovereignty as a field with overlapping interests, faces problems such as data hegemonism, data protectionism, data capitalism, data terrorism, etc. In order to safeguard data security and data sovereignty, the international community should work hard to build a data sovereignty governance system, promote cooperation related to the data sovereignty system, and create a legal system for data sovereignty that meets the needs of development in the world today. By doing so, we will be able to put the global flow of data within the framework of a sound international law system for regulation, so that it can benefit the whole world.

Rise of Data Sovereignty

Cross-border data flow has brought significant impact on the traditional perception of state sovereignty, undermining state sovereignty and giving birth to data sovereignty. Data sovereignty rose out of the concept of cyber sovereignty. At the national level, the concepts of data sovereignty and cyber sovereignty have the same origin, that is, state sovereignty. Both data sovereignty and cyber sovereignty are important components of state sovereignty. As a product of the era of big data, data sovereignty emerges as the data space comes into existence and is a manifestation, extension and reflection of state sovereignty in the data space. Due to the special features of the data space, data sovereignty demonstrates important features, such as contemporaneity, relativity, cooperativeness and equality, among others. The proposition of data sovereignty is of great significance to the protection of data security and to the building of a cyber power.

Origin of sovereignty

In the early stage of human civilization, there was not yet any state polity and people had no idea of sovereignty. With the emergence of war and the establishment of states, the idea and concept of sovereignty gradually took shape and became clear. Scholars of different times and from different countries have elaborated on sovereignty from different perspectives. Now, it is meaningful to review past literature on sovereignty and clarify the characteristics of sovereignty in different periods of time, for this will help us add new connotation to state sovereignty in the age of big data.

Germination of the concept of sovereignty

The concept of sovereignty[1] can trace back to ancient times and it germinated in a specific time and space. It is the result of social changes and

1 Some scholars believe that sovereignty and state sovereignty are two different concepts, "state sovereignty is only one of the manifestations of sovereign subjectivity ... If we do not distinguish sovereignty from state sovereignty, it will be difficult for us to have an accurate understanding of the connotation of state sovereignty." But generally speaking, people do not make too much distinction between sovereignty and state sovereignty, and consider them different expressions of the same concept. At the same time, since the concept of sovereignty is inevitably relevant to the state in terms of its modern significance, the book does not distinguish between sovereignty and state sovereignty.

economic development. Sovereignty is a prerequisite for human activities and leads society from disorder to order. During the period of ancient Greece and ancient Rome, states were separate and troubles abounded in and out of them. Thus, ancient philosophers realized that the only way to prevent internal strife and resist the invasion of enemies was to establish a unified and centralized state. Therefore, they embarked on the strenuous path towards religious power and monarchical power. It can be said that the early philosophers noticed the existence of sovereignty and studied the concept long ago. Although they did not explicitly put forward the political concept of "sovereignty," their research on the origin of states, the types of polities, and the governance of states essentially came very close to our concept of "sovereignty" today, and their efforts had laid the foundation for the proposition of the concept of "sovereignty" in the Enlightenment period.

Aristotle is believed to be the first to have explained the idea of sovereignty. In the book *Politics*, he points out that "a constitution is the arrangement of magistracies in a state, especially of the highest of all." (Aristotle, trans. Wu Taopeng 1996, p. 129). In Aristotle's view, the number of rulers is the main criterion for the classification of government, and the state is the polity with the largest number of rulers and is superior to other forms of government. Therefore, the state has the power to rule. He insists on the rule of law instead of the rule of man, believing that the law is the best ruler and that the formulation of laws must reflect the opinions of the majority to ensure greater consensus and desirability. From then on, the idea that the state has the supreme power was primarily established. Despite the fact that Aristotle did not explicitly use the term of "sovereignty", he had already explained that state sovereignty is the highest authority over domestic affairs.

The earliest form of state sovereignty originated from the thought of ancient Roman jurists that people are the only and final carrier of authority in the state; and a profound understanding that the people are who own and exercise state sovereignty. The idea of sovereignty in ancient Rome is reflected in a famous saying: "*quod principi placuit legis habet vigorem, cum populus el et in eum omne suum imperium et potestatem conferat*" [for that the people have surrender all their rights and powers to the king, the will of the king shall have the force of law] (Chen Xujing, trans. Zhang Shibao 2010, p. 10). This saying has had different interpretations in different times. When the emperor or king enjoys supreme and unrestricted "absolute power", they are considered to have sovereignty, but sovereignty is actually endowed on them through a natural transfer of rights from the people. As an emperor or king is rising towards supreme power or his/her regime is declining, his power is entrusted by the people. Entrustment does not mean giving up, and the people still possess their core rights. Although this kind of thought is very different from modern sovereignty, we can see that the core lies in the belief that sovereignty belongs to the people.

Evolution of the sovereignty theory

French philosopher Jean Bodin was the first in the history to give sovereignty a systematic and specific definition. According to him, sovereignty is the unified, undivided and supreme power over any laws that a country enjoys (Jean Bodin, cited in Zhu Qi 2015). In his *Six Books of the Commonwealth* (*Six livres de la République*), Bodin points out that a commonwealth may be defined as the rightly ordered government of a number of families, and of those things which are their common concern by a sovereign power. Such sovereign power is not subject to the law. It is necessarily perpetual, absolute and supreme. Bodin systematically expounded the concept and characteristics of sovereignty. Although he did not give a sound explanation of the legitimacy of sovereignty, his idea suited the situations in France and the world of his time and laid a solid foundation for further development of the sovereignty theory. Bodin's thought on sovereignty was considered the origin of the modern sovereign state theory, playing a positive role in the proposition of the modern concept of sovereignty.

Thomas Hobbes inherited Bodin's theory of sovereignty and expanded and enriched it. He advocated "natural rights" (*jus natural*), believing that all men are created free and equal and that everyone has equal natural rights to natural resources (Yang Xiaotong 2018). However, resources are limited. Therefore, people accede to a social contract and surrender their power, being thereby bound by the social contract not to be obedient to someone else or some assembly of people, without their sovereign's permission. Because this obedience or personality is formed by mutual consent and the surrender of power is legalized when the contract is signed. Hobbes believed that the "sovereign" is unfettered and supreme, and that the people had only the right to choose whether or not to enter into a social contract: the choice to sign such a contract declares the termination of their political rights. It can be said that Hobbes's theory of sovereignty, which appears to be justifiable, is fundamentally contradictory. Nevertheless, we still acknowledge its value in promoting the development of the sovereignty theory.

Jean-Jacques Rousseau's thought of popular sovereignty represents a great leap in the development of sovereignty theory. It completely overthrew the feudal autocratic monarchy and led people into a new society of freedom and equality. Rousseau held that sovereignty is non-transferable, that popular sovereignty is the embodiment of the "general will," that it is the intersection of the set of everyone's will in signing a social contract, and that power can be transferred but awareness cannot. Based on the idea that sovereignty is not transferable, sovereignty is indivisible because awareness is universal and once divided, it will reduce to nonexistence. When awareness is regarded as the will of the people as an entity, it means the universally acknowledged and open will is a sovereign agreement and constitutes laws (Jean-Jacques Rousseau, trans. Yang Guozheng 2006, p. 20–21). In Rousseau's theory of sovereignty, sovereignty is relatively absolute: It is absolute within the framework of universal agreement, but not so beyond the framework. Rousseau put forward the theory of popular sovereignty on the basis of what his predecessors had achieved. It was a summarization of all previous proposals and a leap forward from there; and moreover, it heralded further development of the sovereignty theory instead of concluding it (see Table 8).

Modern sovereignty

Sovereignty is never a static concept. It is always changing with society and moves forward with innovations in science and technology and economic development. There are two motivations behind the emergence of

Table 8. Several Sovereignty Theories

Time	Figure	Sovereignty Theory
1530–1596	Jean Bodin	The first systematic and specific definition of sovereignty: Sovereignty is a major symbol of a country, and the supreme power towards citizens and subjects free from restrictions of laws; sovereignty is the supreme authority at home and the right to independence and equality in relation to the outside world.
1583–1645	Hugo Grotius	The premise of international laws is state sovereignty. State sovereignty refers to the supreme governing power of a state, that is, the power that enables the sovereign to act without being dominated by the will of others or by law. Grotius opposes to popular sovereignty and advocates sovereignty of the monarch. Sovereignty serves as the foundation of the existence of a state and the precondition for a state to be a subject of international law.
1588–1679	Thomas Hobbes	Individuals transfer natural rights to a sovereign. This theory goes against the divine right of kings, advocates state power, and gives sovereignty a supreme status.
1632–1704	John Locke	State sovereignty is related to political power and the supreme power and it includes legislative power, executive power and federative power. There are two approaches to state sovereignty: parliamentary sovereignty and popular sovereignty. Sovereignty is not equivalent with absolute sovereignty.
1712–1778	Jean-Jacques Rousseau	The earliest complete theory of popular sovereignty: State sovereignty is indivisible and non-transferrable. All expression and application of human rights must reflect popular will and the law is the "general will", which means everyone is equal before the law and the monarch cannot stand above it either.

the modern concept of sovereignty: one is the internal motivation produced as a sovereign state pursues survival, interests and development; and the other is the external force majeure that a sovereign state faces in a changing international environment. Modern sovereignty is a milestone in the development of human civilization in that it has changed the way sovereign states communicate with one another and transformed the international system and international law. Sovereignty cannot be separate from national laws and the theory of sovereignty will surely evolve with time. Therefore, the emergence of the modern sovereignty theory is not only an inevitable result of our efforts to contain chaos and disorder and establish sound legal order, but also a basic requirement for the human society to move from industrial civilization to digital civilization.

Modern sovereignty is a continuation and development of traditional sovereignty. As globalization progresses, traditional sovereignty is confronted with many challenges, such as the establishment and development of international organizations, the more frequent transnational cooperation, and the emergence of a variety of international institutions and mechanisms. These challenges blurred the territorial borders in traditional sovereignty and this was why the modern sovereignty theory came into being, incorporating elements such as communication and cooperation, economic exchanges and resource sharing with international organizations. In the modern sense, sovereignty refers to no longer absolute independence in military, political, economic and technological spheres, but relative independence instead, in an effort to adapt to the trend of globalization. Compared to the traditional concept, the modern concept of sovereignty has a broader scope and richer content in response to the development of new territories. "Traditional sovereignty not only contradicts with practice, but also restricts people's thinking and fetters the state's hands and feet" (Liu Qingjian 2004). All in all, modern sovereignty is a combination of theory and practice, breaks through the limits of traditional sovereignty and solves the predicament that we currently face in relation to sovereignty.

Modern sovereignty is a new form of state sovereignty. It does not create any new rights. As the human world extends from the physical world into the virtual space, we now have a great opportunity to expand and improve the rules of our world. The emergence of the "Fifth Domain" is a result of the continuous evolution of the sovereignty theory in practice. There may not be tangible boundaries in this new territory, but virtual barrier created with technology, knowledge and culture is also sufficient to play the same functions of a physical boundary. The Fifth Domain, carrying the information and data of the physical world, is part of the "global commons" and also a new field that major countries would surely contend for. The emergence of sovereignty over the Fifth Domain is to mitigate the confrontations between different countries in the Fifth Domain, improve the international dialogue mechanism concerning the Fifth Domain, and safeguard the common interests in the "Fifth Domain". Sovereignty over the Fifth Domain is a reflection of modern sovereignty and an externalization of elements of the modern concept of sovereignty that go beyond the traditional sovereignty concept in the sphere of jurisprudence.

From cyber sovereignty to data sovereignty

At present, traditional security and non-traditional security are intertwined, and non-traditional security threats are increasingly prominent, exerting impact on state security. In this context, data sovereignty has become a major part of our efforts to maintain state security. Data sovereignty is a continuation and development of cyber sovereignty and the two overlap to some extent. Data sovereignty aims at dealing with the security problems brought about by massive data, which differ from those related to cyber sovereignty in some way.

State security

State security is a cornerstone of the stability, survival and development of any country. Based on the general understanding of security, state security is first of all a kind of security state, and it also involves the methods and capabilities to maintain and achieve such a state. A country in a secure state is one in which there are stability and order and people are able to pursue and achieve what they desire without any worries. Without state security, there will be no stability or order, and people will have to go all out merely for survival and have no energy at all to pursue self-realization in life. Therefore, safeguarding state security is to safeguard the basic interests of the country and its people. State security is a concern not only for specific countries, but also for mankind as a whole. State security provides important support for building a community with a shared future for mankind.

State sovereignty and state security are intertwined and interdependent, so safeguarding state security is to safeguard the equality, independence, integrity and inalienability of state sovereignty. The complexity, uncertainty and unpredictability of international relations tie state sovereignty and state security close together, and regulations concerning state sovereignty shall be based on adaptation to international relations. In practice, there are cross-regional and cross-cultural interactions between different countries in the sphere of international relations and different types of interactions occur between countries with the same social conditions. It is the external structure of the international system, the consensuses reached between countries in the process of interaction, and the process of the interaction itself that maintain the interaction and determine how it happens. The structure of the international system has great influence on state sovereignty, spurs all countries to do their best to safeguard their state sovereignty, and pushes more and more countries to give high priority to state sovereignty and state security when formulating strategies related to foreign affairs.

At present, state security faces challenges not only in traditional dimensions such as politics, military, homeland and economy, but also non-traditional dimensions such as cyberspace and data. In such a complicated security landscape, how to maintain state security and state sovereignty has become a realistic problem. Innovations in the understanding of sovereignty and the expansion of sovereignty into new fields have become an inevitable trend in our efforts to maintain state security in the era of big data. The emergence of new forms of sovereignty, such as cyber sovereignty and data sovereignty, is perfectly in line with the traditional concept of sovereignty but highly innovative at the same time. It extends and enriches the connotation and denotation of state sovereignty and has important guiding significance for the appropriate handling of state security issues in the era of big data.

Cyber sovereignty

Cyberspace is by no means a place outside of the law, and cyber sovereignty is the natural extension of state sovereignty in cyberspace. In fact, the concept of cyber sovereignty is proposed largely for internal affairs and the central concern is to maintain the peaceful and steady development of cyberspace. "Cyberspace is created by human beings, and its intrinsic characteristics determine that it will inevitably meet with many legal problems. To solve these problems, intervention is required from the national level. If we are to maintain sustainable and healthy development of cyberspace, rules and adjustments must come from the national level. This is bound to extend state sovereignty into cyberspace and thus the concept of cyber sovereignty was born" (Du Zhizhao & Nan Yuxia 2014). Cyber sovereignty, on the one hand, incorporates the virtual space created by the Internet into the overall legal framework so that authorities can find sound legal basis when trying to maintain order in cyberspace and protect the interests of Internet users; and on the other hand, it also provides legal guarantee for free expression and participation in cyberspace.

Cyber sovereignty is an integral part of state sovereignty. In order to build a harmonious cyberspace management system, we need to respect sovereign states' supreme power in internal cyber affairs management as well as the rights to equality, independence, self-defense and their jurisdiction when participating in international cyberspace governance. The right to equality means that all countries can participate in international cyberspace governance as equals, and there must not be inequality in cyber sovereignty based on the size of countries or different endowments of cyber resources. The right to independence means that communication facilities and network equipment located in a country must not be subject to any interference without permission. The right to self-defense means that sovereign states can mobilize all domestic resources to ensure the normal operation of their network infrastructure. Jurisdiction means that the physical platforms that constitute the cyberspace, the data they carry, and the activities related thereto are subject to the judicial and administrative jurisdiction of sovereign states (Fang Binxing, Zou Peng & Zhu Shibing 2016).

Cyber sovereignty has become a consensus of the international community, but the cyberspace, featuring liberalization and borderlessness, differs greatly from the physical world where countries are independent and have fixed borders. Cyber security has become a new element of state security. The fierce competition between the new cyberspace-oriented approach and the traditional approach to security, on the one hand, shows that countries all over the world attach importance to participating in cyberspace governance; and on the other hand, proved the building of a sound, effective and sustainable international cyber security system to be the common goal of the international community and governments of all countries (Yu Zhigang 2016). The concept of cyber sovereignty emerges just in line with the development of the Internet. No country is really out of the cyberspace and we should make good use of the cyberspace to strengthen communication and exchange, promote dialogue, and reduce disputes. Only with mutual respect for equal cyber sovereignty can we truly achieve mutual trust and international consensus and establish a global village for mankind featuring interdependence and integration.

Data sovereignty

Data sovereignty is the core of cyber sovereignty. Both cyber sovereignty and data sovereignty are extensions of state sovereignty in the "Fifth Domain", adding new elements to the traditional concept of state sovereignty and related theories and adapting them to the new situations in a new era. They represent not only an increase in the "quantity" of state sovereignty, but also a major change in the "quality" of it. Data sovereignty is based on the control and use of data as a new kind of resource by the state, while cyber sovereignty emphasizes more on sovereign rights, requiring not only to mastery of Internet technology and information technology, but also the right to possess and manage data in cyberspace. The flow of data affects the exercise of data sovereignty, while the control and management that a data sovereignty holder exerts on data flow affects the exercise of cyber sovereignty (Shi Yuhang 2018).

The proposal of the concept of data sovereignty is an inevitable trend for all countries in the world in the face of massive global data flow, and this is a new trend brought by the rise of the Internet, big data, artificial intelligence and other technologies. Based on the views of experts and scholars at home and abroad, there are data sovereignty in the narrow sense and data sovereignty in the broad sense. "In the narrow sense, data sovereignty only refers to national data sovereignty, while personal data sovereignty can be called data rights, which refer to the right to self-determination and self-control over the personal data of users" (Cai Cuihong 2013). According to Prof. Joel Kinnaman at Tufts University in the United States, data sovereignty in the broad sense includes national data sovereignty and personal data sovereignty. National data sovereignty is the premise of the realization of personal data sovereignty, and national data sovereignty depends on the support and expression of personal data sovereignty in turn.

Data sovereignty is the extension of state sovereignty in cyberspace. With the rapid development of technology, information of people's basic needs and of a country's politics, economy, culture and other aspects have all taken on the form of data. As an indispensable resource in the era of big data, data accounts for a growing proportion of all the resources available, which exerts an important impact on the extension of state sovereignty. State sovereignty is no longer limited to the traditional scope of territorial land, territorial sea, territorial air space, energy and other physical aspects. The virtual space composed of data greatly broadens the scope of state sovereignty. In cyberspace, the dissemination, exchange and replication of data can find applicable principles in the article on "sovereign rights" in the *Convention on the Continental Shelf.* Sovereignty and sovereign rights are closely related and inseparable. Data sovereignty is not only the embodiment of supreme sovereign rights, but also a reflection of state sovereignty. Therefore, the definition of data sovereignty should cover the traditional concept of sovereignty, take state sovereignty as its basis, and serve as an extension of the connotation of state sovereignty.

Features of data sovereignty

Contemporaneity. Each era has a set of concepts unique to it, and the expansion of the content of state sovereignty should keep pace with the time. The rise of the concept of data sovereignty is the realistic foundation and practical requirement of the current era of big data and it should evolve with time so as to identify and deal with the complex problems that may arise. Only by grasping the contemporaneity of data sovereignty and keeping the concept up to date can we control the massive cross-border data flow, meet the demand for the analysis of massive data in a timely manner, and be invincible in the debate over state sovereignty in the era of big data. Data sovereignty is closely connected with the characteristics of the era. It has come into being with the arrival of the era of big data, existed in this era, and developed with the era. Data sovereignty is never out of the picture of our time. Instead, it is a hallmark of the time and moves forward with time. Data sovereignty is technology-based, which is in line with the characteristics of the era. In essence, data sovereignty is the inevitable result of highly mature data technology. Data security and data resources management depend heavily on technology, and to exercise and uphold data sovereignty, we must also rely, to a large extent, on technology. Data sovereignty develops on the sound foundation of progress in science and technology. The definition, connotation and scope of data sovereignty all grow hand in hand with science and technology. Technological innovation and maturity are the basis for the formation and development of data sovereignty theory and the precondition for the exercise of data sovereignty.

Relativity. In the era of big data, data sovereignty comes only at the cost of necessary compromises, so it is relative. State sovereignty is naturally irreversible. It is absolute to the inside and restrictive to the outside, which constitutes relativity. The relativity of sovereignty is justifiable to some extent and widely accepted in the international society today. However, things are different when it comes to data sovereignty. Data sovereignty is relative in that academic understanding of its concept varies greatly, and that there are realistic constraints to it. At present, the realization of data sovereignty faces horizontal and vertical constraints. Horizontal constraints come from how one country's power in the cyberspace compares with that of other countries, while vertical constraints involve the distribution of power between the national, super national, sub-countries, and even down to personal levels (Cai Cuihong 2013). Based on the past evolvement of the concept of relative sovereignty, sovereignty should not be considered absolute, but it should be subject to restrictions. The relativity of data sovereignty is reflected in its definition and constraints. Its definition varies greatly since there is not yet an authoritative, clear and unified definition. Its realization depends on the technological capacity of different countries, but the digital divide between developing and developed countries is not likely to close soon. Therefore, there is a great disparity between counties in terms of the data sovereignty they achieve. In cyberspace, a country's control over data resources is relative, which is different from the absolute possession of physical resources in the real world. Flow and sharing of data creates value, so countries should share data resources in their control (Zhu Yanxin 2017).

Cooperativeness. New rules and mechanisms are needed to control and use data effectively. According to American scholar Adeno Addis, data sovereignty brings two contradictory national missions: globalization and political particularity. Globalization is an important prerequisite for all countries to develop and integrate into the international community, while political particularity serves to ensure the security and interests of different countries. Globalization makes the interests of all countries mutually restrained, and also leads the relevant data of all countries to interact and be mutually dependent, requiring a moderate level of cooperation. This is determined by the characteristics of data itself. Generally speaking, data has higher value when shared. Therefore, to pursue common interests, cooperation should be carried out on the premise of ensuring state security and interests and data sovereignty is thus cooperative. Cooperativeness means that no country should act on their own to solve international problems related to data sovereignty. The emphasis of international cooperation in this aspect lies in monitoring and defending against hegemony in cyberspace, and making joint efforts to build a harmonious, civilized and beautiful data space. "Different from traditional sovereignty protection, data sovereignty protection is not about absolute competition but about a certain degree of cooperation. Data is intangible and flows easily all over the world. No country alone can possibly achieve absolute control over data, and absolute data sovereignty is nothing but a castle in the air. It is much more realistic for us to seek guidance from the 'relative sovereignty theory' when building a data sovereignty system" (Xiao Dongmei & Wen Yuheng 2017). The realization of data sovereignty requires not only support from laws made through international consultation and consensus, but also supervision from relevant international treaties and organizations of various jurisdictions.

Equality. As a pursuit, equality of data sovereignty means that there should be no external authority other than international law to decide on internal data affairs of sovereign states, that sovereign states independent from one another acknowledge equal data sovereignty for one another, and each works independently to manage internal data affairs. The equality of data sovereignty is mainly manifested when a sovereign state deals with other countries. Within one country, data sovereignty is reflected in the hierarchical relationship inside the government; while externally, sovereignty means the recognition of one country as a political entity by other similar countries, establishing a formal and equal relationship with no right or obligation to issue or obey orders between them. Sovereign states have the power to possess, manage and use their own data within themselves, and have the right to keep data confidential, and to maintain independence, and autonomy. In the meantime, they should respect the data of other countries and refrain from interfering and stealing, which is not only the self-demand of countries, but also an international consensus. Theoretically, all countries have equal data sovereignty in cyberspace. However, in reality, there is a huge gap between developing countries and developed countries in terms of the level of data technology, resulting in different influence in cyberspace, and some countries practice data hegemony. These together make it almost impossible to achieve real equality. As a result, data sovereignty is equal merely on paper, that is, in international regulations and consensuses, not in reality. In order to achieve the equality of data sovereignty in the real sense, we need to implement international regulations, observe international standards and eliminate ungrounded discrimination.

Rights of Data Sovereignty

According to the traditional theory, sovereignty is the natural supreme ruling power inside a country and the power to stay independent externally. It includes jurisdiction, the right to self-defense, the right to independence, the right to equality and so on. Data sovereignty also incorporates four basic rights: data jurisdiction means a state has the right to manage and dispose of its data; the right to independence over data refers to the state's independence in the formulation of data laws and policies and the determination of the its data management mode; the right to equality over data means that a state must not claim jurisdiction over data of another country and that is has right to participate in international data cooperation and sharing on equal footing; and data self-defense rights means that a state has the right to resist when it is subject to data theft, monitoring or attack from the outside.

Data jurisdiction

The most important right that a sovereign state exercises internally is jurisdiction, and its scope naturally covers the new territory of state sovereignty – the data space. Data jurisdiction is manifested in the regulation of the data space by the national authority, which is a reflection of the sovereignty principle. Like jurisdiction over other elements, data jurisdiction is part of national jurisdiction. Therefore, data jurisdiction also originates from state sovereignty. Data jurisdiction refers to the right of a country to maintain, manage and utilize its physical equipment and related services for data generation, storage and transmission (Cai Cuihong 2017). Compared with traditional jurisdiction, data jurisdiction is also exercised by those who exercise traditional national jurisdiction, while the objects of data jurisdiction are persons or organizations who use data to carry out various activities and communicate and the property in their possession. In addition, the main legal basis for the exercise of data jurisdiction is the traditional principle of jurisdiction, plus some auxiliary principles derived from the unique nature of data. Data jurisdiction is the same as traditional jurisdiction in that the way of exercising it and the content of it differ greatly according to relevant laws of different countries. How a country exercises data jurisdiction depends on the provisions of its constitution and the international law on jurisdiction (Qi Juxun 2003).

Data jurisdiction is an external manifestation of state sovereignty, and the relativity of state sovereignty determines the relativity of data jurisdiction. The relativity of state sovereignty is reflected in constraints to the exercising of the sovereign rights of a country, as well as in the interdependence and interactions between countries in relation to sovereignty. It is exactly because of the interactions between different sovereign countries that the sovereignty of the countries is maintained. With economic globalization, the interdependence and interaction among all countries in the world intensify, and global problems are ramping up. No country can exist and develop in isolation, for environmental protection, climate change, international finance, energy and food security, etc., are all problems that no country can deal with alone. Therefore, countries must join hands and cooperate in order to overcome difficulties and solve problems relevant to survival and development.

Similar to traditional jurisdiction, data jurisdiction is also practiced by sovereign states generally following the traditional principles of national jurisdiction, namely territorial jurisdiction, personal jurisdiction, protective jurisdiction and universal jurisdiction. Among them, territorial jurisdiction is the foundation of the independence as well as an indispensable right of a country. In accordance with the principle of the territorial jurisdiction, a state has the right to exercise jurisdiction over persons who engage in data transmission and their acts within its territory. Personal jurisdiction, also known as international jurisdiction, provides that a state has jurisdiction over its own citizens whether they are within or out of its borders and over certain cases where a citizen of the state commits certain crimes out of the country. Protective jurisdiction applies to situations where citizens of other countries infringe upon the interests of the country outside of its territory. The act is not committed by any citizen of the said country and occurs outside of the country's territory, but causes seriously detrimental consequences to the said country. Here the harmed country has the right to exercise jurisdiction over the citizens of another country who is beyond its borders. Universal jurisdiction refers to the right of every sovereign state to exercise jurisdiction over certain specific acts that generally endanger the peace and security of mankind or affect the stability and order of the international community. The scope of application of universal jurisdiction is relatively limited. Even in the process of cross-border data flow, it only applies on the basis of explicit provisions in international law.

In the international community, jurisdictional disputes between countries in relation to some international affairs are often resolved through negotiated agreement or through the International Court of Justice or other similar means. In dealing with international disputes, the geographical location where a dispute arises often has an important impact and may even play a key role in specific situations. However, in the data space, it is difficult to define the location and time of a dispute. That is to say, traditional jurisdiction may not apply to the data space, so it is urgent for us to produce dedicated jurisdiction rules for the data space as soon as possible. In the era of big data, national jurisdiction is often ignored by some data citizens who believe that they exist in a space with no restrictions and can do whatever they want. As the data space is virtual, global and borderless, the scopes of data jurisdiction of different countries are likely to overlap, causing difficulties to judicial operation of a country, and closer cooperation and coordination among different countries are needed in the data space. The special characteristics of the data space have caused setbacks in the exercise of national jurisdiction, and the limitations of traditional jurisdiction are gradually exposed in the era of big data. Specifically, it is difficult to apply the territorial jurisdiction principle of the physical world directly to the virtual data space; for personal jurisdiction, the identity of data users is hard to determine; the application of protective jurisdiction also face various obstacles in the data space, and universal jurisdiction also shows its defects in the data space.

Right to independence over data

The right to independence is the most basic part of state sovereignty. It means that "a country can exercise its power independently and completely without foreign interference or restriction from other countries" (Xie Yongjiang 2018). Article 2 (7) of the *Charter of the United Nations* provides: "Nothing contained in the present Charter shall authorize the United Nations to intervene in matters which are essentially within the domestic jurisdiction of any state ... but this principle shall not prejudice the application of enforcement measures under Chapter VII." The purpose is to emphasize the independence of state sovereignty to the outside world and that no country or organization has the right to interfere in the affairs of other countries for any reason. Following the *Charter of the United Nations*, the General Assembly of the United Nations adopted the *Declaration on the Inadmissibility of Intervention in the Domestic Affairs of States and the Protection of Their Independence and Sovereignty* in 1965 (hereinafter referred to as the *Declaration*). The *Declaration* further emphasizes that the independence of state sovereignty is protected and that the external and internal affairs of a country are to be handled independently by the country. At the same time, no state is allowed to interfere in or hamper the handling of the internal affairs of other countries in any form, no state is allowed to directly or indirectly participate in the internal strife of other countries for any reason, and no state is allowed to organize, assist, foment, finance, incite or tolerate activities of subverting the government in other countries. Countries should practice mutual respect in terms of sovereign independence. Accordingly, the purpose of the right to independence is that any country can handle its external and internal affairs independently in accordance with its own will without any form of control and interference from other countries.

State sovereignty "implies, therefore, independence all round, within and without the borders of the country" (Jennings & Watts, trans. Wang Tieya 1995, p. 92). In the era of big data, sovereign states shall be independent to exercise power in the data space. The right to independence over data means that a country has the right to independently manage the data infrastructure and resources within the country, protect data security and prevent other countries from interfering in its data infrastructure and resources arbitrarily. The right to independence over data first includes the right of sovereign states to govern their own data space. The right of governance can take many forms such as moral rules, policies and laws, mainly to maintain the supreme authority of the country in data space. Second, it includes the right to prohibit interference by other countries in its data management. Although there is no border in data space, data management of a country should not be interfered in by other countries. Resisting data hegemony firmly is an effective way to maintain the independence of data sovereignty of all countries (Jiang Ruihao 2016).

The relationship between the right to independence over data and traditional right to national independence is described as follows. First of all, the right to independence over data is the development and extension of independence in the traditional theory of national sovereignty. As the application of national independence in the data space, data independence not only endorses the purpose and essence of the traditional theory of national independence, but also enriches and develops the traditional theory of national sovereignty, and constantly endows it with features of our new era and profound connotation. Second, the traditional theory of national independence is the theoretical basis of the right to independence over data. Like the purpose of traditional independence, the right to independence over data adheres to the spirit of non-interference in internal affairs of the international law, conforms to the provisions of the international law on independence, and complies with the development trends of the international community and international law. Lastly, the right to independence over data and the right to national independence are in a dialectical unity. They are two dimensions of the development of the same thing. The application of national independence in the data space will face some challenges, making it impossible to continue to adjust the ongoing international relations in the era of big data. Compared with the right to national independence, the right to independence over data is better adapted to the environment home and abroad of the data space in the era of big data.

The right to independence over data requires that the data system of a country, including its network and application technology, not be subject to any restraints from any other country or organization. However, from the perspective of domain name resolution, the current operation of the Internet in various countries is highly dependent on the root name server which is located in the United States. This, to a certain extent, affects the exercise of the right to independence over data. The domain name resolution system of adopts a centralized and hierarchical management model. In this model, there are two main risks in domain name resolution: First, domestic domain names may be blocked. If the registration record of the top-level domain name of a country is deleted from the original root name server, no user form any other country would be able to access the websites under domain names of that country. In that case, the multi-level domain name resolution system will also collapse. Second, the risk of not being able to access the Internet. As long as the original root name server and all its slave servers and image servers refuse to provide root name services for the IP addresses of all the recursive DNS servers in one country, the Internet users relying on recursive DNS servers of that country will not be able to access the Internet because they cannot obtain domain name resolution services (Fang Binxing 2014).

According to statistics, there are currently 13 Internet root servers in the world, of which the only primary root server is in the United States, and nine of the remaining 12 secondary root servers are also in the United States. It can be seen that the United States has control over the core and key basic resources of the global Internet. Once it blocks the domain name of a country on the root server, it can make all websites under that top-level domain name "disappear" from the Internet instantly. In this sense, the United States has control over data which no other country can compare and has the ability to deter the data sovereignty of other countries. It can also be seen that except the United State, no country has complete independence over their data on the Internet. To realize the right to independence over data in cyberspace for all countries, we need to transfer the management of the root server of the Internet to an international organization like the United Nations. For a long time, China has been committed to calling upon the United Nations to take over the work of Internet name management and digital address distribution agencies. After being pressed by the international community for many years, on October 1, 2016, the National Telecommunication and Information Administration, a subsidiary of the Department of Commerce of the United States, finally transferred the management power of the Internet digital address distribution agency to the Internet name and digital address distribution agency in California, and concluded the authorization management contract between the two. The transfer of the management power of Internet digital address distribution agencies will help countries get rid of the control of the United States and become more independent (Huang Zhixiong 2017, p. 146).

Right of data equality

"Equality, as a fundamental value in building sound social order, has been what people pursue since the birth of human society" (Wu Shan & Liu Yading 2010). The right to equality is "legalized and standardized equality, representing better order" (Wang Xiangrong 2019). From the perspective of the relations between countries, the right to equality is one of the fundamental rights of a country and the basic expression of the sovereignty of a country. The right to equality refers to the equal status of all countries before international law regardless of their strength, size, political or economic models, culture, social system, and ideology. In 1648, *Peace of Westphalia* clearly stipulated the important legal principles of modern international relations and confirmed the equal status of national sovereignty. The recognition of the principle of sovereign equality in contemporary international law is mainly reflected in the *Charter of the United Nations* which was adopted in 1945. The preamble to it states the belief in "equal rights ... of nations large and small" clearly, and in paragraph 1 of Article 2, it expressly provides that "the Organization is based on the principle of the sovereign equality of all its Members."

Based on international law, all countries, big or small, strong or weak, are equal members of the international community. In other words, although there are differences in territorial area, economic and military strength, there are no difference in terms of their legal status, legal rights and other sovereign rights and interests. Every country is equal before the international law and their legitimate rights and interests are equal and must abide by the basic norms of the international law and international relations.

Ian Brownlie once pointed out that "equality of state sovereignty is the basic constitutional doctrine of the law of nations". It can be concluded that right to equality is of great importance to sovereign countries (Fang Binxing 2017). As one of the basic rights of a country, the right of equality of a country is an important symbol of its sovereignty. As a natural extension of state sovereignty in data space in the era of big data, data sovereignty should be equal.

> The equality of data sovereignty is mainly reflected among sovereign countries, that is, external sovereignty. Data sovereignty is the highest power from the top to the

> bottom internally, while externally, it means that all sovereign state is independent and identified with each other. No country may manage another country on the ground of international affairs; and there are no rights and obligations between countries. Relations between countries shall be equal, which is also the due meaning of national sovereignty. In other words, since a state has the freedom to declare that it is not restricted and controlled by other states within its sovereignty, it must also recognize that other states enjoy equal freedom within their own sovereignty. (Zhang Jinwen 2018, p. 8)

Like the right to national equality, the right to equality over data is an important symbol of data sovereignty. It means that "a country shall not claim data jurisdiction over other countries and the equal rights to participate in international data cooperation and sharing" (Li Aijun & Zhang Jun 2017, p. 34). The right to equality over data requires that the importance of data be accepted by the international community and that data sovereignty be made an important part of national sovereignty, so as to realize the equal exchange of partial data and to allow countries to enjoy the right to equality in the exchange of data in the international community. In practice, the right to equality over data involves three aspects: First, equal access to data resources. Data is the shared wealth of all mankind, and people in any country have the right to use data freely without discrimination under the premise of not infringing on the interests of other countries and people. Second, equal right to make data rules. Countries not only have equal voice in the global data governance system, but also should avoid infringing on the interests of countries that depend on their data services when making their own data rules. Inequality in data rule-making will inevitably lead some countries to face unequal treatment by developed countries. Lastly, the right to equality over data should also emphasize the immunity of state behavior in the data space, which is a continuation from the traditional theory of state immunity in the era of big data and indirectly reflects the equality of national sovereignty.

The right to equality over data is of relativity, which is determined by the data processing ability of each country. With the rapid development of science and technology, it is necessary for the international community to strengthen cooperation and establish unified rules for the data space, so as to reduce the legal differences among countries and promote the establishment of a new global data space order. The right to equality over data concerns not only the direct equality in data resource allocation, but also the equal ability to transform resources after data resource allocation. However, the reality is that the majority of developing countries are far behind developed countries in data technology development and have different influence in the data space. In addition, some developed countries conduct hegemonic behaviors in the data space, so complete equality is basically impossible for the time being. For example, due to their limited technological capacity, many developing countries are not able to store and process data safely, and can only transfer data to developed countries, and even have to accept the hegemonic behavior of them.

The main problem of the right to equality over data is the loss of data equality in different countries. At the present stage, the level of data technology development in different countries in the world is uneven, and there is inequality when countries exercise their rights in the field of big data. On the one hand, the United States and other developed countries have absolute predominance in data technology, while the majority of developing countries are in a disadvantaged position. On the other hand, due to the huge difference in the technological capabilities of different countries, the ability to collect, store, transmit, process and use data is not the same, resulting in imbalance in the process of cross-border data flow. On account of the liquidity and timeliness of cross-border data flow, it is more convenient for data to flow to developed countries that possess more abundant capital and resources. Mastering massive data resources makes it easier for developed countries to expand their data-related advantages, further broaden the gap and grasp the industrial sovereignty and economic development opportunities of less-developed countries. This will lead to further losses of equality in rights. Therefore, the international community should vigorously promote the concept of equality in data sovereignty. In order to realize the equal distribution of data interests, we can learn from the legislative concept of the "principle of common interests of all mankind" in the *Outer Space Treaty*, let all countries in the world enjoy the huge benefits brought by data space, let all countries in the world have equal voice and participation ability in global data governance, and work together to explore a mutually beneficial and win-win data governance model.

Right to self-defense over data

The right to self-defense originates from national sovereignty. According to the principle of national sovereignty, countries have the obligation to respect the sovereignty and independence of other countries. In order to ensure their survival and security and safeguard their sovereignty and independence, all countries have the right to take all measures permitted by the international law for self-preservation. In the traditional international law, a country possesses the right to war, so it can obtain or maintain its own rights and interests with various measures, including war, to realize self-preservation and self-development. In this sense, the right to war is an important part of the right to self-preservation under the traditional international law. In 1928, the signing of the *Pact of Paris* declared war illegal for the first time. After World War II, as the *Charter of the United Nations* came into force, modern international law clearly abolished the right to war, making it no longer a legitimate right of any state to realize self-preservation and development in this way. Such a transition gave rise to the right to self-defense. In the international legal system, the right to self-defense, as a fundamental right of a country, is subordinate to national sovereignty. It is mainly provided for in Article 51 of the *Charter of the United Nations.*[2] In accordance with this article, a state possesses the inherent right to fight against armed attacks, that is, the right to self-defense.

The right to self-defense refers to the right of a state to resist the attacks of external forces by means of force so as to safeguard its inherent or natural right. For a long time, there have been disputes and debates

2 Article 51 of the *Charter of the United Nations* provides that "Nothing in the present Charter shall impair the inherent right of individual or collective self-defence if an armed attack occurs against a Member of the United Nations, until the Security Council has taken measures necessary to maintain international peace and security. Measures taken by Members in the exercise of this right of self-defence shall be immediately reported to the Security Council and shall not in any way affect the authority and responsibility of the Security Council under the present Charter to take at any time such action as it deems necessary in order to maintain or restore international peace and security."

over the right to self-defense in the international community, the focus of which mainly lies in the interpretation of the right to self-defense in the *Charter of the United Nations*. There are two main views on the definition of the right to self-defense: one in the narrow sense and one in the broad sense. In the narrow sense, the right to self-defense refers to the right of a country to carry out individual or collective armed self-defense to fight against the aggressor and to defend itself when attacked by external forces (Zhou Gengsheng 1981, p. 77). In a broad sense, the right to self-defense is inherent to a country as an international personality and the right of a country to defend its own existence and independence (Zhang Naigen 2002, p. 95). The right to self-defense, as Chinese scholars call it, usually refers to the right to self-defense in the narrow sense. They believe that the right to self-defense is a natural right of a country stemmed from its national sovereignty. Based on a summary of relevant points of view, the right to self-defense should be defined as follows: First, it is the inherent right of a state as an international personality. Second, it is the right to defend the survival and independence of a state. Third, in the process of exercising the right to self-defense, there should be no abuse (He Fuyong & Duan Jindong 2005).

Lassa Oppenheim, the famous British scholar of international law, believes that on the basis of customary international law, no country has the obligation to remain passive when another country takes interests that are harmful to its legal protection. If a country is attacked by force, it has the right to use force when necessary to defend itself, repel the attackers and expel them out of its territory. However, when confronted with an attack of data, the right to self-defense against a data attack, which is virtual, is different from the right to self-defense stipulated in general international law. If the data attack causes serious damage to the key data infrastructure of a country, the injured state has the right to exercise the right to self-defense against the attacker, which means to exercise the right to self-defense over data, with certain conditions and limitations. The right to self-defense over data is based on the traditional right to self-defense, which is established to maintain data sovereignty. In addition, it is an important and indispensable right of a country to maintain its data security and development. The right to self-defense over data refers to the right of a country to protect its own rights and interests when its data sovereignty is subject to external data theft, surveillance or attack.

According to Article 51 of the *Charter of the United Nations*, the exercise of a state's right to self-defense must be based on the premise of an armed attack which has occurred or is about to occur. However, Article 51 only refers to the term "armed attack" without defining what it exactly is, let alone clearly providing that data attack can be regarded as an armed attack in the traditional sense. As a new kind of attack, data attacks do not consider mass physical damage as an essential factor, but it can easily interfere with and destroy the battle command system of the enemy due to the increasingly higher dependence of modern war operation mechanisms on data, and then take a heavy toll on physical military facilities, weapons and equipment of the enemy, and even result in fatal damage to combatants. To some extent, a data attack is no different from the tangible military means used in traditional wars. Therefore, if a data attack causes a serious physical damage to the one attacked, it can be regarded as an armed attack as is defined in the *Law of Armed Conflict*, and then sovereign states can carry out data self-defense against such a data attack and exercise their right to self-defense over data.

The international law recognizes the natural right to self-defense of states but limits its exercise. In the Caroline affair, Daniel Webster, then Secretary of State of the United States, made it clear in his reply to the note from a British ambassador that although a state has the right to self-defense, the right to self-defense should be limited to situations where it is "instant, overwhelming, leaving no choice of means, and no moment for deliberation" in self-defense (Can Shang 2019). The same as the restrictions on the exercise of the right to self-defense, the right to self-defense over data is likely to evolve into armed retaliation if necessary restrictions are not imposed. Moreover, armed retaliation is against the purpose of the modern international law and is illegal. As a result, the exercise of the right to self-defense over must be subject to certain limits, namely the principle of necessity and proportionality. The principle of necessity aims mainly to regulate the means and methods use to exercise the right to self-defense over data, as well as the immediate exercise of data self-defense. The principle of proportionality requires that when a state exercises its right to self-defense over data, there must be a reasonable relationship between the extent of the force applied and the damage suffered, and between the specific and direct military interests or the rights protected and the possible collateral damage of civilians and civilian objects.

Game of Data Sovereignty

The status of data as a kind of basic strategic resource is becoming increasingly prominent. Countries rely more and more on data resources for their economic development, construction, social stability. "Competition for data resources is becoming increasingly fierce, data sovereignty has become the focus of the game between multiple parties, and the competition between countries for dominance over data information is becoming more and more fierce" (Zhao Gang, Wang Shuai & Wang Peng 2017). In practice, the absolute independence of data sovereignty leads to multiple jurisdictional conflicts and predicaments related to state security, so the game and confrontation of data sovereignty eventually lead to disorder in the international community in the data space. In this context, to find a way out of the difficult situation of disorder, countries should return to sovereign cooperation and participation, and implement joint regulation and co-governance of the data space commons to ensure the lasting peace, general security and common development of mankind.

Conflicts of data sovereignty

The cross-border flow and storage of data have challenged the traditional theory of absolute independence of sovereignty. It is impossible for an independent sovereign state to fully claim possession and exercise jurisdiction over its data, or completely exclude foreign interference. If a country implements absolute and unilateral control over data and related technologies on the basis of data sovereignty independence, it will lead to spontaneous game and confrontation of data sovereignty, and eventually result in the disorder in the data space of the international community. As a result, overemphasis on the independence of data sovereignty is the main cause of data sovereignty confrontations among countries. At present, based on the independence of data sovereignty, the spontaneous game of data sovereignty mainly results from the conflict of multiple jurisdictions over data and predicament concerning national data security.

The conflict of multiple jurisdictions over data. In the era of big data, international law faces numerous challenges, among which the most lasting and profound one is that data will be governed by the laws of various different countries based on the places of possession, storage and transmission. At the same time, in order to cut down costs and meet the needs of customers, data service providers often outsource some of their services. Then, that part of data is likely to be subject to multiple jurisdictions for they involve different countries, especially given that countries have not clearly defined the jurisdiction of data sovereignty and that all countries exercise their rights in the international community in a completely rational way. Before the establishment of a unified international system or a coordination mechanism, in order to ensure the absolute security and accomplish sufficient monitoring, all countries claim data sovereignty over all the data that they can monitor, and this will inevitably lead to the monitoring of some extraterritorial data, thus forming the situation of multiple jurisdictions. All in all, the current practices based on emphasis on the independence of sovereignty have resulted in anarchy in the international community regarding data jurisdiction (Sun Nanxiang & Zhang Xiaojun 2015).

The predicament of national data security. First of all, compared with developed countries, developing countries and least developed countries are obviously less capable of data control. The majority of developing countries and least developed countries, though having data sovereignty, are usually not able to effectively protect their own data security and national interests owing to the limited level of data technology. Secondly, the revolution in data technology not only enables some developed countries to abuse data sovereignty by making use of their technological advantages, but also imposes serious threats on the data security of other countries. Taking the

United States as an example. In addition to its control over extraterritorial data by applying domestic legislation, the United States also collects and analyzes data under the jurisdiction of other countries through special projects of its state security authorities. In the meantime, the spontaneous game over data sovereignty also makes it difficult for national data security to be effectively guaranteed. On the one hand, the cross-border flow and storage of data has greatly undermined the effective jurisdiction of a country over data and related equipment, forming a serious security loophole. On the other hand, developed countries can collect and monitor data of other countries in secret ways with more advanced technology, thus infringing on the data sovereignty of other countries. As a result, emphasis on the independence of data sovereignty will bring about confrontations between countries and lead some developed countries to arbitrarily implement unilateralism in the data space.

The spontaneous game over data sovereignty. The independence of data sovereignty is closely related to the conflict between multiple jurisdictions and the predicament concerning national data security. This gives rise to a spontaneous game which initiates a state of confrontation over data sovereignty. Firstly, emphasizing the absolute independence of data sovereignty will give rise to conflicts between multiple jurisdictions. Data flow involves at least data producers, receivers and users, the places of transmission, transfer and destination, the location of data infrastructure, the nationality of data service providers and the place of data operation. Due to the indivisibility and integrity of data, every aspect of cross-border data flow can lead to overlapping of jurisdictions and conflicts over data sovereignty. Secondly, to ensure data security, countries are likely to take absolute unilateral control over data and related technologies on account of the independence of data sovereignty. In particular, legal restrictions are imposed on the selection of the location of data centers, requiring them to be established within the scope of security control set by the state. Finally, some developed countries obtain sensitive data by violating data sovereignty of other countries on the basis of protecting their own data sovereignty. For example, the United States has a monopoly over strategic cyber resources of the world and a large number of top network operators and communication service providers in the world as well, making it possible for it to steal confidential data from other countries and posing a threat to global data security.

Against the backdrop of the rapid development and popularization of data technologies, different countries put forward different definitions of data jurisdiction from different perspectives. In particular, based on the independence of data sovereignty, countries continue to claim jurisdiction over extraterritorial data. Furthermore, in the era of big data, countries' control over data is greatly weakened. Under the circumstances of conflicts concerning data sovereignty, the majority of developing countries and least developed countries are not able to ensure their own data security and effectively exercise data sovereignty without the assistance of an effective international coordination mechanism. On the contrary, developed countries can effectively exercise data sovereignty by virtue of advanced technology, and even endanger the security and data sovereignty of other countries. Based on the above, the absolute independence of data sovereignty leads to conflicts of multiple jurisdictions and predicament concerning national data security, and the spontaneous game and confrontation eventually lead to disorder in the international data space. In order to tackle the current disorder, we should explore ways to establish international coordination organizations or mechanisms based on the transferability and cooperativeness of data sovereignty (Sun Nanxiang & Zhang Xiaojun 2015).

Transfer of data sovereignty

At the early days of the sovereignty theory, it was generally believed that sovereignty was absolute, permanent, indivisible and non-transferable. As an American scholar pointed out, globalization destroys sovereign states, connects the world, abuses the political community it establishes, challenges the social contract, and puts forward the useless idea of state-backed social security long before the due time ... From then on, sovereignty is no longer the indisputable basic value as it used to be. It is outdated now to adhere to the absoluteness, indivisibility and non-transferability of state sovereignty and the time has long passed when a country can handle all affairs concerning its sovereignty completely on its own without considering and influence from and implications on other countries. In the new era, the behavior of countries is increasingly influenced and restricted by various other actors. Facing such realities, the idea that sovereignty can be transferred turns up as a new trend. Generally speaking, sovereignty transfer refers to a way to exercise sovereignty in which, in the context of globalization and based on the division of sovereignty into elements related to identity and elements related to power, the sovereign states, in order to maximize national interests and promote positive interaction with other countries and international cooperation, voluntarily transfer part of their sovereign power to other countries or international organizations in accord with the sovereignty principle while reserving the right to withdraw the transferred sovereign power at any time.

"Sovereignty transfer is the product of a collision between globalization and state sovereignty. It is well-grounded and inevitable. Therefore, most people hold a positive attitude towards sovereignty transfer" (Yang Fei 2009). However, the concept of sovereignty transfer has been in dispute since its emergence. The direct reason is that scholars tend to use the term state sovereignty to refer to some specific elements of it, while the root cause is that state sovereignty has multi-facet connotations. State sovereignty contains different elements such as sovereign identity, sovereign authority, sovereign power, sovereign will and sovereign interests. Accordingly, the answer to the question of whether the elements can be transferred is different; some elements such as sovereign power and sovereign interests can be transferred, while other elements such as sovereign will, sovereign authority and sovereign identity cannot. At present, there is not yet any consensus on the term "sovereignty transfer" and scholars sometimes use different wordings such as alienation of sovereignty, transfer of sovereignty, negation of sovereignty, sovereignty concession, etc. (Yi Shanwu 2006).

As the representation, extension and reflection of national sovereignty in the data space, data sovereignty can also be transferred. In fact, no country can possess the data space in the era of big data, because data infrastructure and data exchange centers supporting the operation of the data space should be regarded as "global commons". The openness of the data space naturally requires countries to safeguard their national interests within a unified international framework. Accordingly, if a country desires to fully realize its data sovereignty, it must transfer part of its data sovereignty to some shared mechanism or institution so that the shared mechanism or institution who receive this part the sovereignty can exercise the sovereignty and manage shared property. As an important manifestation of the partial transfer of national sovereignty in the data space, the partial transfer of data sovereignty does not mean giving up national sovereignty. Rather, it is a rational choice in the era of big data. By joining international organizations and transferring part of its data sovereignty for it to be exercised by a collectively accepted organization (Zhang Haibing 2005), countries can share data sovereignty, seek greater long-term national interests, and safeguard national data sovereignty in general.

The transferable parts of data sovereignty consist of data jurisdiction and data ownership. The former means that a country can transfer its data jurisdiction to large companies that abide by the data management laws, regulations and policies of the country and these companies can have relatively independent jurisdiction over data resources and carry out business activities related thereto under the framework of relevant domestic laws and regulations. They can even be foreign multinational companies, but are subject to supervision and inspection by relevant domestic authorities in accordance with laws. The partial transferability of data ownership means that one country does not have ownership over data that is stored or computed within its territory but generated in other countries, and in this case the ownership of such data should be transferred. The key point of the partial transferability of data ownership is that not all data stored or computed in one country can be owned and controlled by the country, because ownership only belongs to the country where the data is generated, and other countries may only compute or store the data, not own it.

The transfer of data sovereignty must adhere to the principle of safeguarding national interests. As American scholar Hans J. Morgenthau pointed out in *Dilemmas of Politics*, as long as the world is made up of countries politically, the ultimate language in international politics can only be national interests. That is to say, national interests determine the basic objectives of a country's foreign policy and international behavior (Cai Gaoqiang 2002). In the era of big data, whether to transfer data sovereignty and how to do it fundamentally depend on national interests. Only on the premise of safeguarding national interests can a country transfer part of its data sovereignty. The transfer of data sovereignty "is to some extent at the expense of temporary and partial interests in exchange for the promotion and maintenance of long-term and overall interests" (Li Huiying & Huang Guiqin 2004). In addition, the transfer of data sovereignty by a country is not unrestricted and unprincipled, nor is it a passive action at the pressure from any power. In terms of the transfer of data sovereignty and autonomous restriction, the extent should be considered carefully so as to maintain the independence of countries and equal rights and status for all countries involved.

Cooperation on data sovereignty

In the era of big data, no country can handle international affairs unilaterally. In view of the conflict of multiple jurisdictions over data and the predicament of national data security among countries in the data space and the problems brought about by the specific conditions of the countries involved, countries should rely on cooperation on data sovereignty to seek solutions, and thoroughly solve the tension between countries over data sovereignty at the very root by reasonably defining jurisdiction, jointly managing data space commons, taking collective actions on data space crimes and other cooperation modes.

Sovereignty cooperation

In the international community, any sovereign state has the freedom and right to act properly. In other words, as long as it does not violate any prohibitive provisions of international laws or any specific treaty obligations undertaken, a state can freely exercise its sovereignty in pursuit of its own interests. However, in an increasingly interconnected world, it is not sufficient for states to exercise their sovereignty and take free actions within the legal framework for problems on the transnational level are increasingly complex and diverse. Additionally, the independent actions of and free exchanges between countries will also lead to mutual infringement (Zhao Zhou 2010, p. 153). Consequently, close sovereignty cooperation is needed, and the ultimate goal of such cooperation is to gain interests. Sovereignty cooperation means "a broad and comprehensive cooperation among countries in order to realize their respective goals on the basis of a full recognition of the differences between their goals and seeking common ground while maintaining differences" (Huang Houwen & Li Quanhui 2009). Besides, sovereignty cooperation "must be based on equality, compliance to international laws, fulfillment of international obligations in good faith, and no interfere in the internal affairs of other countries. Only in this way can we safeguard the common interests of mankind" (Ren Mingyan 2007).

The unique features of data and the data space require a new type of sovereignty cooperation. With the rapid development and spread of data technology, the cross-border flow and storage of data is becoming more common and convenient. At the same time, as data is intangible and flows across the whole world, no country has been able to achieve absolute control over data through unilateral efforts. Therefore, the establishment of absolute state sovereignty is simply not possible. Big data is international by nature, and the problem of data sovereignty it brings about is also international. No country can handle international affairs alone. In light of the problems resulted from the conflict between multiple jurisdictions, the predicament of data security and the different specific conditions of countries in the data space, countries should carry out cooperation of data sovereignty. The current situation can be changed if countries strengthen cooperation on data sovereignty to make global data flow more transparent, better regulated and more orderly. Such cooperation may also enable all countries to better control and make more reasonable use of partners' data, maximize the use value of data and thoroughly solve the tension over data sovereignty among countries.

Ideas of data sovereignty cooperation

Countries shall have the right to participate in the decision-making process of international affairs. This is an important guarantee for cooperation on data sovereignty. As far as the international community is concerned, it is not only the business of the international community, but also the responsibility and obligation of all sovereign states to carry out cooperation to safeguard common interests, security and development space. In the meantime, cooperation is also an important way to exercise data sovereignty. In the era of big data, every country should be fully aware that other countries have the right to manage the data resources, data service providers and data infrastructure within their jurisdictions, and that unilateral pursuit of absolute independence of sovereignty may lead to confrontations between countries. In order to deal with the cross-border flow of data and the many problems it may cause, we should also get back to the issue of how to define data sovereignty. We should attach importance to the right to participate in decision-making in international affairs, which all countries in the world enjoy, whether they are big or small, rich or poor, strong or weak. This is the basis of cooperation on data sovereignty. At the same time, it is impossible for any country to deal with international affairs on its own, so only through sovereignty cooperation can we effectively manage shared property. Sovereignty cooperation is the inevitable approach to data sovereignty.

Cooperation on data sovereignty should adhere to the basic principles of international law, that is, sovereign equality, fairness and mutual benefit. Sovereign equality of all countries is the basic principle stipulated in the *Charter of the United Nations* and it is the premise of cooperation. Fairness is the core of a new international order. Some developed countries implement unilateral control over data and related facilities by virtue of their advantageous technologies, sacrificing the interests of other countries, and thus leading to tensions between countries over data security. Hence, it is critical for cooperation on data sovereignty to avoid a power-oriented approach. The ultimate purpose of cooperation is effective jurisdiction, control and use of the shared data space, and cooperation should be carried out in line with the principles of equality and mutual benefit instead of serving the interests of any one party at the expense of the interests of others. To achieve fairness, the international community should provide data technology support for developing countries, especially least developed countries to improve their ability to govern, control and use their own data, and prevent data security threats such as data hegemony and data terrorism.

Model of data sovereignty cooperation

Balancing and regulating the exercise of jurisdiction is the main content of cooperation on data sovereignty and the core idea is to define jurisdiction appropriately. This definition must be based on sovereignty and the right to governance, and balance between territorial jurisdiction and personal jurisdiction. From the perspective of traditional international law, a state is regarded as an indivisible and unified whole, responsible for all the individuals within the territory, or at least for their actions. Correspondingly, jurisdiction of applicable laws as well as the rights and obligations of all relevant parties shall be determined based upon the location of things or people. Data sovereignty and governance are closely related, and it is impossible for any country to exercise jurisdiction over people or things beyond its control. However, due to the special features of data and the borderlessness of the data space, traditional jurisdiction principles are no longer sufficient here. Therefore, countries should, on the basis of the central spirit of the traditional jurisdiction theory, add the most closely related principle of effect jurisdiction into the picture. If, when a country exercises data jurisdiction, the effect extends to people and locations of other countries, or has a significant impact on the state security, social order and economic interests of other countries, then the impacted countries have the right to exercise data jurisdiction and require the country concerned to refrain from excessively expanding its jurisdiction.

As the most important field of data storage and transport, the data space is regarded as the "global commons", showing similar characteristics as high seas, polar regions, international airspace, outer space. In the era of big data, no country can take possession of the data space alone, and this means that data and related facilities supporting the operation of the data space should be taken as global commons. Since the data space is open, it is natural that countries should safeguard their national interests under the overall framework of the United Nations. Therefore, to fully realize the data sovereignty of each country, we must cooperate on data sovereignty, enjoy and exercise cooperative sovereignty and complete the management of global commons through shared management authorities or mechanisms. Current conflicts are in nature resulted from the fact that some developed countries pursue unilateral jurisdiction over the data space which should be shared by all, with an aim to seek state security and development interests for themselves. The data space is part of the global commons, so data and related facilities supporting the development and operation of the data space, to some extent, should not belong to a certain country but be controlled through some kind of an international condominium.

Since the data space is intangible, virtual, and borderless, the level of data technology of most developing countries, especially least developed countries, is limited, so they are not able to cope with crimes in the data space, especially data terrorism, through effective data jurisdiction within or outside their territory. An effective way to solve this problem is to pursue a security mechanism featuring collective cooperation in the international community on the basis of data sovereignty. At present, although the international cooperation mechanism to combat crime in the data space has become more and more mature, the relevant code of conduct formulated by the international community is still relatively weak in legal terms. Therefore, it is urgent that we act to improve and institutionalize collective actions to deal with criminal activities in the data space. Criminal activities in the data space are relevant to the interests and security of all countries and most major criminal activities are closely connected with data terrorism, which directly threatens the survival, security and development of the whole human society. As a result, it is not only important but also necessary to establish a collective security mechanism for the data space. The idea of allowing a few developed countries to set and enforce rules goes against the idea of cooperation on data sovereignty. Cooperation formed on the premise of the transfer of data sovereignty requires the establishment of a complete code of conduct for the data space within a unified international framework. When confronted with serious data terrorism, transnational actions can even be considered based on the right to collective self-defense.

Governance of Data Sovereignty

The maintenance of data sovereignty is of great significance to state security and development, but in practice, it faces severe challenges. Data hegemonism, data protectionism, data capitalism and data terrorism have been on the rise. Without governance, there is bound to be chaos in the global data space. Therefore, it is urgent to build a governance system to maintain data sovereignty in accordance with relevant principles. In line with the current international political landscape, data sovereignty governance provides an institutionalized and realistic pathway towards cyberspace governance. As data sovereignty is one of the core concepts of China's data rights system, we must clarify its denotation and connotation from a legislative perspective so as to build a system and ultimately materialize data sovereignty within the framework of the rule of law.

Global trend in data sovereignty

At present, data sovereignty has become a new field of competition in the world and some problems in this sphere have even constituted new bottlenecks and risks for global economic growth and social development. Therefore, data sovereignty governance has become a central focus of the world. Anarchy is one of the basic characteristics of the data space, which means that the current data space, like the high seas and outer space, is the anarchic global commons. In an international anarchic state, the data space is facing a series of new challenges, such as data hegemonism, data protectionism, data capitalism and data terrorism.

Data hegemonism. In the era of big data, traditional hegemony has made new development. Some major countries have started to pursue data hegemonism in addition to traditional military hegemony, political hegemony and economic hegemony. They take advantage of people's dependence on data and the vulnerability of the data society, take control of data to achieve the purpose of manipulating or controlling the world. In theory, data hegemonism stands on the opposite side of data sovereignty.

A principle of data sovereignty is that all countries shall have equal rights in international relations. However, in practice, data hegemonism "has posed a serious threat to the sovereignty and state security of all countries as well as to world peace. Some powerful countries not only exceed certain limits in exercising their power, but also extend their power to the sovereignty of other countries" (Key Laboratory of Big Data Strategy 2019, p. 272–273). The existence of data hegemonism is currently the top threat to data sovereignty governance as it hampers the efforts of weak countries in the data space to manage domestic big data effectively and hinders the realization of more effective governance of data sovereignty.

Data protectionism. Cross-border data flow has brought about growth in the global digital economy and has served as the most valuable trade channel in the era of big data. However, countries still impose different restrictions on cross-border data flow. Especially after the Snowden incident, more countries imposed restrictions or bans on cross-border data flow by means of strict management requirements for data localization. Data localization policies provide legal basis for state security and the protection of citizens' privacy in most countries. At the same time, in order to achieve certain economic purposes, some countries have also begun to adopt extreme data localization policies to completely ban cross-border data flow. The extreme practice of data localization has brought threats on account of over-protectionism, that is, data protectionism. Internationally, data protectionism is not only incompatible with the rapid flow of data, capital, technology and talents in the global economy, but also goes against the approach of data sovereignty which is advocated by the majority of countries in the world, showing no respect for the data sovereignty of other countries. Data protectionism cannot effectively prevent the risks brought about by the cross-border data flow. Instead, it is likely to intensify competition and friction, result in extreme egoism and unilateralism, trigger digital trade war and data confrontation, and sink the world into a more serious and widespread crisis.

Data capitalism. Data does not simply mean keeping record and storing information. It is also a treasure of great commercial value. Generally speaking, data is valuable unknown message. People obtain data because they are interested in its use value. An inevitable result of the development of capitalism is that data becomes capital. Data capital is a new kind of capital emerging after monetary capital and knowledge capital. It is a combination of industrial monopoly capital and financial monopoly capital, featuring data monopoly. Data monopoly speeds up capital appreciation to an unprecedented level, thus forming data capitalism. As a form of capitalism, data capitalism "has created a kind of capitalism monopoly that we have never seen since the inauguration of capitalism monopoly, and this form of monopoly has been intensified under the disguise of intellectual property" (Yan Xianjun 2001). Data capitalism cannot completely resolve the basic contradiction of capitalism, which will become more complicated in the era of big data. On the one hand, data capitalism controls and manipulates data production and dissemination in the data space by taking advantage of cutting-edge data technologies, so as to infringe on the data sovereignty of other countries and rake in gains. On the other hand, data capitalism, with control over data technology, seeks political, economic, cultural and other gains, widens the global data gap and sets off the global crisis of data security. Therefore, data capitalism cannot solve the deep-rooted problem of data sovereignty governance effectively, nor does it aim to deal with the new challenges brought by unbalanced development. On the contrary, data capitalism has become an important problem to be solved in the process of the data sovereignty governance.

Data terrorism. In the era of big data, traditional terrorism has not disappeared. It has only realized leapfrog development with the help of big data and extended terrorist activities from the physical space to data space. Big data provides terrorists with new tools and platforms. Terrorists not only use big data as weapons to carry out destruction and disruption, but also use it to recruit terrorists, raise funds, as well as plan and implement terrorist activities. With the development and wide application of big data, data terrorism poses greater threats than traditional terrorism (Key Laboratory of Big Data Strategy 2019, p. 279). Data terrorism shares common features with traditional terrorism, but it sees more serious asymmetry and is more disguised than traditional terrorism. Compared with traditional terrorism, data terrorism does more harm to national sovereignty, world peace and security of the international community by carrying out terrorist activities with the help of data, thus resulting in more devastating consequences. Data terrorism is not only a new method of terrorism, but also “a new global problem in the field of non-traditional security” (Yu Xiaoqiu 2002). At present, data terrorism poses serious threats to economic development, social security and stability in specific countries and even the world and has brought huge challenges to the data sovereignty governance. All in all, it has emerged as a pressing problem for all countries in the world and an urgent solution is urgently needed.

International divergence on data sovereignty

Cyberspace is undoubtedly an important place for data sovereignty. However, “due to the limited understanding of the cyberspace, limited practical experience, and differences and even antagonism in ideology, values and specific national interests” (Huang Zhixiong & Ying Yaohui 2017), there are still varying degrees of divergences in many areas concerning cyberspace in the international community at present. In general, there are divergences in terms of understanding, strategy and governance.

Divergence in understanding: Global commons vs. sovereign territory

At present, there are two sharply different understandings of the cyberspace in the international community. Some believe it to be global commons while others take it as sovereign domain. The former includes the United States, Japan, the European Union and some other countries and organizations who are more developed in the cyberspace. They believe the cyberspace, different from the physical space, is subject to no jurisdiction and domination of any one country, and should be regarded as global commons like the high seas and the outer space. Global commons refer to resources or areas that are not dominated by any country, on which the security and prosperity of all countries depend. The United States, for example, compares cyberspace with oceans, international airspace and the outer space, and classifies cyberspace as global commons beyond the reach of any single sovereign state. "In 2005, the United States classified cyberspace as global commons in the *Strategy for Homeland Security and Civil Support*, and further defined the cyberspace as a global domain within the information environment in *2010 Quadrennial Defense Review*" (Huang Zhixiong 2017, p. 98–99). The United States believes that cyberspace is part of the global commons, and that its management should exceed the boundaries of sovereign states in the traditional sense. That is to say, countries shall not exercise sovereignty in cyberspace. In sharp contrast, the other view, mainly held by Russia, Brazil, the Shanghai Cooperation Organization (SCO), the Council for Security Cooperation in the Asia Pacific (CSCAP) and other emerging countries and organizations in cyberspace, holds that cyberspace clearly has its sovereignty, so in order to protect security and maintain social stability, countries should uphold and exercise their sovereignty in cyberspace. For example, in 2011, Russia, the United Nations, China and other SCO member states submitted the *International Code of Conduct for Information Security* to the 66th session of the UN General Assembly, proposing that the policy authority for Internet-related public issues is part of the sovereignty of states, so the sovereignty of each country in cyberspace should be respected. The CSCAP also holds that cyberspace is by no means part the global commons. Instead, it is an important component of national sovereignty and a new domain for the development of various countries, so to safeguard national sovereignty, security and development interests are realistic issues. At present, although many countries acknowledge that it is necessary to exercise national sovereignty in cyberspace, in practice, due to the significant differences in development level, history, culture and social system (Liu Ying & Wu Ling 2019), there are obvious differences in terms of how they truly understand and deal with the cyberspace. As a result, there is a huge gap concerning the issue of cyberspace sovereignty in relevant international rule-making efforts, and accordingly, data sovereignty, as a subordinate concept of cyberspace sovereignty, is also understood in vastly different ways in the international community. There are even divergences and conflicts as to whether data sovereignty can be justified as a stand-alone concept or is only part of cyberspace sovereignty.

Divergence in strategy: Cyber liberalism vs. a community with a shared future in cyberspace

In terms of values, Western countries unanimously advocate the idea that human rights are superior to sovereignty, upholding the sacredness and inviolability of the basic human rights of citizens. Similarly, in the cyberspace, they adhere to cyber liberalism and oppose the extension of control from the physical space to the cyberspace. Believing that data boundaries bring challenges to democracy, they do not accept any action likely to hinder the free flow of data. For example, the United States holds that the free connection and free flow of data must not be obstructed for any reason and the basic freedom in the cyberspace should be guaranteed. Therefore, in 2011, the United States issued the *International Strategy for Cyberspace* and the *Strategy for Cyberspace* successively for the purpose of promoting the freedom in cyberspace. These two documents constitute the overall framework of the United States' international Internet strategy system and the basis is the theory of autonomy in cyberspace. With cyberspace freedom as a core concept and important component, "the *International Strategy for Cyberspace* is a loyal reflection of the basic principles of the United States: Basic freedom, personal privacy and the free flow of data are the core commitments." After the formation of the cyber liberalism theory, upon its formation, became the official ideology of the U.S. government and was regarded as indisputable universal value. With the strong influence of the Western discourse led by the U.S., the theory has virtually dominated research and discussions related to the cyberspace in the past years (Li Chuanjun 2019). In contrast, developing countries in the cyberspace hold that "cyber liberalism goes contrary to what is needed in cyberspace" (Wang Mingjin, 2016). In cyberspace, we should follow the principles of international relations and the *Charter of the United Nations*, respect the territorial integrity, political independence and freedom of human rights of all countries, and adhere to the principle of balancing between state security and sovereign independence. No country can practice cyber hegemony under the banner of cyber freedom. China, for example, attaches great importance to cyber sovereignty and has been advocating respect for and protection of the cyber sovereignty of all countries as one of its central propositions in regard to international law and international order in cyberspace over the past years. In December 2015, Chinese President Xi Jinping put forward the concept of "building a community with a shared future in cyberspace" and laid out four principles and five paths to realization for it at the 2nd World Internet Conference. This concept is in line with the interests of most countries and was widely accepted soon afterwards. However, some Western countries still have misgivings due to ideological considerations and other factors.

Governance divergence: Multi-stakeholder governance vs. multilateral governance

At present, in terms of the model of cyberspace governance, countries mainly form two categories: one is developed countries in cyberspace headed by the United States and the other is emerging and developing countries in cyberspace represented by China, Russia and Brazil. The former category advocates the model of multi-stakeholder governance, while the latter supports multilateralism governance. The multi-stakeholder approach, which is currently a widely accepted governance model in the global cyberspace, advocates "governance of cyberspace dominated by technical experts, commercial institutions and civil society, while governments and even the intergovernmental organizations such as the United Nations should not intervene too much" (Wang Mingjin 2016). This model attaches importance to the participation of multiple governing bodies, denies national sovereignty and emphasizes individuals, "believing that cyberspace, global and decentralized as it is, has deprived governments of their central position in traditional governance" (Zheng Wenming 2017) and advocating a bottom-up approach instead. The multi-stakeholder governance model may seem to play a somewhat positive role in balancing the interests of all parties, but due to the lack of cooperation and support from sovereign states, it is not likely to achieve effective governance of cyberspace. Moreover, this model also shows a number of defects and faces widespread doubts from emerging and developing countries in cyberspace in terms of its reasonability, legitimacy and reliability. In comparison, the second category of countries tend to support multilateral governance which is dominated by governments, and advocate cyberspace governance within the framework of the United Nations or other international organizations. This is a top-down model for cyberspace governance. It emphasizes "the principle of national sovereignty in cyberspace and pursues solution to disorder in cyberspace with nation-states playing the central role. A state should have the power to protect state security and digital sovereignty in cyberspace and some kind of an organization should be established within the framework of the United Nations, with a state as the main players to coordinate and deal with issues related to cyberspace governance" (Zheng Wenming 2017). There are constant conflicts between the two models. "The divergences between the two are essentially disputes between conservatives and reformers in regard to cyberspace governance mechanism based on their own interests. It can be predicted that the divergences and game around the issue will continue to exist for a long time" (Long Kun & Zhu Qichao 2019).

Legislation on data sovereignty

Data sovereignty is of great practical significance to state security, economic development and social stability, but in practice, many new threats and challenges exist in this aspect. Therefore, there is an urgent need to build a system and explore a path of legislation to safeguard data sovereignty, bringing relevant efforts onto the track of law-based regulation. This will help reduce the risk of data sovereignty abuse and promote sound development in related fields.

Challenges faced by data sovereignty

At present, more and more countries have carried out practices in regard to legislation on data sovereignty, yet the international community has not reached a consensus on the principles to follow in this aspect. On the one hand, Russia, the European Union and the United States hold different views on the exercise of data sovereignty given their different national interests. Russia actively advocates the exercise of data sovereignty for the sake of state security, the EU and its member states also respect data sovereignty for the protection of citizens' personal data, but the United States and some other countries pay more attention to the commercial benefits brought by big data and advocate free cross-border data flow. By comparison, countries with weak control in cyberspace is inclined to accept the concept of data sovereignty in the hope of protecting their rights to data management and use through international cooperation. On the contrary, countries with strong control over data does not worry about their data being plundered or exploited and data sovereignty, therefore, is not really meaningful to them (He Bo 2017). At the same time, as a new right of states, data sovereignty also faces many new challenges and threats, including data hegemonism, data protectionism, data capitalism and data terrorism. Many Western countries, led by the United States, have established relatively complete and mature legal systems for data management, formed the entire industry chains on the basis of their technological advantages provided by domestic giants in the industry, mastered the key points of data management, and actually imposed data hegemony on other countries. For example, with the PRISM surveillance program, the U.S. government allowed its National Security Agency direct access to the huge data resources of nine major companies including Google, Facebook, Microsoft, Youtube and Paltalk, in order to obtain intelligence it needed, which seriously infringed on the data security and national interests of other countries (Du Yanyun 2016).

Data sovereignty system building

At present, laws and policies related to data sovereignty mainly focus on the management and control of data, and the claims and practices of various countries concerning data sovereignty concentrate mainly on the management of cross-border data flow. Internationally, more and more countries and regions have begun to build their data sovereignty systems from the legal perspective for the purpose of data management (He Bo 2017). In the legal system building for data sovereignty, we should not only pay attention to the security of core data from the perspective of risk prevention, but also emphasize the mining and use of big data resources, and be more cautious when dealing with technological risks and economic losses brought by data hegemony. Therefore, in setting relevant rules and building the systems, we should work on three dimensions: transnational data flow based on data classification, localized storage of data resources, and data hegemony elimination by building a community with a shared future (Zhang Jianwen & Jia Zhangfan 2018).

Data control and flow based on classification. In the era of big data, it is in line with the fundamental and long-term interests of most countries to realize free data flow on the premise of state security. This requires countries to manage data on the basis of classification, so as to prevent the leakage of critical data, guarantee the orderly and free flow of non-critical data in accordance with the law, and form a set of rules for cross-border data flow that gives due consideration to both security and freedom. In order to prevent data leakage, we should build models for the dynamic tracking of data flow and the assessment of security risk, establish a multi-facet retroactive accountability mechanism and an emergency response mechanism for security risks. These three together will help us prevent leakage of critical data and minimize the losses brought data leakage when it does occur. To promote the flow of non-critical data, we should introduce the concept of modesty and restraint and the principle of subsidiarity, and support the free exchange and flow of non-critical data, in order to bring benefits to both sides of the game on the basis of giving full play to their respective features and complementary advantages.

Localized storage of data and protection of key infrastructure. Data localization emphasizes localized data collection, processing and storage, requiring all these to be done within the jurisdiction of the country concerned. However, when trying to build a data sovereignty system, we must consider the replicability and mobility of data, so as to prevent the reverse restriction effect and regulatory spillover effect caused by overlapping data jurisdictions. In addition to localized storage of data, we should also set detailed rules as to where key infrastructure such as operators and service facilities should locate. Specifically, operators should be corporate or non-corporate organizations registered within the territory of a country, and the location of servers should be subject to pre-establishment approval and/or post-establishment review. Moreover, infrastructure should be assigned appropriate confidentiality levels and security levels so as to better protect key infrastructure from hacker attacks.

Elimination of data hegemony and the building of a community with a shared future. In order to eliminate data hegemony, developing countries should, on the one hand, strengthen top-level strategic design and offer more support to domestic big data enterprises so as to break hegemonic powers' monopoly on data technologies, and on the other hand, they should also work to build a community with a shared future with a view to undermining the legitimacy of data hegemony. Although data sovereignty covers data generated by citizens of one country in other countries, to truly exercise data sovereignty, it is undoubtedly necessary to secure support and cooperation from other countries. For this purpose, we need to avoid "regulatory spillover effect which may lead to reverse restriction from other countries. Otherwise, it will be difficult to realize the free flow of data and to establish extraterritorial jurisdiction. By strengthening multilateral cooperation, we can promote the formation of new rules for cross-border data flow and build a new system on the basis of equality and mutual benefit. This will effectively remove the inequality in development opportunities brought by data hegemonism and shed light on the formation of new international relations.

Suggestions for legislation on data sovereignty

American scholar Lisa J. Damon pointed out at the end of the twentieth century that theoretically, cross-border data flow should bring people across the world closer, reduce distance in the physical world, make data instantly available, and contribute to an interdependent global economy. However, in reality, cross-border data flow is creating new obstacles between different countries. In order to prevent further harm, it is necessary for us to reach new agreements and establish effective international adjudication bodies (Zhu Gaofeng 2016). "When formulating data sovereignty legislations, we should take a multidimensional and holistic approach and give full consideration to various relevant aspects, for the protection of national data sovereignty is a multilateral and democratic process that involves multiple parties" (Qi Aimin & Zhu Gaofeng 2016).

Domestic laws. At present, there are provisions in some laws and regulations of China concerning the protection of data sovereignty, but no laws or regulations are dedicated to this topic. A preliminary review of the *Compilation of Laws and Regulations on China's Internet Industry* (2018) reveals that at present, the protection of cyber and data security in China mainly focuses on the protection of network infrastructure, data systems and data vulnerabilities, and that no laws or regulations focus on national data sovereignty. Therefore, it is urgent for us to put in place regulations for network and data security and the maintenance of national data sovereignty. For this, at the national level, China should actively improve laws and regulations related to data sovereignty, move faster to establish the legal status of data sovereignty, work hard to design a specific framework for legislation on data sovereignty, exercise data sovereignty on sound legal basis, and protect data security and national interests. At the international level, China should make full use of the experience and methods it has obtained from cooperation with other countries in various fields, and learn from Western countries for better data protection. This will, despite the lack of sound data sovereignty legislation, enable us to build a systematic legal framework of data rights, improve our data review mechanism, and enhance our technological capability for data-related legislation in accordance with our specific conditions.

International laws. Data sovereignty shows clear features of an international issue. In the era of big data, all countries face threats in relation to their data sovereignty and no country can stay completely out of it. Therefore, in the principle of seeking common ground while reserving differences, countries should take an actively part in the formulation of international rules on data security and the formation of relevant treaties. These treaties can take diverse forms so that they can be comprehensive, have a full coverage, and reflect the holistic approach to security. They can be regional, bilateral, or multilateral treaties. Data sovereignty is inseparable from national sovereignty and national sovereignty covers data sovereignty. Therefore, the basic principles of national sovereignty should apply to the data security treaties to be concluded, which should have well-defined objectives and purposes, and concrete content, and clearly stipulate the obligations and responsibilities of each party to them. Specifically, these treaties should intend mainly to steer the international community towards data security, guide countries and regions to strengthen international co-operation to combat the abuse of data and infringement on and damage to the data sovereignty of various countries, eliminate non-security risks to political, economic and social data security, ensure fair and just distribution of data resources, and maintain secure, stable and free data operation (Qi Aimin & Zhu Gaofeng 2016).

Bibliography

Aristotle. 1996. *Politics*. Trans. Wu, Taopeng. Beijing: Commercial Press.

Cai, Cuihong. 2013. "The Concept of Data Sovereign and Its Application Prospects in the Cloud Era." *Contemporary International Relations*, 12th issue.

Cai, Gaoqiang. 2002. "On the Transfer of Sovereignty Power in Globalization." *Journal of Hunan Political-legal Cadre College*, 5th issue.

Can, Shang. 2019, March 12. "Caroline Massacre: How Can a Country Exercise the Right to Self-Defense?" March 12. <http://www.sohu.com/a/300675149_120094707>.

Chen, Xujing. 2010. *Recent Theories of Sovereignty*. Trans. Zhang, Shibao. Beijing: Tsinghua University Press.

Du, Yanyun. 2016. "National Data Sovereignty in the Big Data Era." *International Review*, 3rd issue.

Du, Zhichao, and Nan, Yuxia. 2014. "Researches on the Relationship Between Network Sovereignty and National Sovereignty." *Journal of Southwest Petroleum University (Social Sciences Edition)*, 6th issue.

Fang, Binxing. 2014. "The Autonomous Root Name Resolution System Based on National Alliance from the Perspective of State Network Sovereignty." *Information Security and Communications Privacy*, 12th issue.

Fang, Binxing. 2017. *On Cyberspace Sovereignty*. Beijing: Science Press.

Fang, Binxing, Zou, Peng, and Zhu, Shibing. 2016. "Research on Cyberspace Sovereignty." *Strategic Study of CAE*, 6th issue.

Gu, Dexin. 2001. "Conflicts in the Laws of War." *International Forum*, 1st issue.

He, Bo. 2017. "Study on the Legal Practices and Suggested Countermeasures on Data Sovereignty." *Information Security and Communication Privacy*, 5th issue.

He, Fuyong, and Duan, Jindong. 2005. "On the Right to National Self-Defense in Anti-Terrorism Actions from the Perspective of International Laws." *Forum of World Economics & Politics*, 2nd issue.

Huang, Houwen, and Li, Quanhui. 2009. "Cooperation is the Cornerstone of Sustainable Development and A Harmonious Society." *The South of China Today*, 12th issue.

Huang, Zhixiong, and Ying, Yaohui. 2017. "The Impact of the United States on Cyberspace International Law and Its Inspiration for China." *Fudan International Studies Review*, 2nd issue.

Huang, Zhixiong. 2017. *On Cyber Sovereignty: Jurisprudence, Policy and Practice*. Beijing: Social Sciences Academic Press.

Jennings, R. Y., and Watts, A. 1995. *Oppenheim's International Law*. Trans. Wang, Tieya et al. Beijing: Encyclopedia of China Publishing House.

Jiang, Ruihao. 2016. "Brief Analysis of Cyber Sovereignty." *Legality Vision*, 13th issue.

Key Laboratory of Big Data Strategy. 2019. *Block Data 5.0: Theories and Methods of Data Sociology*. Beijing: CITIC Press.

Li, Aijun, and Zhang, Jun. 2017. *The Legal Nature and Attributes of Data Right*. Paper presented at the Summit for Big Data under the Rule of Law, Beijing.

Li, Chuanjun. 2019. "Order Change and Model Construction of Global Governance in Cyberspace." *Journal of Wuhan University of Science and Technology (Social Science Edition)*, 1st issue.

Li, Huiying, and Huang, Guiqin. 2004. "On the Transfer of State Sovereignty." *Hebei Law Science*, 7th issue.

Liu, Qingjian. 2004. "An Analysis on Theory of State Sovereignty." *Journal of Renmin University of China*, 6th issue.

Liu, Ying, and Wu, Ling. 2019. "Global Governance in Cyberspace: Chaos, Opportunities and China's Propositions." *Cognition and Practice*, 1st issue.

Long, Kun, and Zhu, Qichao. 2019. "Rule-making for Cyberspace: Consensus and Discord." *Global Review*, 3rd issue.

Qi, Aimin, and Zhu, Gaofeng. 2016. "On the Establishment and Improvement of the National Data Sovereignty System." *Journal of Soochow University (Philosophy & Social Science Edition)*, 1st issue.

Qi, Juxun. 2003. "Jurisdiction on the Internet." *Lanzhou Academic Journal*, 5th issue.

Ren, Mingyan. 2007. "A Study on Informational Sovereignty under the Background of Internet." *Hebei Law Science*, 6th issue.

Rousseau, J. 2006. *The Social Contract*. Trans. Yang, Guozheng. Xi'an: Shaanxi People's Publishing House.

Shi, Yuhang. 2018. "The Network Boundary of Sovereignty: From the Perspective of Regulating the Cross-Border Transmission of Data." *Journal of Intelligence*, 9th issue.

Sun, Nanxiang, and Zhang, Xiaojun. 2015. "On Data Security: An Examination of Game and Cooperation in Cyberspace." *Pacific Journal*, 2nd issue.

Wang, Mingjin. 2016. "The Future of the Global Cyberspace Governance: Sovereignty, Competition and Consensus." *Frontiers*, 4th issue.

Wang, Xiangrong. 2019. "On the Right to Equality in the Constitution of Our Country." *Legal System and Society*, 18th issue.

Wang, Yuan, Huang, Daoli, and Yang Songru. 2017. "Study on the Nature and Ownership of Data Right." *Information Security and Communications Privacy*, 5th issue.

Wu, Shan, and Liu, Yading. 2010. "The Integration Process of Sovereignty and Equality." *Contemporary World & Socialism*, 1st issue.

Xiao, Dongmei, and Wen, Yuheng. 2017. "Defending National Data Sovereignty in Global Data Deluge." *Red Flag Manuscript*, 9th issue.

Xie, Yongjiang. 2018. "Study on Principles of Cybersecurity Law." *Jinan Journal (Philosophy & Social Science Edition)*, 6th issue.

Yan, Xianjun. 2001. "Information Capitalism is a New Stage in the Development of Capitalism." *Finding*, 6th issue.

Yang, Fei. 2009. "Analysis of the Definition of State Sovereignty Transfer." *Journal of University of International Relations*, 2nd issue.

Yang, Xiaotong. 2018. "Hobbes's Theory of Evil Human Nature and Contract State." *Literature Education*, 32th issue.

Yi, Shanwu. 2006. "A New View on Sovereign Transfer." *Journal of Chongqing Jiaotong University (Social Sciences Edition)*, 3rd issue.

Yu, Xiaoqiu. 2002. "Trends and Features of Global Information Network Security." *Contemporary International Relations*, 2nd issue.

Yu, Zhigang. 2016. "Adhering to Cyber Sovereignty and Data Sovereignty, Building an International Internet Governance System." *Procuratorial Daily*.

Zhang, Haibing. 2005. *Research on European Integration System*. Shanghai: Shanghai Academy of Social Sciences Press.

Zhang, Jianwen, and Jia, Zhangfan. 2018. "Interpretation Logic and System Construction of Data Sovereignty from the Perspective of Law and Economics." *Journal of Chongqing University of Posts and Telecommunications (Social Science Edition)*, 6th issue.

Zhang, Jingwen. 2018. *Research on the Regulation of Data Sovereignty in the International Law*. Hohhot: Inner Mongolia University.
Zhang, Naigen. 2002. *Research on Contemporary International Law*. Shanghai: Shanghai People's Publishing House.
Zhao, Gang, Wang, Shuai, and Wang, Peng. 2017. "Exploration of Big Data Governance Technology Solutions for Data Sovereignty." *Cyberspace Security*, 2nd issue.
Zhao, Zhou. 2010. *On Sovereign Responsibility*. Beijing: Law Press China.
Zheng, Wenming. 2017. "China's Choice in Internet Governance Model." *Chinese Social Sciences Today*.
Zhou, Gengsheng. 1981. *International Law (I)*. Beijing: The Commercial Press.
Zhu, Gaofeng. 2016. "The Establishment and Legislation Suggestions of National Information Sovereignty in the Big Data Era." *Jiangxi Social Sciences*, 7th issue.
Zhu, Qi. 2015. "On the Concept of Order in Bodin's Views on Sovereignty." *Guizhou Social Sciences*, 12th issue.
Zhu, Yanxin. 2017. "Network Sovereignty from the Perspective of the International Law." *Journal of Xi'an Politics Institute PLA*, 1st issue.

CHAPTER 5

Data Rights System: An International Comparison

Data rights are a common major issue in the world, and their protection constitutes a major strategy of legislation in various countries. The United States regards the protection of data rights as part of its efforts to protect the right to privacy in the broad sense. The European Union demonstrates the necessity of the protection of data rights from the perspective of personality rights. Japan combines the advantages of the Anglo-American law system and the civil law system. Based on the concept of a community with a shared future for mankind and in cyberspace, China advocates that "different countries need to strengthen cooperation, deepen exchanges, grasp the opportunities of digital, Internet-based and intelligent development, and properly address the legal, security and governance challenges in the development of the big data industry". On the basis of summarizing the latest technological advances, trends, and modes of data rights legislation in foreign countries, and guided by the vision of an international legal community, we did relevant research to put forward a roadmap for data rights legislation and point out that data rights law is a grand idea aimed at understanding how life will be in the future. This is a major discovery in the study of digital civilization and an important jurisprudential tool for our participation in global governance.

Data Rights Systems of Foreign Countries

Data rights legislation is a national strategy in the era of big data and an important move to gain an upper hand in the effort to have our voice heard in the international arena for data rights legislation. The legislation for personal information protection in the 1970s marked the start of a prime time in legislation for the protection of data rights in foreign countries. Countries all over the world have been making plans and taking strategic moves towards data rights-related legislation. According to statistics available, the number of countries or regions that have enacted laws to protect data rights has exceeded 110. Here, we focus on comparing the practices and explorations of foreign data rights systems in terms of law, security, and governance, in order to find out some patterns, models and experience from their data rights legislation practices.

Comparison of legal protection of data rights

Personal data protection is a new challenge to global data governance and has become a focus of legislation in various countries (see Table 9). Obviously, Europe is in the forefront of the world in legislation for personal data protection since most European countries have already established personal data protection laws and have been making improvements to relevant systems. For example, some countries such as Switzerland and Germany put personal data protection laws in place as early as in the 1970s. As for American countries, the United States took the lead in establishing privacy laws in the 1970s and extended the coverage of such protection to children. Countries in Oceania established personal data protection laws around the end of the previous century. The vast majority of African countries have not set up any data rights system so far, with only a few exceptions like South Africa and Tunisia. Israel is the first of the nine Asian countries who have established personal data protection laws, while Japan has the most detailed personal data protection laws with careful and refined categorization.

In the legislative practices of foreign countries for data rights protection, there are mainly three basic legal concepts, namely, personal data, personal information and privacy. Personal data is the most widely used one among the three, as can be seen in legislations of the European Council, the European Union and its member states, as well as many other countries that borrowed heavily from the EU *Directive on the Protection of Personal Data* (1995). "In common law countries such as the United States, Australia, New

Table 9. Data Rights Legal Systems in Major Countries and Regions

Continent	Country (Region)	Year	Law
Europe	Sweden	1973	Data Act
		1998	Personal Data Act
	Finland	1999	Personal Data Act
	Denmark	1978	Private Registers Act
		1987	Public Authorities' Registers Act
		2000	Act on Processing of Personal Data
	Norway	1978	Personal Data Registers Act
		1978	Public Data Registers Act
		2000	Personal Data Act
	France	1978	Data Protection Act
		2016	Digital Republic Law
	Austria	1978	Data Protection Act (amended in 2012)
	Germany	1977	Federal Data Protection Act (amended in 1990, 1994, 1997, 2001, and 2009 respectively)
	Belgium	1992	Data Protection Act (amended in 1998)
	Luxembourg	1979	Law on Restricted Use of Data Processed by Electronic Computers
		2002	Law on the Protection of Persons with Regard to the Processing of Personal Data
		2005	Specific Provisions for Protection of the Individual in Respect of the Processing of Personal Data in the Electronic Communications Sector
	Switzerland	1992	Federal Act on Data Protection

(To be continued)

Table 9. Continued

Continent	Country (Region)	Year	Law
	Spain	1992	Organic Law on Regulation of the Automated Treatment of Personal Data
		1999	Organic Law on Protection of Automated Processing of Personal Data
	Portugal	1991	Law on Protection of Personal Data Processed by Automated Means
		1998	Act on the Protection of Personal Data
	Italy	1996	Data Protection Act
	Greece	1997	Law on the Protection of Individuals with Regard to the Processing of Personal Data
	United Kingdom	1984	Data Protection Act
		1998	Data Protection Act
	Ireland	1988	Data Protection Act
		2003	Data Protection (Amendment) Act
	Russia	2015	Personal Data Protection Act
	Romania	2001	Law on the Protection of Individuals with Regard to the Processing of Personal Data and the Free Movement of Such Data
America	United States	1970	Fair Credit Reporting Act
		1974	Privacy Act (state-based)
		1998	Children's Online Privacy Protection Act
		2014	Data Privacy and Smart Grid: A Voluntary Code of Conduct
		2015	Consumer Privacy Act

(To be continued)

Table 9. Continued

Continent	Country (Region)	Year	Law
	Canada	1983	Privacy Act
		2000	Personal Information Protection and Electronic Documents Act
		2003	Personal Information Protection Act
	Argentina	1998	Personal Data Protection Act
		2000	Personal Data Protection Act
	Chile	1999	Law on the Protection of Private Life
	Uruguay	2002	Data Protection Act
	Brazil	1997	Data Protection Act
	Paraguay	2000	Personal Data Protection Act
	Bahamas	2003	Data Protection (Privacy of Personal Information) Act
Asia	South Korea	1997	Act on Personal Information Protection of Public Agencies
		2011	Personal Information Protection Act
	Japan	1988	Act on the Protection of Personal Information Pertaining to Electronic Data Processing Held by Administrative Organs
		1989	Act on the Protection of Personal Information Pertaining to Electronic Data Processing Held by Non-Public Service Organs
		2003	Act on the Protection of Personal Information Held by Incorporated Administrative Agencies, etc.
		2003	Information Disclosure and Personal Information Protection Review Committee Setting Law

(To be continued)

Table 9. Continued

Continent	Country (Region)	Year	Law
		2003	Act on the Protection of Personal Information
	Singapore	2002	Law on the Protection of Information in Private Institutions
		2012	Personal Data Protection Act
	Israel	1981	Protection of Privacy Law (amended in 1985)
	Thailand	1997	Official Information Act
	Armenia	2002	Law of the Republic of Armenia on Protection of Personal Data
	United Arab Emirates	2007	Data Protection Act
	China	2016	Cyber Security Law
	Hong Kong SAR	1995	Personal Data (Privacy) Ordinance
	Macao SAR	1995	Law on the Protection of Computer Personal Data
		1996	Detailed Rules for the Implementation of the Law on the Protection of Computer Processing Personal Data
		2005	Personal Data Protection Act (Privacy Act)
	Taiwan, China	1995	Computer-Processed Personal Information Protection Act
		1996	Detailed Rules for the Implementation of the Computer-Processed Personal Information Protection Act

(To be continued)

Table 9. Continued

Continent	Country (Region)	Year	Law
Oceania	Australia	1988	Privacy Act (amended in 2000)
		1998	National Principles of Fair Handling of Personal Information
		2002	Privacy (Private Sector) Amendment Regulations
	New Zealand	1993	Privacy Act
Africa	South Africa	2014	Protection of Personal Information Act
	Tunisia	2004	Law on the Protection of Personal Data
	Senegal	2008	Personal Data Protection Act
	Mauritius	2004	Data Protection Act

Zealand, Canada, as well as many APEC member states heavily influenced by the United States, the concept of 'privacy' is more popular. In Japan, South Korea, Russia and other countries in the same region, 'personal information' is favored term" (Zhou Hanhua 2005). In addition, other basic concepts such as personal life (e.g. in Chile's *Personal Life Protection Act*) and personal data and privacy (e.g. in OECD's *Guidelines on the Protection of Privacy and Transborder Flows of Personal Data*). "Conceptual differences are mainly rooted in different legal traditions and usage practices but do not affect the connotation of the legal concepts in their substantial meaning" (Zhou Hanhua 2005).

According to the specific provisions, the legislations for personal data protection of various countries, regions and international organizations generally share three common features: First, the laws protect individuals as natural persons, not enterprises, governments or other organizations, nor robots or gene-edited men. Second, legal protection for personal data adopts the principles of legality, legitimacy, necessity, limited purpose and data minimization to protect the maximal legitimate rights and interests of data rights holders. Third, the goal of the laws is to prevent infringement on personal data rights by preventing identifiable personal information from being collected, stored, transmitted and illegally used at will. Therefore, the focus of legislation for personal data protection is not personal data itself, but the behaviors or activities related to personal data processing. For such reasons, many countries, regions or organizations specifically highlight the concept of processing in their legislations, and examples include the European Council, the European Union, San Marino, Iceland, Greece, Denmark, and Taiwan of China.

Constitution is the fundamental and supreme law of a country and has the highest authority in the legal system of a country. The legal protection of personal data is not a new topic, but it is indeed new to compare and examine the different paths, models and methodologies adopted in different countries for data rights protection from the perspective of the constitution. The United States, Germany and Japan have more mature constitutional protection for data rights. France is the most likely to enshrine personal data protection in its constitution.[1] Due to the different histories, cultures and legal traditions, there are great differences in the concepts, methods and effects of the constitutional protection of data rights in different countries, and it is highly significant to make comparisons here for the improvement of the constitutional protection of data rights in China (Yao Yuerong 2011, p. 70–76).

United States

In the context of US laws, the right to personal data is equal to the right to privacy. Although the Privacy Act of 1974 is has the word "privacy" in the title, its content is centered on personal data, and it is regarded as a classic law on the protection of citizens' personal data

1 The France-based *European Times* reported on July 23, 2018, that the French National Assembly on the night of July 18 local time voted to adopt an amendment to include a personal data protection clause in the bill of constitutional amendment. The clause, entitled "combating the extension or unreasonable use of personal data", shall be included in Article 34 of the Constitution.

against infringement from public power in administration. Therefore, to discuss the protection of data rights in the United States, we must start from the right to privacy.[2] Privacy was first discussed in the field of civil tort, but with the concern of privacy protection, the U.S. Supreme Court began to interpret the right to privacy in the Constitution on the basis of the Fourth and Fifth Amendments to the Constitution, and then the justices extended their interpretative power to the First and Fourteenth Amendments. Any unlawful infringement of the right to personal privacy on the part of the state shall be deemed as violations of the Fourth Amendment to the Constitution. Another example is the extension of freedom of association in the First Amendment to the protection of privacy of association members. The U.S. Supreme Court recognized the right to privacy as a right granted by the Constitution. Although it is not expressly provided for in the Constitution, it is still a right endowed by the Constitutional Amendment in its ramification sphere, which falls within the scope of constitutional rights and must be subject to necessary requirements of due process of law. However, treating the right to privacy as an independent constitutional right is

2 It is generally believed that privacy, as one of the recognized types of rights, began with the right to be let alone in *The Right to Privacy* by Warren and Brandeis (1890). It was a belief of the two justices that no other has the right to publish his productions in any form, without his consent. In order to proceed, the common example of preventing the publication of manuscripts or works of art by others is used to argue that this right undoubtedly has the nature of a property right. But where the value of the production is found not in the right to take the profits arising from publication, but in the peace of mind or the relief afforded by the ability to prevent any publication at all, it is difficult to regard the right as one of property, in the common acceptation of that term. The principle which protects personal writings and all other personal productions, not against theft and physical appropriation, but against publication in any form, is in reality not the principle of private property, but that of an inviolate personality. The right of one who has remained a private individual, to prevent his public portraiture, presents the simplest case for such extension. The protection of the right to privacy is expressly included in the last volume of the first Restatement of Tort of 1939. In 1960, Dean Prosser wrote one of the most influential papers of the twentieth century, which was titled "Privacy", confirming the existence of privacy in the American legal system through combing more than 300 cases decided by the Courts of Appeals involving privacy disputes.

Table 10. Data Rights Acts of the United States

Year	Act	Description
1970	Fair Credit Reporting Act	It gives consumers the right to correct mistakes and ensures that mistakes in consumers' credit reports will not be used to harm consumers.
1974	Privacy Act	It gives individuals the right to consult, ensuring the accuracy of personal information files and the accuracy of information collection purposes. Secret files are not allowed to be kept, and individuals may have access to civil litigation remedies.
1978	Financial Privacy Act	It prohibits financial institutions from disclosing customers' financial records to the federal government without informing customers or obtaining customers' consent. The federal government must follow certain procedures and provide corresponding supporting documents to obtain customers' financial records.
1980	Financial Privacy Act	It regulates financial institutions' inquiry about bank records.
1980	Privacy Protection Act	It provides standards for law enforcement institutions to use information recorded in newspapers and other media.
1984	Cable Communications Policy Act	It stipulates that a notice must be provided to obtain personal information, and that individuals have the right to review what is documented and refuse to provide irrelevant information.
1986	Electronic Communications Privacy Act	It stipulates the circumstances and liabilities of infringement on personal privacy through interception or disclosure of preserved communication information.
1988	Video Privacy Protection Act	It prevents what it refers to as "wrongful disclosure of video tape rental or sale records".
1994	Driver's Privacy Protection Act	It imposes restrictions on the use and disclosure of personal vehicle records by state transportation departments.

(To be continued)

Table 10. Continued

Year	Act	Description
1996	Health Insurance Portability and Accountability Act	It protects personal health and privacy information and prevents unauthorized use and disclosure.
1999	Financial Services Modernization Act	It requires financial institutions to protect the privacy and personal information of consumers.
2000	Children's Online Privacy Protection Act	It protects personal information processed by online service providers. Without consent from parents, federal laws and regulations restrict the collection and use of children's personal information.
2008	Genetic Information Nondiscrimination Act	It provides enhanced protection for privacy and genetic information.
2010	Consumer Financial Protection Act	It authorizes the Consumer Financial Protection Bureau to supervise and protect financial privacy.
2018	California Consumer Privacy Act	The scope of application has been greatly expanded, and a series of consumer privacy rights relating to the access to, deletion of, and sharing of personal information collected by businesses have been created, requiring enterprises to take stronger measures to protect personal data.

derived from the interpretation of the Ninth Amendment.[3] It is worth mentioning that in the United States, constitutional cases directly concerning data rights are rare, but the practice of protecting data rights through legislative procedures has seen great achievements.

3 The Ninth Amendment is a general provision of the Constitution of the United States, which states that "The enumeration in the Constitution, of certain rights, shall not be construed to deny or disparage others retained by the people."

Germany

As an important branch of the traditional civil law system, the legal tradition of Germany is obviously different from that of the United States. Personal data protection has never flourished in Germany as it did in the United States. There is no "right to privacy" in the civil law or constitution of Germany. The German equivalent to privacy of the US legal system is "private sphere" or "the private nature". The right to privacy does not has its place in the legal tradition of Germany, but Germany does not ignore the theories, doctrines and precedents related to the right to privacy that has been gaining more recognition in the United States. Generally speaking, in Germany the concept of personality rights protection in the private sphere in its civil law system is what corresponds to the concept of protection of privacy in the field of civil tort in the United States (Wang Tze-chien 2007);[4] and the protection of personal data and the protection of general freedom of action corresponds to the protection of privacy in the Constitution of the United States. The right to self-determination of information established by the German Federal Constitutional Court and protected by specific provisions of the *German Federal Personal Data Protection Act* is seen as the German counterparts of protection of the right to privacy in the United States. The Federal Constitutional Court of Germany proceeded on the basis of endorsing the sphere theory adopted by the Federal Court to reinforce the constitutional interpretations to the privacy domain in the private sphere which is the core part for absolute protection. It emphasizes that human dignity shall be inviolable and that to respect and protect it shall be the duty of all state authority as is provided for in Paragraph 1 of Article 1 in the *Basic Law* (Wang Tze-chien 2007).[5]

4 The German academia has long been upholding what is known as the "sphere theory", in which information related to individuals belongs either to the private sphere or the public sphere. Those in the private sphere here is similar to privacy. The German Federal Constitutional Court also used to divide things into three categories: those in the privacy sphere, those in the private sphere and those in the public sphere. This theory features a concentric structure where different spheres of private life forms circles of different radiuses and protection is afforded based on distances to the center.

5 The *Basic Law*, or the *Basic Law of the Federal Republic of Germany*, is the constitution and fundamental law of Germany.

Table 11. Data Rights Acts of Germany

Year	Act	Description
1970	Data Protection Act of the State of Hesse	As the world's first data protection law, it ushered in a new era of data protection through legislation.
1976	Federal Personal Data Protection Act	The Act, which entered into force in 1977, is officially known as the Act on the Protection against the Misuse of Personal Data in Data Processing, and more commonly known as the Personal Data Protection Act
1977	Federal Data Protection Act	It is the first in the world to stipulate a unified regulation model for public and private institutions. It requires public institutions as well as private ones to protect personal data so as to achieve comprehensive coverage of personal data protection.
1997	Act on Information and Communication Services	Also known as the "multimedia law", it is the first law in the world to concerning communication on the Internet. Its influence on Internet supervision in Germany is mainly reflected in three aspects: First, it has strengthened the determination of liabilities for illegal content communication; second, it mandates specific "cyber police" to monitor the spread of harmful content through laws and regulations; and third, it makes it an unlawful act if a person makes or disseminates statements harmful to children on the Internet.

(To be continued)

Table 11. Continued

Year	Act	Description
1997	Telecommunications Act	Internet service providers are responsible for the content they provide according to substantive laws. Under the condition that the service provider does not violate the provisions of the Telecommunications Act on keeping telecommunication secrets, it is obliged to prevent the communication of illegal content according to law. If there is evidence that the information known by the service provider contains illegal content which can be prevented from dissemination technically but was not, it constitutes "intentional violation" and the service provider "must bear the joint and liabilities for the illegal activities."
1997	Telecommunications Data Protection Ordinance	It lays out strict provisions for possible infringements on personal information during Internet operation.
2007	Telemedia Act (Revised in the year of 2010/2016/2017 successively)	As a core piece in Germany's Internet legislation, this act is commonly known as Germany's "Internet Law". "Telemedia" is a unique concept in Germany's media law and it covers almost all kinds of Internet services in the country.

Different from the US approach to privacy represented by claims such as the right to be let alone, non-interference in private life, or keeping quiet, Germany approaches it from the theoretic perspective of private sphere protection, which means that the inviolability of freedom of the person under Article 2 and the freedom of faith and of conscience under Article 4, the inviolability of the privacy of correspondence, posts and telecommunications under Article 10, and the inviolability of the home under Article 13 are all regarded as basic rights. At the same time, the freedom of press, science and art under Article 5, special protection of family under Article 6, freedom of assembly under Article 8 and freedom of association under

Article 9 could be availed of for protecting the private sphere to some extent, but these are not all the protection of fundamental rights in the private sphere at the constitutional level. In German theory and practice, the human dignity in Paragraph 1 of Article 1, and the personality rights in Paragraph 1 of Article 2 of the *Basic Law* are availed of for interpreting and protecting fundamental rights that are not listed but still regarded as basic rights in the private sphere. It could be said that the protection of the private sphere in the *Basic Law* is virtually loophole-free, with a dense and extendable system for the protection of basic rights.

Japan

Japan introduced the Western legal system back in the Meiji era in its reforms, and its legal system has therefore been deeply influenced by continental Europe, especially the German political, military and legal systems which have been almost completely copied. After World War II, the United States "took over" Japan, and put it under its sole control. The Japanese Constitution was thus drafted by the Americans but promulgated in the name of the Japanese government. The whole process was directed by the Americans (Li Wei 2009). This can also be seen in the Japanese legal system today, which features an integration of traditional elements from both Germany and the United States. Personal data of citizens were initially protected from the perspective of privacy. In 1970, Professor Koji Sato published *The Constitutional Position on Privacy*, which was based on the American privacy theory and seeks constitutional basis for the right to privacy from the "right to pursue happiness" guaranteed by Article 13 of the Japanese Constitution. "In Japanese law, the right to privacy is mostly protected from the perspective of emphasizing the right of refusing to disclose one's own personal information or personal affairs, as for other personal interests including names, portraits, areas of personal life and self-determination, the law makes it clear that those interests and rights shall be protected to some extent through the interpretation of the right to pursue happiness." Article 13 of the Constitution of Japan states: "All of the people shall be respected as individuals. Their

Table 12. Data Rights Regulations of Japan

Year	Regulation	Description
1973	Regulations of Tokushima City Concerning Personal Data Protection Management on Computers	It upholds respect for personal privacy rights and interests involved in the government's processing of personal data.
1988	Act on the Protection of Personal Information Pertaining to Electronic Data Processing Held by Administrative Organs	The scope of protection is limited to personal data information processed by computers and does not involve data information processed manually.
1997	Directives on Computer Processing and Protection of Personal Information in the Private Sector	Issue privacy certification marks (P-MARK certification) to enterprises with effective protection measures
2003	Personal Information Protection Act and supporting laws such as the Act on the Protection of Personal Information Pertaining to Electronic Data Processing Held by Administrative Organs, Act on the Protection of Personal Information Held by Incorporated Administrative Agencies, etc., Information Disclosure and Personal Information Protection Review Committee Setting Law, Law on Improving Relevant Laws Involved in the Implementation of the Act on the Protection of Personal Information Held by Administrative Organs	The "Personal Information Protection Law" is called the Basic Law governing the protection of personal information in various fields, and is commonly called the "Five Coordinating Laws on the Protection of Personal Information" with the other four laws.
2015	Personal Information Protection Law (Revised)	It further expands the scope of personal information protection and of law application, and promotes the application of anonymous personal information.

right to life, liberty, and the pursuit of happiness shall, to the extent that it does not interfere with the public welfare, be the supreme consideration in legislation and in other governmental affairs." This provision is often referred to as the "personal dignity" provision and personal dignity is considered one of the basic rights outlined in the Japanese Constitution. The right to pursue happiness was initially a general term for the human rights of individuals, from which no other rights could be derived directly. Up to the 1960s, with more challenges brought about by social and economic turmoil, the interpretative significance of this provision shall be reassessed. "As a result, the right to pursue happiness, based on the principle of respecting the individual, has gradually been interpreted as a generalized right that underpins new human rights not enumerated in the Constitution" (Nobuyoshi Ashibe, trans. Lin Laifan 2006, p. 104).

Comparison of data security legislations

Data security is an important foundation and component of data rights protection. The European Union, the United States, Japan, Australia, Russia, Singapore and other countries with well-developed data security protection system have all put in place a number of laws and regulations in this regard (see Table 13). Although they have different strategies and approaches, the elements contained in their relevant laws and regulations are basically the same. Examining the relevant laws and regulations of the European Union, the United States, Japan and other countries, analyzing the basic principles embodied in their legislations will help us deepen our understanding of the different legislative models and concepts and then give advice for data security legislation as well as the formulation of specific data security laws, regulations, administrative rules, and industry standards in China.[6]

6 See National Information Security Standardization Technical Committee, Special Working Group – Big Data Security: White Paper on Big Data Security Standardization (2018 Edition), April 2018. <http://www.cesi.cn/201804/3789.html>.

Table 13. Data Security Laws and Regulations of Major Countries

Country (Region)	Laws, Regulations and Departmental Rules	Year	Category
European Union	General Data Protection Regulation	2018	Law
	EU Data Retention Directive	2006	Law
	Privacy and Electronic Communications Directive	2002	Law
	EU Data Protection Directive	1995	Law
United States	Privacy Shield Protocol	2016	Law
	California Online Privacy Protection Act	2014	State law
	Federal Privacy Act	2014	Law
	Digital Accountability and Transparency Act	2014	Branch regulation
	Digital Government Strategy	2012	Law
	Open Government Directive	2009	Law
	California Security Breach Notification Law	2002	State law
	Financial Services Modernization Act	1999	Branch regulation
	Health Insurance Portability and Accountability Act	1996	Branch regulation
	Federal Trade Commission Act	1914	Branch regulation
Japan	Act on the Protection of Personal Information (Amendment)	2017	Law
	Act on the Protection of Personal Information	2005	Law
	Act on the Protection of Personal Information Pertaining to Electronic Data Processing Held by Administrative Organs	1988	Law
	Guidelines for the Protection of Computer-Processed Data	1976	Law

(To be continued)

Table 13. Continued

Country (Region)	Laws, Regulations and Departmental Rules	Year	Category
Australia	Telecommunications Act	1997	Branch regulation
	Federal Privacy Act	1988	Law
Russia	Article 152-FZ of the Russian Federation Law on Personal Data of 2006	2015	Law
	Article 149-FZ of the Law of the Russian Federation on information, information technology and data protection in 2006	2006	Law
	Strasbourg Convention	2005	Law
Singapore	Personal Data Protection Act	2012	Law

Source: See National Information Security Standardization Technical Committee, Big Data Security Standards Work Team: *White Paper on Big Data Security Standardization (2018 Edition)*, April 2018. <http://www.cesi.cn/201804/3789.html>.

European Union

Data security legislation of the European Union adopts a state-led approach. Member states believe that personal data has the characteristics of personality rights in nature, reflects the connotation of personality rights, should be covered by basic rights endowed by the constitution, and should also be governed and protected as part of the substantive rights represented in specific laws of different branches. As an organization of regional political and economic integration, the European Union is highly integrated in legislation, but allows space for independent development of its member states, forming a pattern of EU laws plus member state laws. First of all, guidelines for data security-related legal issues are formulated at the EU level and such legal documents include conventions, directives, guidelines, framework agreements and so on. The content of these legal documents may not be directly applicable to specific judicial practices, but it establishes the basic framework and basic principles for the data security legislation in member states. Following this pattern, each member state then formulates its own laws and regulations on data security protection. Because of its comprehensiveness, strictness and feasibility, the legal protection for personal data security in the European Union has great influence across the world. At the EU level, since 1981, the *Convention for the Protection of Individuals with Regard to Automatic Processing of Personal Data* (1981), Council Decision of March 31, 1992 in the field of security of information systems (92/242/EEC), *Data Protection Directive* (1995), *Privacy and Electronic Communications Directive* (2002), *Data Retention Directive* (2006), the COMPACT Internet Governance principles of the European Union (2011), Strategic European Initiative (2012), *Cyber Security Strategy* (2013), *General Data Protection Regulation* (2018), as well as other legal documents have been successively put into force in a bid to enhance data security in this region. The legal framework and basic norms of data security protection have thus been erected, cross-border data flow is gradually put under legal regulation, and relevant regulatory and supervisory agencies have also been put in place to better protect the personal data of Internet users (Ran Congjing & Wang Bingjie 2019), laying solid foundation for the construction of the "strictest" EU data security legal protection system.

United States

Data security legislation in the United States is different from that in the EU. The United States does not have a uniform legal framework for personal data protection. Instead, protection is specific to different areas or matters involved. Personal data and data on privacy are protected by the Constitution, privacy laws and other legal documents, while important data in important industries and fields are protected by special legislation, and general data are covered by industry-specific self-regulation and market regulation rules, forming a general pattern where multiple parties are engaged in the governance of data security. The right to privacy is the legal basis of legislation for the protection of personal data security in the United States. To some extent, the connotation of the right to privacy in the United States is close to that of personality rights in the civil law system. It can be said that the United States' legal system on data security protection is a comprehensive system that protects the personality of data rights holders, which is reflected in the country's personal data security laws and regulations as well as its industrial self-regulation rules. Personal data protection in the United States can be divided into public sphere protection and private sphere protection. Legislation is decentralized in the public sphere and represented by industrial self-regulation rules in the private sphere. In the public sphere, there are the *Fair Credit Reporting Act* (1971) that deals with the collection, processing and storage of personal information by private organs, the *Privacy Act* (1974) that deals with the processing of personal information by state organs, the *Family Education Rights and Privacy Act* (1976) which protects the personal information of students and their parents, the *Electronic Communications Privacy Act* (1986) and the *Computer Matching and Privacy Protection Act* (1988) which deal with the processing of electronic information, the *Children's Online Privacy Protection Act* (2000) which protects children's personal information, and the *USA Freedom Act*, which was adopted and entered into force on June 2, 2015. The industrial self-regulation in the United States, government-led, is the result of dialogues between and joint innovation efforts by governments, companies, universities and research institutes. It is flexible and supplementary to legislation. This model is also known as "guiding legislationism" (Zhao Qiuyan 2005). Specifically, there are three main forms of such self-regulation: technology protection, industrial guide, and commercial certification. For example, it is pointed out in the *Framework for Global Electronic Commerce* issued by the United States Government in 1995 that the government supports the efforts of commercial organizations to establish a self-regulation-based system to facilitate the effective protection of privacy of their clients.

Japan

Legislation on data security in Japan started later than in Europe and America, but Japan is still one of the first countries in Asia to make laws for the protection of personal data security and has one of the best developed legal system in this regard. Japan has drawn lessons and borrowed the legislative framework from the European Union. The comprehensive personal data protection system thus formed centered around citizens' personality rights and property rights, including their right to privacy, governs the personal data processing behavior of both government authorities and private enterprises. At the same time, Japan has also learned from the pragmatism of the United States in its legislative efforts. On the basis of the personal data protection law, it pays attention to special legislation, self-regulation and third-party supervision for key industries, so as to pursue balance between personal data rights protection and data application. It is worth noting that Japan drew much reference from foreign countries, while not ignoring its own specific conditions, and that it pays due attention to balance between the protection of the legitimate rights and interests of individuals and the promotion of the free flow of data. Reviewing Japan's legislative process in the field of personal data protection, we can see that relevant efforts began with some local and industrial laws and regulations in the 1980s, as well as laws specifically designed to protect personal data held by the executive branch. For example, in Japan Information Processing Development Center (JIPDEC) formulated the *Guidelines for the Protection of Personal Data in Financial Institutions* in March 1987 and the *Guidelines for the Protection of Personal Information in the Private Sector* in March 1988; then in 1989, the Ministry of Economy, Trade and Industry formulated the *Guidelines for the Processing and Protection of Personal Information by Computers in the Private Sector* (Xie Qing 2006). Entering the twenty-first century, Japan formally promulgated the *Act on the Protection of Personal Information* in 2003,[7] and decided to amend it in 2013. On May 30, 2017, the newly

7 Five laws related to the protection of personal information, including Act on the Protection of Personal Information, Act on the Protection of Personal Information of Administrative Organs, Act on the Protection of Personal Information Held by Independent Administrative Legal Persons, Act on the Opening of Information--Act on the Establishment of Personal Information Protection Review Conference, Act on the Protection of Personal Information Held by Administrative Organs, are collectively referred to as the Act on the Protection of Personal Information.

amended *Personal Information Protection Act* came into force. "This latest version provides for more detailed protection of the right to personal information and changes related to the use of anonymous information processing, the certification of enterprises for using information, the third-party certification system, and the transfer of power over practitioners who obtain personal information from the Minister of General Affairs to the Personal Information Protection Commission are all new achievements in improving personal information protection legislation" (Wei Jianxin & Song Renchao 2018).

Comparison of government administration systems

Data is becoming an important driving force behind innovations in government administration, pushing for transformations in the concept, model, content and means of governance. Digital government will become an important manifestation of concepts such as open government, collaborative government, service-oriented government and smart government. Data-driven government will bring about historical changes in government administration and provide strong support for and serve as the path towards its modernization. In the era of big data, governments of both developed and developing countries are thinking about government transformations and the building of governance systems (see Table 14). The European Union, the United States and Japan are the forerunners and leaders in big data plus government administration and they also benefit a lot from such efforts. It is of great practical significance for China and other developing countries to promote the digital, Internet-based and intelligent development of government administration by comparing and carefully studying the data-driven government administration systems of these three countries, in a bid to find the differences and produce a set of new mechanisms that base information disclosure, decision-making, management and innovation all on data.

Table 14. Digital Government Strategies of Major Countries

Country	Strategy	Year	Description
Japan	i-Japan Strategy 2015	2009	The letter "i" in *i-Japan Strategy 2015* has two meanings: inclusion and innovation, inclusion represent the vision that ICT should be integrated into all aspects of economic and social development like sunshine, water and air, while innovation calls for creativity and the innovative spirit. The main thrust of *i-Japan Strategy 2015* is to focus on three areas of digitalization, namely, e-government, healthcare and education.
South Korea	Smart Government Plan	2011	The goal is to build a smart government by 2015. Its implementation strategy includes four aspects: openness, integration, coordination and sustainable and green growth.
United Kingdom	Government Digital Strategy	2012	The strategy expounds the current situation, obstacles, achievements and future action plans of digital services in the United Kingdom, and guides various departments to formulate their own digitalization strategies so as to promote the improvement and development of digital services. Its core is to regard digital service provision as the preferred way for the government to provide public services, aiming at providing conditions for people who choose to use digital channels and creating conditions for people who cannot use them.

(To be continued)

Table 14. Continued

Country	**Strategy**	**Year**	**Description**
United States	Digital Government: Building a 21st Century Platform to Better Serve the American People	2012	The goal is to make more innovations at lower cost and to enable entrepreneurs to make better use of government data to improve the quality of services provided for the American people.
Singapore	Smart Nation 2025	2014	To help the citizens, government and public services of Singapore get connected in an unprecedented way, so that institutions and citizens can benefit from access to data. Smart Nation is of great significance to citizens, enterprises and their partners.
France	Digital Republic Action Plan	2015	First, it promotes the data economy by creating the concept of data of universal interest; second, it is to establish alliances for open innovation by encouraging cooperation between traditional enterprises and start-ups; and third, it encourages open science with open access to publications and research data.
Germany	Digital Strategy 2025	2016	It introduces goals in key areas of digital government development, and puts forward specific and highly targeted implementation measures, which play an important role in accelerating progress towards Industry 4.0 in Germany.

(To be continued)

Table 14. Continued

Country	Strategy	Year	Description
Denmark	Digital Strategy 2016–2020	2016	It is a continuation and development of the Digital Government Strategy 2011–2015 and defines the process of digitalization in Denmark's public sector and its interaction with enterprises and industries, aiming at laying the foundation for a strong and secure digital Denmark.
Sweden	Digital Strategy: Sweden's Sustainable Digital Transformation	2017	It outlines the key points of the government's digitalization policy and expresses Sweden's vision of achieving sustainable digital transformation. The overall goal is to make Sweden a world leader in seizing the opportunities of the digital transformation.
Australia	Digital Transformation Strategy	2018	The main task is to improve the delivery of public services through a central database that stores open government data and create new values for users and the whole society. The strategic vision is to build Australia into one of the world's Top 3 in digital government development by 2025 for the benefit of all Australians.

Source: See *2019 Digital Government Development Report* by the E-Government Research Center of the Party School of Central Committee of CPC (National Academy of Governance), July 2019.

European Union

E-governance is a way to represent the new features of e-government in its later development stage[8] (Dong Lisheng 2012). It also stands for new explorations on the part of the European Union for the modernization and governance capacity of its government administration system. Compared with technology, system building plays a more important role in the development of e-governance. In December 2005, the *Manchester Ministerial Declaration on eGovernment* introduced by the Council of Ministers of the European Union proposed four priorities for the early development of e-governance: No citizen left behind, effective and efficient government, high impact European services, simple and secure access to online public services. In 2006, the European Commission issued the *i2010 Action Plan for eGovernment-Accelerating eGovernment in Europe for the Benefit of All*, which is part of the EU's overall strategy for informatization, i2010. This action plan pushed e-government building on the pan-Europe level onto the track of systematic development.[9] The European Union's law on e-governance is basically a regulatory system. In addition to the general legal documents such as the *e-Commerce Directive*, the Directive on the Legal Protection of Databases and the Directive on Certain Legal Aspects

8 As a Dutch scholar pointed out, e-governance refers to the governance model which uses information technology to simplify the process of government administration and public affairs and promote democratization in the interaction between government and civil society, government and enterprises, and government operation. The interpretation offered by the main report of the 26th International Conference on Administrative Sciences was as follows: E-governance is not a simple application of new information and communication technologies in the field of public affairs, but a kind of society that is more related to the ways of organization and use of political power and social power – ways of political organizations and their activities, and is the manifestation of governance in the information age.

9 i2010 eGovernment Action Plan-Accelerating eGovernment Development in Europe for the Benefit of All. The five core perspectives of fighting the digital divide, improving efficiency, implementing eProcurement, establishing a Europe-wide e-service channels, enhancing participation and democratic decision-making, as set out in the Action Plan can be seen as concretization of the Manchester Ministerial Declaration on eGovernment of the Council of Ministers of the European Union of December 2005.

of Information Society Services, in Particular Electronic Commerce, in the Internal Market (Directive on Electronic Commerce), this mainly aims at areas of e-governance development that requires strict regulation. For example, in view of the health of the cyberspace, the United Kingdom introduced the "R3 Safety-Net" in September 1996, which intended to remove illegal, especially pornographic and obscene materials from the cyberspace through the basic measures of "rating, reporting, and responsibility". Cyberspace management in France attaches great importance to the protection of minors. For example, the law on the protection of minors was promulgated in 1998, stipulating heavy punishment for the use of the Internet to seduce juvenile delinquency. Through the adoption of the *Convention for the Protection of Individuals with regard to Automatic Processing of Personal Data*, the *Directive on the Protection of Individuals with Regard to the Processing of Personal Data and on the Free Movement of Such Data*, the *First Directive on the Transmission of Personal Data to Third Countries-Possible Programmes to Assess Adequacy* and the *Protection of the Collection and Transmission of Personal Data on the Information Superhighway*, it set strict standards for the protection of the privacy of individuals on the Internet.

United States

Open government data represents a breakthrough in the governance reform of the United States. In July 1966, the US government adopted the *Freedom of Information Act*, which provides for the right of the public to obtain administrative information and the obligation of the administrative organs to provide administrative information to the public (National Information Security Standardization Technical Committee and Task Force on Big Data Security Standards 2017). In September of 1993, *Building the Information Superhighway* was released, which launched the information technology revolution and established a comprehensive information service system with the Internet at the core. In December 2009, the US government issued the *Open Government Directive*, launched data.gov for access to public data, established the three principles of open government, that is, transparency, participation and collaboration, and required the government to publish data through the website, so that the public know more about government affairs, there are public dialogues, and the public has more trust in the government. Since then, the US government has creatively introduced the concept of big data into the field of government administration. In March 2012, the US government issued the *Big Data Research and Development Initiative* to formally launch its Big Data Development Program, announcing that it would spend more than $200 million on big data research. Then, in May of the same year, the federal government issued the *Digital Government Strategy*, which aims to delivers better digital services to the American people. A series of measures around data soon followed and the impact of big data on the US government were gradually seen (Liu Yeting & Tang Sisi 2014). The three objectives of digital government development in the United States are as follows: First, to enable the American people and an increasingly mobile workforce to access high-quality digital government information and services anywhere, anytime, on any device; second, to ensure that as the government adjusts to this new digital world, we seize the opportunity to procure and manage devices, applications, and data in smart, secure and affordable ways; and third, to unlock the power of government data to spur innovation across our Nation and improve the quality of services for the American people (E-Government Research Center of the Central Party School 2019).

Japan

Japan is a global leader in national governance. As the Meiji Restoration progressed, Japan caught up with and even surpassed European and American powers within a short time and became the first country in Asia to start and complete the modernization process, serving as a typical case for modernization research. The government of Japan established the IT Strategic Headquarters in 2000 and launched the *e-Japan Strategy* in 2001, with the aim of upgrading Japan's overall ICT infrastructure and making Japan the world's number one power IT development. In 2003,

Japan adopted *e-Japan Strategy II*, adjusting the focus and direction of Japan's informatization development drastically in order to promote the application of information technologies, especially in the seven areas of health care, food, life, finance for small and medium-sized enterprises, education, employment and administration. Meanwhile, it proposed to expand the efficient use of information technologies in five horizontal projects, namely, new-generation infrastructure, confidentiality, research and development, human resources and international strategy (Liu Ziheng & Zhou Jiagui 2013). In December 2004, the u-Japan policy[10] was launched, which aims to build the Japan government into a ubiquitous existence which provides public services to anyone on any matter at any time in any place. Subsequently, in January 2006, the government again issued the New IT Reform Strategy, and e-government building was an important part of it. In July 2009, the *i-Japan Strategy 2015*,[11] as a continuation from e-Japan, u-Japan, and the New IT Reform Strategy, painting new blueprint for the future of informatization in Japan (Yao Guozhang & Lin Ping 2009). "The main thrust of *i-Japan Strategy 2015* is to focus on three areas of digitalization, namely, e-government, healthcare and education." (Hai Qun & Wu Rina 2010) In order to promote IT development and bring maximal benefits to the people and society, in 2013, the Japanese government formulated the *Declaration to Be the World's Most Advanced IT Nation Basic Plan for the Advancement of Public and Private Sector Data Utilization* which took flexible IT application as a development strategy with relevant infrastructure reinforced under the guidance of the chief information officer of the government. A variety of policy measures have also been introduced for the 2020 Tokyo Olympic and Paralympic Games (Lian Cheng, Yang Fei & Zhang Hengye 2018).

10 The letter U here has four connotations: ubiquitous, universal, user-oriented and unique. Japan's announcement of the u-Japan policy marks a new stage in the building of its e-government network, that is, from the e stage to the u stage.

11 The letter "i" in *i-Japan Strategy 2015* has two meanings: inclusion and innovation, inclusion represent the vision that ICT should be integrated into all aspects of economic and social development like sunshine, water and air, while innovation calls for creativity and the innovative spirit.

China's Data Rights System

The protection of data rights has become a major topic that no one can avoid today. Most countries in the world strengthen the protection of such rights through domestic legislations in order to achieve the purpose of protecting the rights of the data rights holders. At a key point of the new round of technological revolution and industrial transformation, China firmly grasps the opportunities of digital, Internet-based and intelligent development, and actively responds to the challenges brought about by big data development in law, security, government administration and other aspects. A legal system for data rights protection has gradually taken shape in China spanning criminal law, civil law, and administrative law with laws made by National People's Congress as well as with departmental regulations and industrial standards, and covering sharing of and open access to data, data security management, digital government administration and more. All these together constitute a legal system for rights protection with clear Chinese characteristics.

Legal system for the protection data rights

At the national level, the provisions concerning the protection of data rights are mainly seen in different branches of law like the Constitution, criminal law, civil law and other laws (see Table 15). However, at present, no law or regulation concerning the protection of data rights contains a feasible definition data rights, nor is there a clear boundary of the protection. Also, we can see a lack of systematic structure and consistency, as well as other limitations in terms of the scope of protection and the standards for applicability.

Constitutional protection

The Constitution is the basis for the protection of the right to personal information and data, and the personal dignity clause, or Article 38 of

Table 15. Legal Provisions on the Protection of Data Rights in China

Category	**Law**	**Date of Implementation**	**Relevant Provisions**
Constitution	Constitution	March 11, 2018	Articles 33, 37, 38, 39, 41
Criminal Law	Criminal Law	November 4, 2017	Articles 253(1), 286, 286(1), 287, 287(1), 287(2)
Civil Law	Tort Law	July 1, 2010	Articles 2, 36
	Law on the Protection of Consumer Rights and Interests	March 15, 2014	Articles 14, 29, 50
	General Provisions of the Civil Law	October 1, 2017	Articles 110, 111, 127
Other Laws	Passport Law	January 1, 2007	Articles 12, 20
	Law on Practicing Doctors	August 27, 2009	Articles 22, 37
	Statistics Law	January 1,2010	Articles 9, 25, 37, 39
	Law on Guarding State Secrets	October 1, 2010	Articles 23, 24, 25, 26
	Law on the Identity Card of Residents	January 1, 2012	Articles 6, 13, 19, 20
	Law on the Prevention and Treatment of Infectious Diseases	June 29, 2013	Articles 12, 68, 69
	Postal Law	April 24, 2015	Articles 7, 35, 36, 76
	National Security Law	July 1, 2015	Articles 51, 52, 53, 54
	Law on Commercial Banks	October 1, 2015	Articles 6, 29

(To be continued)

Table 15. Continued

Category	Law	Date of Implementation	Relevant Provisions
	Cybersecurity Law	June 1, 2017	Articles 10, 18, 21, 22, 27, 37, 40, 41, 42, 43, 44, 45, 66, 76
	Lawyers Law	January 1, 2018	Articles 38, 48
	Law on Electronic Signature	April 23, 2019	Articles 15, 27, 34
	Cryptography Law	January 1, 2020	Articles 1, 2, 7, 8, 12, 14, 17, 30, 31, 32

the Constitution, provides room for the interpretation in regard to new fundamental rights of individuals, including the right to information and data. The "state respect and preservation of human rights" clause, which is Article 33 of the Constitution, states that the state respects and preserves human rights. This is regarded as a general right clause in the Constitution of China and also the main basis for the existence of the right to information and data as a fundamental right that is not explicitly listed. Other relevant clauses include Article 37 on the inviolability of freedom of the person, Article 39 on the inviolability of residences, Article 40 on the protection of freedom and privacy of correspondence provided, and Article 41 on the right to criticize and make suggestions, complaints, charges or exposures. These specific provisions on fundamental rights are directly or indirectly linked to the right to the protection of information and data and the realization of these concrete fundamental rights provides strong guarantee for the realization of the right to self-determination over information. Essentially, the right to protection of information and data is part of the core content of fundamental rights, namely, human dignity and personality independence. The protection of information and data is a must for social democracy, the premise of citizen autonomy and the strong guarantee for the realization of individual freedom in a democratic society. At the same time, it is also the inevitable result of the adaptation of the fundamental rights system to the development of the information society (Li Aijun 2018).

Criminal law protection

Infringement of citizens' right to personal information is far beyond the control of civil law and administrative law. Amendment VII and Amendment IX to the Criminal Law, adopted respectively in 2009 and 2015 contains provisions regarding crimes related to personal information and data. Article 253 of the revised Criminal Law contains the newly added crime of selling or illegally providing personal information on citizens, and illegally obtaining personal information of citizens. Amendment IX to the Criminal Law has greatly revised and improved the provisions about personal information security. First of all, Article 253A was partially amended, removing the crimes of selling and illegally providing personal information and illegally obtaining personal information of citizens, and adding the crime of infringing on personal information of citizens (Supreme People's Court and Supreme People's Procuratorate 2015). More specifically, this represents an expansion of the scope of possible perpetrators on the basis of Amendment VII, extending it beyond the personnel of state organs or financial, telecommunications, transportation, education, medical and other institutions, and increasing the penalties on the above-mentioned personnel who commit the crime of infringing upon citizens' personal information. In addition, Article 286 adds the crime of failing to perform the information network security management obligation, and Article 287 adds the crime of using information network illegally and assisting criminal activities by means of information network (Yao Yuerong 2011, p. 22–23), offering vigorous protection for citizens' right to data. In the era of big data, it is absolutely necessary to strengthen the protection of personal information from the perspective of criminal law, and efforts in this aspect shows China's commitment to human rights and the protection of citizens' personal information.

Civil law protection

In 2010, the *Tort Law* was promulgated and implemented, and the right to privacy was established for the first time as a kind of civil right. Article 36, a provision for liability for network infringement, moves forward from the previous indirect protection of citizens' right to privacy in cyberspace, and clarifies the legal liability of Internet users and Internet service providers for infringement upon other people's right to privacy. The newly revised *Law on the Protection of Consumer Rights and Interests* of 2014 is the first specialized laws in China to protect personal information with detailed provisions. Articles 14, 29 and 50 provides respectively for "the right to protection of personal information in accordance with the law," "the principles and obligations that operators shall follow when collecting personal information" and "the right relief for the parties". These are direct and specific provisions for the protection of consumers' personal information. *The General Provisions of the Civil Law* adopted in March 2017, included the right to "personal information of natural persons" as a civil right for the first time. Article 110 provides that a natural person enjoys the right to name, portrait, reputation and honor, as well as the right to privacy; Article 111 provides that personal information of a natural person shall be protected by law. Any organization or individual needing to obtain the personal information of other persons shall legally obtain and ensure the security of such information, and shall not illegally collect, use, process or transmit the personal information of other persons, nor illegally buy, sell, provide or make public the personal information of other persons. Article 127 directly responds to the legal status of data by providing that "where any law provides for the protection of data and network virtual property, such law shall apply." This move marks the formal entry of data information into the scope of civil law regulation and protection, and highlights the fact that the *General Provisions of the Civil Law* is keeping up with the time.

Other legal protections

The protection of data rights is a complicated and systematic project, which involves not only the constitution, criminal law and civil law, but also many other laws. There are three categories of these. The first is generally applicable legal protection, such as that provided by the *Passport Law, Statistics Law, Law on Guarding State Secrets, Law on the Identity Card of Residents, National Security Law*, etc., which provide general guidance, framework and principles for the protection of personal information. The second category protects personal information of specific groups, and examples include the *Law on the Protection of Minors* and the *Law on the Protection of Rights and Interests of Women*, which, by protecting the personal information of specific population groups, protect their personality, dignity and freedom and uphold their legitimate rights and interests. The third category targets at specific fields and examples are the *Law on Practicing Doctors*, the *Lawyers Law*, the *Law on the Prevention and Treatment of Infectious Diseases*, the *Postal Law*, the *Law on Commercial Banks*, the *Cybersecurity Law*, the *Law on Electronic Signature*, and the *Cryptography Law*. This category has the largest number of laws and has the largest coverage in terms of fields and industries. The provisions of these laws are highly professional, enforceable and operable, and play an irreplaceable role in the legal system for the protection of data rights in China. It can be said that these three categories of laws protect data rights at different levels, effectively safeguarding the legitimate rights and interests of citizens, legal persons and other organizations, and helping to promote the healthy and orderly development of the economy and society.

Legislative practice related to data security

There could be no state security without data security and legislation plays a fundamental role in our efforts to ensure data security. Only on the track towards the rule of law can we achieve balance between the application and security of big data and ensure security for the state, public interests and individuals while putting big data in to its best use. At present, China is striving to seize the opportunity of big data development and making active attempts at data security legislation. A sound system has been formed in this aspect with the state pushing things forward, local authorities serving as pioneers, and experts calling for progress.

National legislative practices

In the era of big data, data security not only has great bearing on the healthy development of the big data industry, and may also constitute serious threats to state security. Therefore, data security is one of the most urgent problems for us to tackle in the field of information security in the era of big data.

According to the *Action Outline for Promoting the Big Data Development* issued by the State Council on September 5, 2015, the legal and standards systems shall be improved to make use of big data in a scientific and standardized manner and effectively protect data security. On December 8, 2017, President Xi Jinping pointed out during the second collective study session on the implementation of the National Big Data Strategy of the Political Bureau of the CPC Central Committee that "efforts should be made to effectively ensure national data security. We should strengthen the security protection of key information infrastructure, build our capacity to protect key data resources, and enhance our capability for early warning and tracing of data security. Coordination should be improved between policies, supervision, and laws, and the building of legal systems should be sped up. Systems should be established for the confirmation, open access, circulation and trade of data resources, and the system for protecting data property rights should be improved." This requires us to adhere to the holistic approach to state security, establish an appropriate attitude towards cyber security, attach equal importance to security and development, and accelerate the building of our big data security system, and ensure smooth implementation of our national big data strategy.

The *Cybersecurity Law* is a powerful tool for China to meet the security challenges in the international cyberspace, uphold our sovereignty in cyberspace and protect citizens' legitimate rights and interests in cyberspace. As the first law in the field of cybersecurity in China, the *Cybersecurity Law* has clear provisions on data security, information security in cyberspace and other aspects, which lays a legal foundation for promoting data use, ensuring data security and safeguarding national data sovereignty. Article 21 of the *Cybersecurity Law* requires network operators to take measures such as data classification, backup and encryption of important data to prevent stealth or tampering. Articles 37 and 38 stipulate that where it is indeed necessary for the personal information and important data stored by critical information infrastructure operators within the territory of the People's Republic of China to be stored or provided overseas, security assessment shall be conducted in accordance with the provisions. Articles 40 to 45 provide that network operators shall strictly keep confidential users' personal information collected by them, and establish and improve the system for the protection of users' information, shall not collect, use or process personal information in violation of the provisions of any law or the agreement, and shall take measures to prevent data of citizens' personal information from being illegally obtained, leaked or illegally used. Article 47 expressly stipulates the obligation of network operators regarding the disposition of illegal information: If any operator finds any information of which the release or transmission is prohibited by any law or administrative regulation, it shall immediately cease the transmission of such information, take deletion or any other handling measure to prevent the information from spreading, preserve relevant records, and report it to the competent department (Li Anjun 2018). It can be said that such the *Cybersecurity Law* has left space for the development of data circulation and transaction in China, and also provides a strong guarantee for personal information protection.

Cryptograms are an important national strategic resource with direct bearing on national data security. On October 26, 2019, the Cryptography Law of China was formally promulgated, establishing cryptography as a core technology for data security in China and pushing it to a central position in the field of data security. With 44 articles in five chapters, the *Cryptography Law* present clear provisions on the leadership and management system for cryptography, the principles for the classified management of cryptography, the scenario-based application of cryptography, and the promotion of and support for the development cryptography. The *Cryptography Law* is well-connected with the *Cybersecurity Law*, the *Law on Guarding State Secrets* and other related laws and regulations; and it has also laid the foundation for the *Data Security Law* and the *Law on the Protection of Personal Information* that are to follow. As the first law in the field of cryptography in China, the *Cryptography Law* offers sound legal basis for the protection data encryption and protection, putting to an end the time when data go unprotected and is widely abused. As all kinds of cryptographic applications for data encryption and protection are put into wider use, the Internet will be more secure and controllable in China. This will provide strong momentum for the healthy and sustainable development of the Internet in China and offer great help for our efforts to strengthen and promote data security protection.

On May 28, 2019, the *Measures for the Administration of Data Security* (draft for comment) were officially released. These measures were formulated in accordance with the *Cybersecurity Law* and other relevant laws and regulations. In terms of the content, these measures mainly make adjustments in regard to the security management and protection of important data and personal information, clarifying the standards for the collection, processing and use of personal information and important data as well as relevant security supervision and management, and proposing that network operators collecting important data or sensitive personal information for the purpose of operation shall register at local cyberspace and information authorities, and network operators collecting and using personal information through websites, applications and other products shall formulate separate rules for the collection and use. In 2018, the European Union introduced the *General Data Protection Regulation*, which was considered the strictest data protection law in history. It not only details the protection of personal data rights, but also specified severe penalties for violations. After the aforementioned measures were issued in China, some believed them to be even stricter. Moreover, in September of 2018, the *Data Security Law* was formally included in the legislative agenda of the Standing Committee of the 13th National People's Congress, and data security legislation became a national strategy. On March 4, 2019, Zhang Yesui, spokesperson, said at the press conference of the Second Session of the 13th National People's Congress that work to make the Data Security Law will move forward in the year 2019 in a bid to enhance the ability of preventing and resisting security risks.

Legislative attempts at the local level

Local legislations have the unique advantages of high flexibility, low trial-and-error cost and distinctive features. They not only provide strong institutional guarantee for the exploration of innovative experiments and the promotion of social development within the territory, but also accumulate a lot of valuable experience with which we can blaze the trail towards governance of China. This is extremely important and plays an irreplaceable role in the process of fully implementing the basic national strategy of the rule of law. Data security is the premise of the development and application of big data. Without data security, the development and application of big data will not be sustainable, and the big data industry will not be able to develop in a healthy way. Guizhou Province and Tianjin Municipality are the vanguards and leading forces in legislations on big data at the local level. They are also designated as national big data comprehensive pilot zones. As of November 2019, these two places have formulated six local laws and regulations on big data, five by Guizhou and one by Tianjin. Such local legislative efforts have provided scientific guidance and legal support for the development of the big data industry in Tianjin and Guizhou, especially for the management of data security. Other places, such as Shanghai, Chongqing, Zhejiang, and Fujian have also formulated governmental rules to enhance data security management, data sharing, data application and data services (see Table 16). These legislative practices at the local level concerning data rights have made some contributions to management of the collection, use and processing of data, and to data security and the protection of the legitimate rights and interests of data rights holders.

Guizhou is among the first provinces in China to develop the big data industry. Plans were made in 2013 and concrete programs were officially launched in 2014. Guizhou Province successfully positioned itself as one of the forerunners in the big data development, standing shoulder to shoulder with Guangdong, Beijing and Tianjin. In January 2016, Guizhou Province formulated China's first local regulation on big data, *Regulations of Guizhou Province on Promoting the Development and Application of Big Data*, setting out principles, general provisions and guidelines for the management of big data security (articles 4, 29, 31, 32, and 33). "Amid rapid development, big data security issues have become increasingly apparent: First, there are a large number of big data security risks; second, the conflict between requirements of big data security and demand for open access and sharing grow prominent; and third, big data security laws and regulations still need to be improved" (The Legislative Affairs Commission of the Standing Committee of the People's Congress of Guizhou Province 2019, p. 4). Therefore, it was pointed out at the Legislative Work Meeting of the Standing Committee of the 13th People's Congress of Guizhou Province specially that "we should study and formulate local laws and regulations concerning the security of big data in Guizhou Province." In August of 2019, Guizhou Province pioneered again to formulate China's first provincial big data security regulation, the Regulations on the Guarantee of Big Data Security of Guizhou Province. On the basis of the *Regulations of Guizhou Province on Big Data Security Control*. On the basis of the previous regulations, this document refines provisions on big data security control, defines big data security responsibilities, supervision and management, and legal liabilities, and embodies the concept of paying equal attention to development and security, ensuring development through security, and promoting security through development. The *Regulations* aim at building eight systems[12] for data security protection, focusing on improving the comprehensive defense and governance capability of big data security in the whole society, and respond to three core issues in the development of big data industry: First, facing up to the problem of prioritizing development over security in the previous development of the big data industry, we put in place dedicated legislation to ensure big data security; secondly, in response to the problem of multiple regulators for the development and application of big data without clear division of labor, we clarified who is in charge of big data security and defined their specific responsibilities; thirdly, we made clear the relationship between open access & sharing and security (He Xinghui 2019). The *Regulations* is of great significance

12 The eight systems of big data security protection are the organization system, the prevention system, the supervision and regulation system, the emergency response system, the comprehensive protection system, the technical service system, the talent education and training system, and the work support system.

to big data security and personal information security, and to the clarification of big data security responsibilities and the promotion of the big data development and application. They also and laid a solid theoretical and practical foundation for big data security legislation and personal information protection legislation at the national level.

Guiyang, as the core area of the National Big Data (Guizhou) Comprehensive Pilot Zone, has always attached great importance to innovations in systems in its drive to fulfill the important key strategic task of building China Data Valley. It introduced the 1+1+3+N top-level design[13] for big data security development and committed itself to the building of a national big data and cybersecurity pilot and demonstration zone. In May of 2017, officially approved by the Ministry of Public Security, Guiyang became the country's first Big Data and Cybersecurity Demonstration Pilot City, and this marked the start of the city's new efforts in the field of big data security to create a new urban model for big data security. In 2018, Guiyang compiled the *Regulations of Guiyang City on Big Data Security Management* in accordance with the provisions of the *Cybersecurity Law* and other relevant laws and regulations. The *Regulations* were put into force on October 1, 2018. There are 37 articles in the six chapters respectively titled general provisions; security support; monitoring, early warning and emergency response; supervision and inspection; legal liabilities; and supplementary provisions. In terms of security support, the *Regulations* clearly state that "the legal representative or main person in charge of an entity with security responsibilities is the first responsible person for big data security in the entity. An entity with security responsibilities shall formulate and improve access control policies, adopt authorized access,

13 In 1+1+3+N, the first 1 indicates Guiyang's intention to become Big Data and Cybersecurity Demonstration Pilot City, which has been realized, lending momentum to the development of big data security; the second 1 stands for the plan to build a big data security shooting range in Guiyang, which is a place for both commercial and civilian use and provide certification and security verification for different products, technologies and services, meeting the demand for Internet security and big data security in the future; the 3 indicates Guiyang's intentions to build the Urban Security Situation Awareness Center, Urban Security Supervision Center, and Big Data Security Innovation Center; and the N refers to the different platforms to be built for data security and cybersecurity in different fields and industries.

Table 16. Local Legislations on Data Rights across China

Legislation	**Issuer**	**Time of Issuance**	**Time of Implementation**
Local Regulations			
Regulations on Promoting Guizhou Province's Big Data Development and Application	Guizhou Provincial People's Congress (including the Standing Committee)	January 15, 2016	March 1, 2016
Regulations of Guiyang City on Open and Shared Government Data	Guiyang Municipal People's Congress (including the Standing Committee)	April 11, 2017	May 1, 2017
Regulations of Guiyang City on Big Data Security Management	Guiyang Municipal People's Congress (including the Standing Committee)	August 2, 2018	October 1, 2018
Regulations of Guiyang City on the Application and Development of Healthcare Big Data	Guiyang Municipal People's Congress (including the Standing Committee)	October 9, 2018	January 1, 2019
Regulations of Tianjin Municipality on Promoting the Development and Application of Big Data	Tianjin Municipal People's Congress (including the Standing Committee)	December 14, 2018	January 1, 2019
Regulations of Guizhou Province on Big Data Security Control	Guizhou Provincial People's Congress (including the Standing Committee)	August 1, 2019	October 1, 2019
Regulations of Guizhou Province on Open and Shared Government Data (Draft)	Guizhou Provincial People's Congress (including the Standing Committee)	--	--

(To be continued)

Table 16. Continued

Legislation	**Issuer**	**Time of Issuance**	**Time of Implementation**
Local Government Rules			
Measures of Zhejiang Province for the Administration of Geospatial Data Exchange and Sharing	People's Government of Zhejiang Province	May 4, 2010	July 1, 2010
Measures of Qinghai Province for the Administration of Geospatial Data Exchange and Sharing	People's Government of Qinghai Province	October 14, 2015	December 1, 2015
Measures of Fujian Province for the Administration of Government Data	People's Government of Fujian Province	October 15, 2016	October 15, 2016
Measures of Hunan Province for the Administration of Geospatial Data	People's Government of Hunan Province	March 3, 2017	April 1, 2017
Measures of Zhejiang Province for the Management of Public Data and E-Government	People's Government of Zhejiang Province	March 16, 2017	May 1, 2017
Measures of Guiyang Municipal Government for the Management of Government Data	Guiyang Municipal People's Government	November 23, 2017	January 1, 2018
Measures of Jiangxi Province for the Administration of Geographic Information Data	People's Government of Jiangxi Province	December 26, 2017	March 1, 2018

(To be continued)

Table 16. Continued

Legislation	Issuer	Time of Issuance	Time of Implementation
Measures of Guiyang City for the Open and Shared Government Data	Guiyang Municipal People's Government	January 12, 2018	March 1, 2018
Regulations of Chengdu Municipality on the Application and Management of Public Data	Chengdu Municipal People's Government	June 6, 2018	July 1, 2018
Interim Measures of Guiyang City for Assessment of Open and Shared Government Data	Guiyang Municipal People's Government	June 27, 2018	September 1, 2018
Measures of Ningxia Hui Autonomous Region for the Sharing of Government Data Resources	People's Government of Ningxia Hui Autonomous Region	September 4, 2018	November 1, 2018
Regulations of Shanghai Municipality on the Management of Public Data and Handling Affairs through All-in-one Online Account	Shanghai Municipal People's Government	September 30, 2018	November 1, 2018
Interim Measures of Hainan Province for Big Data Management	People's Government of Hainan Province	May 21, 2019	May 21, 2019
Measures of Tianjin Municipality on the Management of Data Security (Provisional)	Tianjin Cyberspace Administration Office	June 26, 2019	August 1, 2019
Interim Measures of Chongqing Municipality on the Management of Government Data Resources	Chongqing Municipal People's Government	July 31, 2019	July 31, 2019
Interim Measures of Shanghai Municipality for Public Data Opening	Shanghai Municipal People's Government	August 29, 2019	October 1, 2019

identity authentication and other technical measures to prevent unauthorized queries, replication, modification and transmission of data. Personal information and important data shall be protected through encryption and other security measures, and data relevant to state security, social and public interests, trade secrets and personal information shall go through decryption and masking processes in accordance with the law (Guiyang Daily 2018). As the first local regulations of big data security management in China, the *Regulations* not only refine the responsibilities of the government and competent authorities at the institutional level in accordance with the *Cybersecurity Law*, but also realize the real-time and dynamic monitoring of the security risks for important big data, which is of great significance to the development of the big data industry of China and the development of the rule of law in relation to big data security. In addition, articles 24 and 25 of the *Regulations of Guiyang City on Open and Shared Government Data* (2017), Article 26 of the *Regulations of Guiyang City on the Application and Development of Health and Medical Big Data* (2018), and Articles 46 to 51 of the *Regulations of Tianjin Municipality on Promoting the Development and Application of Big Data* (2018) all contain clear stipulations on data security management. The formulation and implementation of these local regulations are of great importance to building the awareness of data security in the whole society, enhancing the ability of data security protection in the whole society, and promoting the formation of a sound legal environment in which data security is a responsibility shared among all members of society. It provides a useful reference for the formulation of data security laws and regulations at the national level.

Experts' legislative recommendations

As conditions become better for data security legislation on the national level, louder voices come from all walks of life calling for data security legislation. During the annual meetings of the National People's Congress (NPC) and the Chinese People's Political Consultative Conference (CPPPCC) in recent years, many participants have been calling vigorously for the introduction of data security law on the national level. For example, NPC deputy Zheng Jie said that data security has great bearing on cybersecurity, state security, citizens' privacy, and social security and stability so the formulation of a data security law should be accelerated. His proposal was that "we should establish data sovereignty, define the scope of data security law, make it clear that personal information and important data collected and generated in the course of operations within the country shall be stored within the territory of the People's Republic of China; improve the security assessment mechanism for data exit, and expand the application of this mechanism from key information infrastructure operators provided for in the *Cybersecurity Law* to other network operators; and incorporate data-related activities relevant to the interests of the state, enterprises, organizations and citizens into the scope of the data security law" (Zhao Yingying 2019).

CPPCC member Lian Yuming submitted the *Proposal on Legislation on Data Security* (March 2018) and the *Proposal on Speeding up the Legislation Process of Data Security Law* (March 2019), calling on the relevant national authorities to intensify theoretical research on data rights, data rights system and data rights law, actively carry out consultations for the making of the data security law, move faster to organize the drafting of the data security law, strengthen cross-border jurisdiction over data, hold firmly in hand the right to make data security rules and have our voice heard in the international community, providing China's wisdom and proposal for the rule of law in global cyberspace governance. Lian's proposals also describe the elements to be covered by data security legislation: "First, the purpose of legislation shall include safeguarding state security, upholding social and public interests, protecting the legitimate rights and interests of citizens, legal persons and other organizations, promoting open access to and sharing of data as well as the development and application of data. Second, we should attach equal importance to security and development, and follow the principles of government leadership, prudent regulation, innovation in protection, unity of powers and responsibilities, and controllable risks. Third, we should make adjustments to the scope, focus and supervisors. The adjustments should cover security support in data collection, storage, circulation and application, with priority given to data concerning national interests, public security, trade secrets, personal privacy and military research and production. Different from the problems encountered din the making of the *Cybersecurity Law*, the lack of regulatory bodies is the major difficulty for legislation on data security. The fourth point is the standard system, for which relevant stakeholders should be mobilized to first establish four feasible standards, namely the basic standard, technical standards, management standards, and application standards for data security. The fifth point is classified protection, which involves a classified security protection system in which confidential and sensitive data receive a higher level of protection and key information infrastructure is put into a dedicated class and under an appropriate level of protection. The sixth is risk assessment. A mandatory data security risk assessment system shall be established, and data security certification and institutionalized data security testing shall be launched. The seventh point is about restrictions. Attempts should be made to impose restrictions on four categories of data. The first category can be stored on overseas servers, the second category must be stored on controllable servers within the country, the third category must be backed up, and the fourth category is not allowed to leave the country" (Zhong Guangping 2018).

In addition, Qi Aimin and Pan Jia proposed a set of legal support mechanisms for big data security, suggested the basic principles and a specific structure (including general provisions, private law mechanisms, criminal law mechanisms, administrative law mechanisms, and international law mechanisms), and maintained that to ensure data security, "the point is not only to give full and effective protection of data, but also to promote the development, flow and use of data resources, so as to achieve a reasonable balance between the two" (Qi Aimin & Pan Jia 2015). A literature review finds that researchers approach data security legislation mainly from three directions: First, they study basic concepts and fundamental rights such as information, privacy, data, data rights, and database rights; second, they study the major problems and challenges in the field of data security, as well as how to prevent and deal with them; third, they study the necessity, feasibility, timing, conditions and possible obstacles of data security legislation. These research efforts have built the theoretical ecosystem of data security legislation and laid the theoretical and jurisprudential foundation for data security legislation at the local and national levels.

Governance by a digital government

The Chinese government attaches great importance to cybersecurity and informatization, and has made a series of important arrangements to speed up the building of a digital China. *The 13th Five-Year Plan* proposed to the strategy of building China's strength through network-based development and speed up the development of a digital China. In the *Outline of National Informatization Development Strategy*, the development of information economy and digital China is regarded as the top priorities in China's informatization process. *The 13th Five-Year Plan for National Informatization* refined the goals of digital China development. The report to the 19th CPC National Congress laid out further requirements for promoting the building of a digital China (E-Government Research Center of the Party School of the Central Committee of CPC 2019). Then, at the Fourth Plenary Session of the 19th CPC Central Committee, which has just concluded, a clear proposal was made to promote the building of a digital government. As an integral part of the digital China campaign, digital government offers strategic support to the modernization of the national governance system and governance capacity. Digital governance is an important part of the governance of China. Governance by a digital government is a new model of public governance that aligns administration with modern science and technology, and it is also a form of public governance in line with the basic service needs and pursuit of rights of the public in the era of digital civilization. Compared with the traditional governance model, governance by a digital government represents a series of changes and new features: Governance shifts from an enclosed model to an open one, from one-way efforts to collaboration, and from power-based governance to data-based governance.

With the further implementation of the digital China strategy, Guangxi, Guangdong, Zhejiang, Hubei, and Fujian successively issued digital government development plans or relevant policies and regulations (see Table 17). The People's Government of Guangxi Zhuang Autonomous Region issued the *Guangxi Three-Year Action Plan to Promote Digital Government Development (2018–2020)* in August 2018, proposing the working objective of "initially establishing a digital government featuring science-based decision-making and analysis, refined internal management and highly efficient public service provision by 2020", and making specific arrangements for seven main tasks, namely, promoting the building of an integrated basic support system, promoting open access to and sharing of data resources, promoting the Internet Plus government services model, promoting big data application for macro decision-making, promoting digitalized market supervision, promoting digitalized supervision of natural resources, and promoting digitalized ecological environment governance. The Guangdong Provincial People's Government published the *Master Plan of Guangdong Province for Digital Government Building (2018–2020)* on October 26, 2018, proposing that by the end of 2020, Guangdong shall have established a digital government administration system featuring a holistic approach, government-enterprise cooperation and separation of management and operation, and a digital government business system featuring overall operation, sharing, collaboration and service integration, build a unified and secure government cloud and government network, an open and integrated big data center and an integrated online government service platform, and form a digital government that is connected to all upper and lower levels of the government system and covers all aspects and fields. On December 28, 2018, the People's Government of Zhejiang Province issued the *Reform of Zhejiang Province for One-stop Government Services and Overall Plan for Government Digital Transformation*. The overall objective proposed is to initially form a digital government system that is vertically well-connected and horizontally coordinated, featuring connection to all upper and lower levels of the government system and coverage of all aspects and fields by the end of 2020. The overall framework of the digital government is a data platform with four horizontal and three vertical lines, and the hierarchical structure is proposed with a balance between integration and division of labor. In January 2019, the People's Government of Hubei Province issued the *Guiding Opinions of Hubei Provincial People's Government on Promoting Digital Government Development* and the *Implementation Plan of Hubei Province for Promoting Digital Government Development*, which made specific arrangements in five aspects: intensive support of infrastructure, integration of government services, smart and collaborative office work, science-based government decision-making for governance, and systematic support with sound working mechanisms. On March 20, 2019, the People's Government of Fujian Province introduced *Key Work Points of Digital Fujian in 2019*, which put forward specific requirements in five aspects: making every effort to ensure the success of the Second Digital China Summit, improving and upgrading information infrastructure, comprehensively improving e-government services, implementing the action plan for leadership in the digital economy, and strengthening support for effective implementation (E-Government Research Center of the Party School of the Central Committee of CPC 2019).

Table 17. Local Digital Government Plans in China

Plan	**Publisher**	**Time of Release**
Guangxi Three-Year Action Plan to Promote Digital Government Development (2018–2020)	People's Government of Guangxi Zhuang Autonomous Region	August 29, 2018
Master Plan of Guangdong Province for Digital Government Building (2018–2020)	People's Government of Guangdong Province	October 26, 2018
Reform of Zhejiang Province for One-stop Government Services and Overall Plan for Government Digital Transformation	People's Government of Zhejiang Province	December 28, 2018
Guiding Opinions of Hubei Provincial People's Government on Promoting Digital Government Development	People's Government of Hubei Province	January 15, 2019
Implementation Plan of Hubei Province for Promoting Digital Government Development	People's Government of Hubei Province	January 15, 2019
Implementation Plan for Digital Government Development of Shandong Province (2019–2022)	People's Government of Shandong Province	March 13, 2019
Key Work Points of Digital Fujian in 2019	People's Government of Fujian Province	March 20, 2019
Work Plan on Accelerating Digital Government Development in Ningxia Hui Autonomous Region	People's Government of Ningxia Hui Autonomous Region	June 24, 2019

Open access to and sharing of government data is one of the most urgent tasks in governance by a digital government. At the national level, China formally issued the *Regulations on Open Government Information* on April 5, 2007, requiring all administrative authorities to disclose government information to the public in accordance with statutory procedures. On August 31, 2015, the State Council issued the *Action Plan for Promoting Big Data Development,* proposing to "accelerate the building of a unified national open government data platform, and make plans for public institutions to make their data public." On September 5, 2016, the State Council issued the *Interim Measures for the Administration of Sharing of Government Information Resources*, laying out uniform provisions for the sharing of government information at the national level, breaking the separation between different administrative organs who act in isolation, and requiring solid basis is any resources is not to be shared so that administrative authorities can no longer refuse to share resources without a reason. In October 2019, it was proposed at the Fourth Plenary Session of the 19th CPC Central Committee that we should "accelerate the building of a nationwide integrated government service platform" so that government bodies can provide enterprises and the public with public services covering whole processes in a better integrated way, contributing to the modernization of government administration. With the improvement of national governance capacity and the rapid development of social informatization, the *Regulations on Open Government Information* (2008) encountered problems in the new situation in the implementation process. Therefore, efforts to revise it started in 2019 and revised edition came into force on May 15, 2019 with changes mainly involve three aspects: First, we will adhere to the principle that all government information is open unless it is necessary to keep some confidential in only special cases, and the scope of open government information shall be clearly defined and expanded constantly. Second, we will improve procedures for disclosure at request so as to effectively protect the legitimate rights and interests of applicants and other stakeholders, and at the same time, take necessary measures to prevent a small number of applicants from improperly exercising their right to request information so that the normal operation of open government information will not be hampered. Third, we will raise stricter requirements for services that provide convenience for the public so as to enhance the effectiveness of government information disclosure through the use of information technology, and give full play to the role of the government as a service provider, offering access to information concerning people's production, daily life, economic and social activities (Wu Shan 2019).

At the local level, Beijing, Wuhan and Shanghai, respectively issued their measures for open government information in 2008, 2015 and 2016 (see Table 18) and Guiyang introduced the *Regulations of Guiyang City on Open and Shared Government Data*, the first of its kind at the local level in China, requiring the government to make public government data and manage the work, funds and target-based performance assessment in the field of open access to and sharing of government data in a law-based manner so as to ensure the sustainable development of open government data. The implementation of the *Regulations* means that the sharing of and open access to government data is no longer a matter of choice, but a must according to law. Encouraged by the Regulations, as of November 13, 2019, there were a total of 117,29,739 data entries, 3,078 datasets, and 480 application programming interfaces (APIs) from 51 municipal authorities and 13 districts and counties on Guiyang Open Government Data Platform, the first prefecture-level integrated open government data platform in China.[14] Anyone can retrieve government data from the platform by subject, industry, field, department, or district/county. In May of 2019, Guizhou Province released a draft for comments of the *Regulations of Guizhou Province on Open and Shared Government Data* which have 44 articles in eight chapters, laying out clear provisions on the management, sharing, openness, application, supervision, and legal liabilities of government data resources. In terms of data sharing, the *Regulations* clearly stipulate that data sharing shall follow the principle of "sharing as a principle and no sharing as an exception" and data is divided into three categories respectively for unconditional sharing, conditional sharing and no sharing. Similarly, access to government data is also offered based on the three categories: unconditional access, conditional access and no access. By doing so, Guizhou has grasped the key to big data legislation on open government data. Open access to and sharing of government data leads the way towards society-wide open access and sharing, providing the experience of Guizhou that can be copied and disseminated all over China.

14 Data are available from the Guiyang Open Government Data Platform at <http://www.gyopendata.gov.cn/city/index.htm>.

Table 18. Local Government Programs for Open Government Data

Place	Document	Key Points	Year
Beijing	Several Opinions on Strengthening the Sharing of Government Information Resources	It is a general plan for the development and maintenance of the information resource databases. It avoids repeated work through shared search engines, make clear rules about the responsibilities for data collection; require timely sharing of all information resources free of charge based on confidentiality agreements signed between the provider and the user.	2005
	Regulations of Beijing Municipality on Promoting Informatization	It sets rules for the management of government information, the integration of existing informatization projects, the building of a unified platform for the sharing and exchange of government information, guidance on and standardization of the use of information resources for value creation, better application of information technology, and the effective implementation of classified information security management.	2007
	Measures for the Management of Beijing Municipal People's Government's Information Resources Sharing and Exchange Platform	It requires all municipal authorities to share resources through the municipal sharing and exchange platform, and various district and county sharing platforms are connected to the municipal platform. It stipulates that those who request data must not provide the shared data to any third party without permission, and emphasizes the requirements for safe operation and maintenance of the sharing platform.	2008

(To be continued)

Table 18. Continued

Place	Document	Key Points	Year
	Implementation Opinions on Promoting Information Consumption and Expanding Domestic Demand	It is to promote information consumption and supply capacity of the city, promote the upgrading of the information industry, improve next-generation information infrastructure, promote the sharing of public information resources, and encourage progress that creates new value.	2014
	Action Plan of Beijing Municipality on Big Data and Cloud Computing	It sets objectives for open data development: By 2020, 90 percent of authorities will provide open access to 60 percent of their data, and the relevant quality and efficiency will be improved.	2016
	The 13th Five-Year Plan for Informatization of Beijing Municipality	It provides plans and lists for public data sharing, decides to offer access to public data in order to encourage open access to and integration of more data resources across society, and decides on the building of a data trade center.	2016
	Three-Year Action Plan of Shanghai Municipality for Promoting Big Data Research and Development (2013–2015)	The plan analyzes the advantages and disadvantages of Shanghai: The advantages are abundant data resources, strong research capability, and a sound structure of the data industry. The disadvantages are inadequate development of the data industry, shortage of key technology reserves, and the lack of a complete industry chain. It also proposes to promote standardized data sharing by signing relevant agreements.	2013

(To be continued)

Table 18. Continued

Place	Document	Key Points	Year
Shanghai	Implementation Opinions of Shanghai Municipality on Promoting Open Access to and Use of Government Information Resources	Application-oriented, active, prudent and gradual measures shall be taken to promote open access to data generated and collected with fiscal funds. For data that should but cannot be made public due to immature conditions, efforts should be made to create the conditions needed, and social forces should be encouraged carry out development activities for added value.	2014
	Work Plan of Shanghai Municipality for Government Affairs-Related Data Resources Opening and Sharing (2015)	It requires efforts to improve the three basic databases, asks all municipal authorities to sort out their data resources and make lists of open-access data according to the key areas set for 2015, requires efforts to solicit and analyze social needs, improve the quality of data services, and expand available channels for access to public data other than the data service network.	2015
	Work Plan of Shanghai Municipality for Government Affairs-Related Data Resources Opening and Sharing (2016)	New informatization projects that do not share data will not be approved. Real-time data will be accessible mainly through interfaces. Sensitive data will be made public after desensitization. Data with higher security levels such as security-related data will be provided at request. Sharing and open access will be included in performance evaluation. Urban security is the key area of the year for data sharing.	2016
	Implementation Opinions on Big Data Development in Shanghai	It sets standards for open data systems, strengthens quality management and cross-check, takes openness and sharing into performance evaluation, encourages open access to and sharing of social data, and promotes flow of commercial data.	2016

(To be continued)

Table 18. Continued

Place	Document	Key Points	Year
	Measures of Shanghai Municipality for the Management of Government Affairs-Related Data Resources Sharing	It defines responsibilities in data sharing, requires administrative institutions not to collect data repeatedly, sets rules for classified sharing based on three categories of data: shared, shared at request, and not shared.	2016
Guiyang	Several Opinions on Accelerating the Development of the Big Data Industry	It proposes to build the world's first block data public platform by 2017.	2015
	Information Disclosure Regulations of Guiyang Municipal People's Government (Revised)	It sets out new requirements for government authorities at different levels to boost information sharing	2015
	Measures to Promote Big Data Technology Innovation in Guiyang National High-tech Industrial Development Zone	It encourages and gives rewards for enterprises to develop and use open data, invites users to share their unpleasant experience so as to expedite improvements and secure satisfactory services	2016
	Work Plan of Guiyang Municipal People's Government for Replicating Experimental Practices of China (Shanghai) Pilot Free Trade Zone	It requires gathering, communication and use of government data; and establishment of a joint meeting system for sharing work	2016

(To be continued)

Table 18. Continued

Place	Document	Key Points	Year
	Regulations of Guiyang City on Open and Shared Government Data	Shared data of licenses and permits can be used as for administrative purposes, lists of shared and open data shall be provided, open data should be provided on open data platform in a machine-readable and reproducible manner, and data that should be but are not made public, in or out of the lists can be open at request.	2017
Wuhan	Opinions on Promoting Big Data Application and the Development of the Big Data Industry	It proposes to keep record of the city's government data assets, build data exchange platforms and trading markets, implement application demonstration projects, guide the society to collect open data, improve government regulations and the security system.	2014
	Action Plan of Wuhan on Big Data Industry Development (2014–2018)	The city should take the lead in open government data, manage government data assets in a centralized manner, establish data transaction rules, and form a big data industry chain on the basis of trading platforms.	2014
	Interim Measures of Wuhan City for the Management of Government Affairs-Related Data Resources Sharing	Administrative institutions are to carry out digital transformation and structured data processing. Data of licenses and permits should be stamped with electronic seals and updated in real time. Data are divided into three categories: unrestricted sharing, restricted sharing and no-sharing.	2015

(To be continued)

Table 18. Continued

Place	Document	Key Points	Year
Taiwan, China	Freedom of Government Information Act	Government information should be made public voluntarily or provided upon request. Government agencies may charge fees according to the purpose of applying for government information. The fee standard shall be formulated by each agency. Those who apply for government information for academic research or public welfare purposes shall be eligible for rate cut or exemption.	2005
	Open Government Data Operating Principle	Following the principle of openness, sensitive information and other special circumstances may be exceptions on the basis of formally giving the reasons and grounds and with approval from relevant responsible persons. Second-level central authorities are to serve as the centers for overall planning and list the data on the government's open data platform. A set of data, if made public, shall not be arbitrarily divided into parts so as to ensure their integrity, correctness and timeliness. Based on the principle of free provision, but for those with special business needs, the charging method and amount shall be agreed upon through consultation. All agencies shall, based on the principle of use for added value, set standards and restrictions for the use of data. Each authority shall establish a performance management and promotion mechanism of its own.	2013

(To be continued)

Table 18. Continued

Place	Document	Key Points	Year
	Essential Requirements for Government Open Data Datasets	Ministries and commissions shall serve as the centers for overall planning of dataset management of all subordinate agencies.	2013
	Regulations for the Use of Government Open Data Platform	Authorization by way of free and non-exclusive authorization does not apply to trademark rights and patent rights, and shall not constitute any restriction on the user's time, location and way of use; users who find errors and omissions should provide information free of charge to help government agencies correct them. The user shall bear the liability for compensation for damages to the interests of any third party; government agencies do not guarantee the completeness and correctness of the data.	2013
	Open Government Data License Taiwan 1.0	Users are not allowed to sub-authorize; users shall declare the use of the data by name and clearly indicate the original data providing authority.	2015

In Taiwan of China, data sharing among government data among agencies has long been in operation and policies in this regard has been coming out since 2013, including the *Open Government Data Operating Principle*, the *Essential Requirements for Government Open Data Datasets*, the *Regulations for the Use of Government Open Data Platform*, and the *Open Government Data License Taiwan 1.0*. On December 9, 2015, the Open Knowledge Foundation (OKF) released the results of the international comparison of open government data, and Taiwan ranked first (Lian Yuming 2017, p. 88).

Significance of the Data Rights System to Global Cyberspace Governance

The data rights law is an important jurisprudential tool for a country to participate in global governance and a golden key to problems in global cyberspace governance. At present, the development of the global cyberspace governance system is unbalanced, relevant rules await improvement, and the cyberspace is in poor order and of an abnormal structure where hegemony prevails and the rule of law is underdeveloped (Zhi Zhenfeng 2017). The technological community seems to be making rules on its own initiative, but is in fact manipulated by hegemonic powers from the very beginning. Therefore, there is power monopoly under the cover of pseudo-decentralization in cyberspace. The cyberspace is not a place outside of law, and the international community calls for a fair system the rule of law in cyberspace. Therefore, based on the theoretical framework of data rights, data-rights system, and data rights law, we will hereby elaborate on the building of a community with a shared future in cyberspace and delve into the special significance of data rights law to global cyberspace governance, with a view to blazing the trail towards the rule of law in cyberspace with a Chinese approach.

Significance of data rights law to the world

Change of approach: From boundary management to sovereign governance

Sovereignty is the core issue in global cyberspace governance of the Internet. Cyber sovereignty[15] is an important cornerstone of the reform of

15 Cyber sovereignty is rooted in modern jurisprudence, and is regarded as a natural extension and representation of national sovereignty in cyberspace. It is an important part of national sovereignty.

the global cyberspace governance system and of good governance. Respect for cyber sovereignty is to oppose cyber hegemony. In terms of global cyberspace governance, traditional legal and technological approaches emphasize boundary management in cyberspace and the establishment of independent and controllable methods for route authentication. However, in the era of big data, the competition between different stakeholders for control over data is becoming increasingly fierce, the traditional boundaries between states, enterprises, and individuals for cyberspace management are broken, and what is urgently needed is a set of global legislations based on sovereign governance, which redefine, reconcile and improve relationships concerning data ownership. As the core element and key point of the data rights law, cyber sovereignty is an important guarantee for the global cyberspace governance system featuring respect for the sovereignty of all relevant countries, dialogue on an equal footing, and ultimately joint contribution and shared benefits in cyberspace. The data rights law emphasizes that global cyberspace governance must be based on sovereignty. Sovereign states enjoy jurisdiction, right to independence, right to defense, right to equality and so on in cyberspace under the premise of compliance with relevant laws and regulations. Only when cyberspace governance is based on sovereign governance can it be truly just and fair.

Institutional change: From hegemony to consultative democracy

Unilateralism is a key problem in global cyberspace governance. Developed countries in cyberspace use their advanced technologies and strong voice to trample wantonly on international justice, advocate cyber liberalism, implement the cyber deterrence strategy, and promote ideological hegemony in cyberspace. Upholding the principles of extensive consultation, shared benefits and joint governance in cyberspace, China advocates multilateralism and wide participation in global cyberspace governance, instead of unilateralism, hegemonism, and dictatorship. This means that cyberspace governance should be based on consultation among various sovereign states, giving full play to the role of governments, international organizations, Internet enterprises, the technology community, non-governmental organizations, citizens and other parties. Data rights, in nature, are the rights to share. The data rights law is a legal instrument formed based on the basic data rights system. It is naturally altruistic and show the characteristics of consultative democracy. While upholding cyber sovereignty, the data rights law advocates multilateralism, consultative democracy and international cooperation, supports the United Nations to coordinate global cyberspace governance, fully reflects the interests of all stakeholders around the world, and aims to "find the greatest common divisor and draw the largest concentric circles", and jointly build a community with a shared future in cyberspace.

Structural change: From decentralization to recentralization

The Internet was born in the United States. Internet technologies and architecture are believed to endow the Internet with the unique characteristic of decentralization. However, this is actually a misunderstanding. The "decentralization" here is not decentralization in the real and absolute sense. Rather, it is US-centered "decentralization" merely in structure. For example, major Internet operators and management institutions in the world are almost all in the hands of Western countries, especially the United States. This is likely to silence many stakeholders, leaving their legitimate interests unprotected and depriving them of the autonomy in choosing their own Internet development path and management model. The data rights law, aiming at building a community with a shared future in cyberspace, offers a solution to law-based global cyberspace governance. The data rights law emphasizes that the Internet has a decentralized and polycentric structure rather than an absolutely decentralized one, and that sovereign states can realize identity authentication and account management on different nodes based on its own cyberspace sovereignty. In the decentralized and polycentric structure, all centers are equal and have the same weight, there is no hegemony or domination, and no one has absolute authority any other party.

Model change: From technological governance to good law and good governance

The Internet has its origin in the United States, and the mechanisms and models of its governance are mostly based on the spontaneous organization by the technological community. However, this technological community is comprised mainly of American organizations, and their core management staff and scientists are almost all from major developed countries in Europe and America. They advocate freedom and technology-based cyberspace governance. Technology has no borders, but scientists have their nationalities. The nationalities of the scientists who control the core technologies and have the loudest voice in global cyberspace governance will directly affect the future of science and technology and cybersecurity of the country. In contrast, the data rights law does not advocate governance that is based solely on technology. Instead, it emphasizes that global cyberspace governance needs a combination of legal rules and technical rules.[16] The essence of this combination is remixing, and the goal is to achieve "technology-based governance backed by legislation". There are three core points: adaptation to the needs of Internet technology architecture and business model innovation, balance and coordination between various stakeholders and different values, and the necessity to guide and promote the healthy development of the Internet industry and maintain fairness and justice. On this basis, the data rights law can serve as a common code of conduct and value orientation of the Internet society, help achieve good law and good governance, and expedite the emergence of the Internet of order.

Predicament of the rule of law in global cyberspace governance

Cyberspace governance is not only an important part of global governance, but also an important aspect of the game between big powers. At present, global cyberspace governance faces insufficient supply of systems and a predicament in its rule of law formed by the following four

16 The technological rules are composed of software, protocols, programs, algorithms, supporting facilities and other technical elements, forming a hybrid architecture. In essence, the technological rules are a series of machine-readable computer code with irreversible execution characteristics. Legal rules are composed of legal framework, provisions, industrial policies, etc. Any violation will lead to corresponding legal liabilities.

difficult points that remain unsolved: The first is unbalanced Internet development, imperfect rules and poor order in the global cyberspace; the second point is that threats of infringements on personal privacy, intellectual property rights and information resources continue to grow; third, cybersecurity incidents such as sniffers, cyberattacks and cybercrimes remain highly frequent; and fourth, common hazards in the cyber world, such as cyber terrorism, cyber hegemonism and cyber militarism, remain to be tackled (Zhi Zhenfeng 2016). Simply put, the global cyberspace governance system is plagued with serious problems, lacking the rule of law, and in urgent needs of more governance efforts.

Imbalance in global Internet operation and management

The cyber world, just like the real world, depends on resources and their allocation for its operation. IP addresses, domain names, ports, protocols and the like are the necessary core resources for Internet operation. These resources can neither be generated out of thin air nor used at will, but need to be allocated and managed by specialized agencies. According to statistics available, major Internet operation and management organizations in the world include ICANN, RIRs, ISOC, IAB, IETF, IRTF, ISO, W3C, INOG, etc.[17] (see Table 19). These organizations provide strong technical support for the operation of the Internet itself and exerts absolute control and dominance. As such, these organizations control almost all the core standards and key protocols in regard to key information infrastructure and core technologies of the Internet, serving as the backbone of global cyberspace governance. However, from the membership

17 The institutions and organizations that play a role and participate to some extent in the operation of the global Internet include: Asia-Pacific Economic Cooperation (APEC), the Association of Southeast Asian Nations (ASEAN), the Council of Europe, the European Union, Forum of Incident Response and Security Teams (FIRST), the Group of Eight (G8), Institution of Electrical and Electronics Engineers (IEEE), International Telecommunication Union (ITU), Internet Governance Forum (IGF), the International Criminal Police Organization (INTERPOL), the Meridian Process, the North Atlantic Treaty Organization (NATO), Organization of American States (OAS), the Organization for Economic Co-operation and Development (OECD), etc.

Table 19. Major Global Internet Operating Organizations and Their Responsibilities

Internet Operation Organization	Major Responsibilities
Internet Corporation for Assigned Names and Numbers (ICANN)	It is responsible for the Internet unique identifier system and its safe and stable operation worldwide, including the spatial allocation of Internet protocol addresses, the assignment of protocol identifiers, the management of generic top-level domain names, national and regional top-level domain name systems, and the management of root server systems. The management team is composed of ISOC members, and staff members come from many countries around the world, many from the United States.
Regional Internet Registrations (RIRs)	They are responsible for allocating and registering Internet digital resources in their respective region, undertaking ICANN allocation, and allocating IP addresses and autonomous system (AS) numbers to economies. Members include Internet organizations such as ISP and national (or regional) Internet registrations (NIRs), which are non-profit member organizations.
Internet Society (ISOC)	The objective is to create beneficial and open conditions for the development of the Internet worldwide, and to formulate relevant standards, release information and conduct training on Internet technology. In addition, ISOC is also committed to social, economic, political, moral, legislative and other work that has bearing on the development direction of the Internet. The directors are of outstanding Internet elites selected from all over the world. It is a non-governmental, non-profit, industrial international organization with its headquarters in the United States.

(To be continued)

Table 19. Continued

Internet Operation Organization	Major Responsibilities
Internet Architecture Committee (IAB)	It defines the structure and sets long-term development plans of the entire cyberspace, carries out technical supervision and coordination, and appoints and supervises various Internet-related organizations. Members are elected by IETF participants and appointed by ISOC directors. There are 15 professional researchers from different professions in the world. The committee was founded in 1979 by the U.S. Department of Defense and its Advanced Research Projects Agency. It was affiliated to ISOC in 1992 and changed from a US government entity to an international public entity.
Internet Engineering Task Force (IETF)	It is responsible for the research, development and formulation of Internet-related technical specifications. It is spontaneously participated and managed by experts and is open to all those who are interested in the industry. The organization belongs to ISOC and is an open international non-governmental organization.
Internet Research Task Force (IRTF)	Authorized and managed by IAB, it has several groups under it to carry out theoretical research on different Internet technology issues.
International Organization for Standardization (ISO)	It aims to promote the development of standardization work worldwide in order to facilitate international material exchange and mutual assistance, and to expand cooperation in knowledge, science, technology and economy. The main task is to formulate international standards, coordinate standardization work worldwide, and cooperate with other international organizations to study standardization issues. Participants included national standards bodies and major companies from member states. The highest authority is the ISO General Assembly. All members of ISO groups, correspondents and international organizations with ties to ISO are represented at the assembly. It is a global non-governmental organization in nature.

(To be continued)

Table 19. Continued

Internet Operation Organization	**Major Responsibilities**
World Wide Web Consortium (W3C)	It aims to study and formulate relevant Internet standards such as those for Internet open platforms and wireless Internet technologies. The organization is led by Tim Berners Lee, father of the World Wide Web, and Jeffrey Jaffe, chief executive officer. It is jointly operated by a global team set up at four global headquarters of Massachusetts Institute of Technology, the European Union for Mathematics and Informatics, Keio University in Japan and Beijing University of Aeronautics and Astronautics in China. In nature, it is an international neutral technology standards agency developed as a project of CERN.
Internet Operators Alliance (INOG)	It discusses and exerts influence on matters related to the operation of the Internet. Its members mainly include Internet service providers and Internet switch centers.

Source: See Zhi Zhenfeng, "The Rule of Law in Global Cyberspace Governance," *Law and Social Development*, 1st issue, 2017.

of these institutions, especially their core bodies, we can see that they are mainly in the hands of Western technological powers led by the United States, and this promises serious imbalance from the very root. Such imbalance gives rise to the predicament that some stakeholders have no voice or influence in the system. Specifically, this is manifested mainly in two aspects: First, the governing bodies and their members are mainly European and American countries or their citizens, and the rights and interests of countries with underdeveloped Internet technologies and their citizens are not adequately protected. Second, with power monopoly in the global cyberspace governance system, the autonomy of developing countries in choosing their own Internet development path and Internet governance model is likely to be hampered.

Table 20. Cyber Hegemony and Cyber Domination

Category	Manifestation
Cyber management hegemony	A few Western developed countries led by the United States have monopoly on the core parts of the Internet. The lifeblood of the Internet is the root server and domain name system. At present, there are 13 root servers supporting the operation of the Internet in the world, of which the only one primary root server and 9 out of the 12 secondary root servers are located in the United States, one in the United Kingdom, one in Sweden and one in Japan. At present, ICANN, authorized by the US government and actually controlled by the United States, is responsible for the unified management of the global Internet root server, domain name system and IP address system. The U.S. Department of Commerce has veto over ICANN's decisions at any time and can interfere in other countries' Internet systems at any time. In addition, a few Western developed countries led by the United States also dominate the formulation of Internet rules.
Cyber technology hegemony	The United States is the birthplace of computer and information technology. Americans made the world's first electronic computer and create the Internet. The United States is far ahead of other countries in the world, including other Western developed countries, in the IT field. The United States controls the core computer and Internet technologies. Every key link on the Internet industry chain, such as chips, operating systems and search engines, is basically dominated by American companies. Among them, Microsoft and Google are obvious monopolies in nature.

(To be continued)

Table 20. Continued

Category	Manifestation
Language Hegemony and Monopoly on Network Information Content	Computer assembly language, operating system and software and hardware standards are all in English. More than two-thirds of the information flow on the Internet comes from the United States, with Japan taking the second place with a share of only 7 percent, and Germany in the third place with 5 percent. China has only 0.1 percent of the information input traffic and 0.05 percent of the output traffic of the entire Internet. It can be seen that English is the dominant language in the Internet, and developed countries are the main producers of information on the Internet. Among them, the United States is the most important one, and truly the "suzerain of network information"
Cyber Ideological Hegemony	A few Western developed countries, led by the United States, vigorously promote and whitewash Western values such as freedom, democracy, human rights, equality, fraternity and justice on the Internet. They advocate Western political models, and have long regarded the Internet as an important tool to spread democracy. Cyber liberalism has become one of the main excuses for the West to carry out cyber hegemonism. In fact, the so-called "free flow of information in cyberspace" that the United States vigorously promote actually means "free" flow according to the needs of the United States.

Source: See Wang Zhengping and Xu Tieguang, "Western Cyber Hegemonism and Cyber Rights in Developing Countries," *Thinking*, 2nd issue, 2011.

Cyber hegemony and cyber domination

As the birthplace of the Internet, the United States has monopoly on the most advanced Internet technologies and key Internet infrastructure in the world, controls the production of major global information products and the management of Internet address resources and root servers, and has unparalleled control over other technologically less advanced countries. At the same time, the cyberspace is also in the hands of the United States. China and other countries are basically in the gray area of cyberspace sovereignty, actually holding only part, or none of their cyberspace sovereignty in a cyberspace that is in almost complete chaos. In addition, the United States follows double standard,[18] advocates technological liberalism, and creates technological dictatorship, leaving room for terrorism and militarism in cyberspace. "Although the new scientific and technological revolution undermines and constrains the national sovereignty of all countries, this affects developed and developing countries to vastly different degrees, which is highly unbalanced and unequal (Zhao Xudong 1997). Such imbalance and inequality are actually a manifestation of the international relations featuring domination and being dominated and cyber hegemony. This greatly undermines international justice, and put third-world countries in seriously disadvantaged positions (see Table 20).

Cybersecurity and cybercrimes

Cybersecurity and cybercrimes are another difficult problem in the global governance of the cyberspace. The Internet is a virtual world that is open and decentralized where participants are anonymous, countries have no borders between them, and interactions occur in real time. These characteristics make it possible and somewhat easy for criminals to anonymously carry out cyberattacks, cyber fraud, cyber pyramid selling and other criminal activities. Cybersecurity incidents and cybercrimes occur from time to time all over the world, and threats such as cyber terrorism, cyber hegemonism and cyber militarism have become common hazards of the world. In general, there are two types of cybercrimes. The first type is trespassing and sabotage, such as sniffers, website attacks and the spread of viruses. Examples include the Snowden Incident, the Five Eyes surveillance incident, Stuxnet, etc. The second type is traditional crimes committed on the Internet, such as online financial fraud, illegal Internet financing, cyber theft, etc. Other forms of traditional crimes, such as false advertising, cyber manhunt, insulting and defamation, and online espionage, exert serious impact on the existing global security system. Compared with traditional crimes, cybercrimes have three obvious

18 Double standard refers to the application of different standards in terms of cyber freedom and security, that is, one set of standards for oneself and for allies and another for developing countries.

characteristics: First, they tend to be more destructive and committed by younger perpetrators. Second, the cost is low but the number of victims can be large and economic losses high. Third, the damage can be widespread and the political, economic and social security and stability of countries may even be at stake.

Data rights as a solution to the Internet global governance

The rule of law is an important means of global cyberspace governance and here he core is the law. "The law originates from human nature. It is created by the people and exists for the people. It starts from the people and ends serving the people" (Qin Ying 2009). Aimed at global cyberspace governance, we hereby extend basic hypotheses of human nature and attempt to approach the problem with the "data man" hypothesis. "Rights derived from 'data man' are called data rights; order constructed on the basis of data rights is called data rights system; and the legal norms thus formed on the basis of the data rights system is called data rights law. Thus comes the legal framework of data rights, data rights system, and data rights law" (Key Laboratory of Big Data Strategy 2018).

Data rights, data rights system and data rights law

The data rights law is a legal norm formed based on the data rights system. It re-allocates and improves the distribution of responsibilities, rights and obligations in order to regulate various relationships and conflicts of interests that arise in cyberspace. Different from traditional laws such as civil law, commercial law, criminal law, administrative law, and property law, the data rights law regulates new types of social relationships and right-obligation relationships in the cyberspace with data at the core. As data has wide coverage and the regulation of data can occur across various boundaries, the data rights law may include content that can be seen in civil law, administrative law, and criminal law by nature, involving multiple categories of legal relations. The data rights law is a collection of legal norms that regulate various rights and obligations in cyberspace, the core of which is to regulate data ownership, data rights, data use, and data protection. For example, the new types of legal rights that have arisen in cyberspace, such as data asset rights, data personality rights, the right to share data, and the right to be forgotten of data, exert constant impact on the traditional legal definitions of human rights, property rights, and intellectual property rights, and trigger changes in the operation mechanisms of traditional legal systems concerning finance, trade, contracts, torts, etc. Despite all these, the data rights law is necessary for the orderly flow of data in cyberspace, a premise of data reuse and balance between personal privacy and data use, and a basic component of the legal empire in cyberspace.

Table 21. Internet Rule of Law 1.0, 2.0 and 3.0

Stage	Features
Internet Rule of Law 1.0 (1994–2000)	The Internet mainly transmitted information which is mostly in static forms. The way of information transmission was relatively simple, and the Internet did not exert profound influence on society, economy and life. Therefore, the Internet rule of law at this stage was mainly based on the governance of Internet infrastructure, including IP address management, domain name management and computer information system security management.
Internet Rule of Law 2.0 (2000–2013)	The Internet mainly transmitted value. E-commerce, social media and search engines became the three pillars of the Internet. Information flow gradually transformed into value flow. Users became the core of Internet services. At this stage, the Internet rule of law was mainly management of the Internet industry, Internet information services, classified security protection and online transaction management.
Internet Rule of Law 3.0 (2013–Now)	The cyberspace witnesses chaos as it develops rapid and is in urgent need of good order. At this stage, with the rapid rise of new-generation information technologies such as big data, artificial intelligence and blockchain, information economy, cyber economy and digital economy have established themselves into new economic forms. At the same time, the negative impact of personal information leakage, cross-border data flow and cyber terrorism have emerged and sounded the alarm bell. Issues such as cybersecurity, data security and data rights protection need to be tacked through legislation.

Data rights law as an approach to rule of law in global cyberspace governance

Cyberspace is not a place outside the law, and the international community needs a fair and just system of law-based cyberspace governance. Since China officially connected to the Internet in 1994, the Internet rule of law has gone through stages 1.0, 2.0 and 3.0 (see Table 21). At the 3.0 stage, the global cyberspace developed and prospered like never before, but risks and threats also abounded, which calls for a fairer and forward-looking legal system. Focusing on the key issues concerning the rule of law in cyberspace like data sharing, data security, data rights protection and data sovereignty, the data rights law came into being exactly when it should and became a core part of Internet rule of law 3.0. The ultimate purpose of the data rights law is to lay down the rules, discipline and bottom line for cyberspace and cyber society. It is the legal norm that regulates various relationships and conflicts of interests in cyberspace, offering important support for safeguarding cyberspace sovereignty and promoting innovations in the Internet industry, and relevant technologies and business models. If the property law is a must in the era of the industrial civilization, the data rights law is a must for the rule of law in cyberspace in the era of big data. It sets the basic framework for legal order in cyberspace, represents law-based cyberspace governance by the state, and offers important support and a legislation-based solution to global cyberspace governance.

Data rights law for the building of a community with a shared future in cyberspace

A community with a shared future in cyberspace is what we envisage for the future of the cyberspace, and it enables the cyberspace to bring more benefits to mankind. As a system of rules created on the basis of human rationality, legal systems always exist in specific time periods and spaces (Huang Zhirong 2017). Since the era of big data, China has never stopped its efforts towards the establishment of data rights, the data rights system and the data rights law. With the data rights laws as the overarching project, we have made achievements in the rule of law in cyberspace, forming a pattern of good law and good governance.[19] Aimed at redefining the rights and obligations concerning resource allocation in cyberspace, the data rights law embodies the ideology, values and philosophy of the Internet era. The digital civilization is the value justification and driving force of the creation of the data rights law, while the data rights law offers basis for the existence of the digital civilization, helping maintain its systems and improving its order. The data rights law is highly meaningful in that it serves as the order paradigm of the digital civilization and lays the foundation for maintaining order in this civilization (Key Laboratory of Big Data Strategy 2018). In this sense, the data rights law is the product of a leap of our civilization and its order, and the legal basis for the building of a community with a shared future for mankind in cyberspace. It, together with the property law, constitute the legal foundation of the era of digital civilization, and form a synergy that pushes for the leap of the human world from the industrial civilization to the digital civilization.

Bibliography

Dong, Lisheng. 2012. "An Institutional Analysis of the Development of eGovernance in the European Union." *Journal of the Party School of the CPC Hangzhou Municipal Committee*, 5th issue.

E-Government Research Center of the Party School of the Central Committee of CPC (National Academy of Governance). 2019. *Digital Government Development Report.*

19 The development of Internet rule of law, which has the data rights law as its overarching project, has a dual structure with dedicated legislations for the cyberspace and traditional laws that continue to be used in cyberspace. This legal system includes laws that protect key Internet infrastructure, oversee the Internet industry, and manage Internet content and Internet crimes, as well as Internet-oriented judicial interpretations. It covers all the important areas and key parts of cyberspace, and features a hierarchy of laws, regulations, rules and other legal instruments. All the legal documents in this system are well grounded in existing legislations, all rules are clearly written, and the system belongs to the realm of public law in nature.

Guiyang Daily. 2018. "Regulations of Guiyang City on Big Data Security Management." *Guiyang Daily*.

Hai, Qun, and Wu Rina. 2010. "E-Government Strategy in Japan's i-Japan Strategy 2015." *Office Operations*, 4th issue.

He, Xinghui. 2019. "China's First Local Law on Big Data Security Protection Formally Implemented and Guizhou's Big Data Industry Enjoys More Effective and Efficient Management." *Science and Technology Daily*, 14 October, p. 7.

Huang, Zhirong. 2017. "Research on China's Internet Legislation." Diss. Party School of the Central Committee of CPC.

Key Laboratory of Big Data Strategy. 2018. *Data Rights Law 1.0: The Theoretical Basis*. Beijing: Social Sciences Academic Press.

Legislative Affairs Commission of the Standing Committee of the People's Congress of Guizhou Province. 2019. "Interpretation of the Regulations on Big Data Security of Guizhou Province." *Guizhou Daily*, September 26.

Li, Aijun. 2018. *China Big Data Rule of Law Development Report*. Beijing: Law Press.

Li, Wei. 2009. "Success and Regret: Formulation of Japan's Postwar Constitution." *Dushu,* 4th issue.

Lian, Cheng, Yang Fei, and Zhang Hengye. 2018. "Evaluation of E-Government Development in South Korea and Japan." *Management Observer,* 19th issue.

Lian, Yuming. 2017. *Big Data Blue Book: China Big Data Development Report No. 1.* Beijing: Social Sciences Academic Press.

Liu, Yeting, and Tang Sisi. 2014. "Big Data's Impact and Challenges on Government Governance." *E-Government*, 6th issue.

Liu, Ziheng, and Zhou Jiagui. 2013. "u-JAPAN and Development in Japan." *Journal of University Libraries*, 3rd issue.

National Information Security Standardization Technical Committee and Task Force on Big Data Security Standards. 2017. *White Paper on Big Data Security Standardization*.

Nobuyoshi, Ashibe. 2006. *Constitution (3rd ed.)*. Trans. Lin Laifan et al. Beijing: Peking University Press.

Qi, Aimin, and Pan Jia. 2015. "Research on Legal Support Mechanism for Big Data Security." *Journal of Chongqing University of Posts and Telecommunications (Social Sciences Edition)*, 3rd issue.

Qin, Ying. 2009. "Understanding Law from the Hypothesis of Evil Human Nature." *Theoretical Observation*, 3rd issue.

Ran, Congjing, and Wang Bingjie. 2019. "Research on International Strategic Models of Cyber Sovereignty Security." *Journal of Information Resources Management*, 2nd issue.

Supreme People's Court and the Supreme People's Procuratorate. 2015. "Supplementary Provisions on the Implementation of the Crimes Defined in the Criminal Law of the People's Republic of China (VI). *Judicial Interpretation (2015) No. 20*. October 30.

Wang, Tze-chien. 2007. "Privacy Rights in Protection of Personality Rights: Issues and Prospects (3)." *Law of Taiwan, No. 96*.

Wei, Jianxin, and Song Renchao. 2018. "Experience and Reference of Legislation Protection of Personal Information Rights in Japan." *Journal of Shenyang University of Technology (Social Sciences Edition)*, 4th issue.

Wu, Shan. 2019. "Li Keqiang Signs Decree of the State Council to Promulgate Revised Regulations of the People's Republic of China on Open Government Information." *People's Daily*. April 16.

Xie, Qing. 2006. "The Legal System of Personal Information Protection in Japan and Its Enlightenment." *Journal of Politics and Law*, 6th issue.

Xu, Tieguang. 2011. "Western Cyber Hegemonism and Cyber Rights in Developing Countries." *Thingking*, 2nd issue.

Yao, Guozhang, and Lin Ping. 2009. "Planning and Deployment of E-government and E-government Development in Japan." *E-government*, 12th issue.

Yao, Yuerong. 2011. "Personal Information Protection from the Constitutional Perspective." Diss. Shanghai: East China University of Political Science and Law.

Zhao, Qiuyan. 2005. "Construction of Network Privacy Protection Model." *Qiushi*, 3rd issue.

Zhao, Xudong. 1997. "The Impact of the New Technological Revolution on National Sovereignty." *Europe*, 6th issue.

Zhao, Yingying. 2019. "NPC Deputies Propose to Speed up Data Security Legislation and Make Public Traffic and Other Relevant Data Under the Premise of Data Protection." *Beijing Evening News*. March 7.

Zhi, Zhenfeng. 2016. "Global Vision of the Community with a Shared Future in Cyberspace and China's Responsibility." *Guangming Daily*, November 27.

Zhi, Zhenfeng. 2017. "The Rule of Law in Global Cyberspace Governance." *Law and Social Development*, 1st issue.

Zhong, Guangping, and Lian Yuming. 2018. "Member of the CPPCC National Committee: A Proposal Suggesting Accelerating Data Security Legislation." *China Radio, Film and Television*, 6th issue.

Zhou, Hanhua. 2005. "Notes on Some Issues Concerning the Personal Information Protection Law (draft version based on experts' recommendations)." *China Yearbook of Science & Technology Law*, 1st issue.

Postscript

The term "data rights law" was first proposed by Professor Lian Yuming, director of the Key Laboratory of Big Data Strategy in March 2017, and was then officially recognized by China National Committee for Terms in Sciences and Technologies. In July 2017, the Data Rights Law Research Center of China University of Political Science and Law was officially established, with Professor Lian Yuming as the director. This is the first data rights law research institution in China.

On May 28, 2019, China University of Political Science and Law and Guiyang Municipal People's Government jointly convened the Inaugural Meeting of Digital China Think Tank Alliance and Symposium on *Data Rights Law 1.0* (Simplified and Traditional Chinese, English Versions). Zhao Deming, member of the Standing Committee of the CPC Guizhou Provincial Committee and Secretary of CPC Guiyang Municipal Committee, attended the meeting and delivered a speech. He commended *Data Rights Law 1.0* as a major theoretical innovation. *Data Rights Law 1.0* drew wide attention from the world upon its release. It was covered by more than 170 Chinese and over 200 foreign media agencies in English, French, German and Spanish, as well as Chinese. One foreign media agency commented: "Its publishing provides a jurisprudential basis for the transformation of human society from the industrial civilization to the digital civilization, and gives us a key to the future of digital civilization." *Data Rights Law 1.0* marked the entry of Chinese laws to the world stage. It is also a powerful jurisprudential tool for China's participation in global governance. *Data Rights Law 1.0* reveals the theoretical logic, value logic and legal logic of data rights, and discusses ten fundamental viewpoints: a. human rights, real rights, and data rights are the three categories of fundamental rights of mankind in the future; b. data rights are a combination of personality rights and property rights; c. the subjects of data rights are specific right holders, while the objects are specific datasets; d. data rights break through the limitations of "one ownership for one object" and "properties are tangible," and are often manifested as "multiple ownerships for one data." e. data rights have the characteristics of private rights, public rights, and sovereign rights; f. the data rights system have five basic dimensions: the system of data rights legalization, the data ownership system, the system of usufructuary right of data, the system of usufructuary right of public data, and the sharing system; g. the rights to share is the essence of data rights; h. the data rights law provides legal norms governing data ownership, data rights, data use, and data protection; i. the data rights law reshapes the digital civilization; and j. the data rights law is an important step stone on the path from industrial civilization to digital civilization. This is the starting point for us to understand and study the data rights law.

Data Rights Law 2.0 is a continuation from *Data Rights Law 1.0*, delving deeper into the matter. First, it proposes for the first time the data man hypothesis as the logical starting point for studies on the data rights law, with altruism at its core. Second, centered around data rights, it puts forward three major rights in the era of big data, that is, the rights to data, the rights to share, and data sovereignty. Third, it is a response to President Xi Jinping's instructions in his congratulatory letter to 2019 China International Big Data Industry Expo that we should "handle the challenges in big data development in the fields of law, security and government administration." This book is firmly based on discussions and exchanges, and in-depth research efforts organized by the Key Laboratory of Big Data Strategy, and was written with all authors working together. The core ideas and the general structure of the book came from Lian Yuming and a more detailed outline as well as the main points were worked out mainly by Long Rongyuan and Zhang Longxiang. Authors include Lian Yuming, Zhu Yinghui, Song Qing, Wu Jianzhong, Zhang Tao, Song Xixian, Long Rongyuan, Zhang Longxiang, Zou Tao, Shen Xudong, Chen Wei, Yang Guanhua, Yang Lu and Yang Zhou, and Long Rongyuan serve as the coordinator. Chen Gang offered many important forward-looking and guiding ideas for this book. Meaningful and forward-looking inputs also came from Zhao Deming, member of the Standing Committee of the CPC Guizhou Provincial Committee and Secretary of the CPC Guiyang Municipal Committee; Yan Aoshuang, Vice Chairman of the Standing Committee of Beijing Municipal People's Congress and

Director of the Beijing Municipal Committee of Zhigong Party; Chen Yan, Deputy Secretary of the CPC Guiyang Municipal Committee and Mayor of Guiyang; Xu Hao, member of the Standing Committee of the CPC Guiyang Municipal Committee and Executive Vice Mayor of Guiyang; Liu Benli, member of the Standing Committee and Secretary General of the CPC Guiyang Municipal Committee; and Professor Li Zheng, Secretary General of the Academic Committee and Dean of the Institute of Artificial Intelligence and Rule of Law of China University of Political Science and Law. Special thanks go to the leaders and editors of Social Sciences Academic Press. Its president Xie Shouguang, with his profound insights, unique vision and great courage, spoke highly of the book and offered support for its publishing. He organized a group of high-caliber editors to make careful plans, work conscientiously on the editing, and present an excellent design for the book. Without these, the book would not have come out as scheduled.

During our research and compilation of this book, a number of high-level academic seminars were held and over 30 experts from the law, science, and translation circles had rounds of discussions. They are Wu Dahua, Liu Hongyu, Qu Qingchao, Kong Qingjiang, Xie Quan, Zhang Qing, Zhou Xuefeng, Tian Linan, Li Youxing, Ma Jing, Zhang Jiyu, Zhu Yinghui, Song Qing, Zhang Zhuhong, Pan Shanbin, Sun Zhiyu, Qi Jun, Xu Yan, Zhu Xiaowu, Wang Hao, Xiao Yu, Fu Yao, Wang Liping, Zhang Biao, Gao Xiangyu, Dai Jiajia, Zhang Chunyang, Wang Jing, Wu Yueguan and Zhu Jingjie. Among them, Wu Dahua (Guizhou Academy of Social Sciences), Xie Quan (Guizhou University), Pan Shanbin (Guizhou Minzu University), Wang Hao (Guizhou Xiaoi Robot Technology Co., Ltd.), Xiao Yu (Guizhou ZhongChuangLian Law Firm) and Wang Jing (Guiyang Global Big Data Exchange) believed that with the advancement of science and technology, laws must also keep pace with the times, and we should be inclusive and broad-minded in the face of various new things that come out one after another; and that the concept of "data rights law" was legally valid and future-oriented. Zhang Jiyu (Renmin University of China), Zhu Xiaowu (China University of Political Science and Law), Sun Zhiyu (Guizhou University), and Xu Yan (China University of Political Science and Law) pointed out that the propositions of "data man" and "the rights to share" were necessary and forward-looking, that the data man hypothesis broadened the vision of the legal community, while the rights to share is of great significance to the coordination and balance between the private rights and public power over data. Liu Hongyu (Jincheng Tongda & Neal), Qu Qingchao (Long Institute), Kong Qingjiang (China University of Political Science and Law), Zhou Xuefeng (Beihang University) and Li Youxing (Zhejiang University) believed that the data rights law, as a pioneering concept put forward within the Chinese discourse, marked a new breakthrough in the jurisprudence research concerning big data in China as well as in the world. Zhu Yinghui (International Institute for Urban Development, Beijing) and Song Qing (Guiyang Institute for Innovation-Driven Development Strategy) believed that research on the data rights law actually studied the development trends of technology, law and human society; that the data rights law was a modern solution to technology-based governance and governance capacity in the era of remixing; that it offered oriental wisdom to hold firmly onto our right to formulate data rights rules and to have our voice heard in the international community; and that it is how we approach future legal systems with our rationality from the perspective of human civilization. Translation experts Zhang Qing, Tian Linan, Ma Jing, Qi Jun, Fu Yao, Wang Liping, Dai Jiajia and Zhang Chunyang from China University of Political Science and Law stated that the data rights law is a topic of innovative and cross-disciplinary research, which is creative, attractive and influential; that the translation of this book series on data rights law provided an important window for exchanges between Chinese and foreign legal experts; and that it greatly broadened the vision of and opened a new chapter in data rights studies worldwide.

The three books on digital civilization: *Block Data*, *Data Rights Law*, and *Sovereignty Blockchain* by Key Laboratory of Big Data Strategy are milestones in the development of big data theories, and are hailed as the three major pillars of the new order of the digital civilization. They have great influence both at home and abroad. Our laws are never faced with greater challenges like the ones posed by science and technology development today. We should pay close attention to cutting-edge technologies and actively respond to these challenges, control possible risks, balance between the development of law and science, and actively promote interactions between laws, the rule of law, and jurisprudence in response to the social transformation. The proposal of data rights law has laid a legal foundation for maintaining national data sovereignty, firmly holding in our hands the right to formulate rules and having our voice heard in the international community in terms of data rights, as well as promoting the rule of law for global cyberspace governance. It is of special importance to the establishment of a community with a shared future in cyberspace. The research on data rights law is a ground-breaking theoretical exploration oriented towards both the present and the future. It will definitely have a positive impact on the development of the digital economy, digital government, the governance of the digital society, and the progress of the digital civilization. We will continue with our work and produce *Data Rights Law 3.0: The Legislative Foresight*, *Data Rights Law 4.0: Rights to Share and Rights to Privacy*, and *Data Rights Law 5.0: Data Rights Theory and New Ethics*, in order to further build and improve the theoretical system of data rights laws.

During the writing and editing of this book, we tried our best to collect information on the latest studies and absorb the latest ideas. However, as this book covers various complicated fields, there will always be limitations and our understanding may not be completely accurate. For any possible errors and mistakes and particularly any omission of quotations in the book, we apologize and welcome comments from all readers. The first steam engine of the world could not be used and the first car was not truly able to go on the road. Whatever is new is definitely imperfect. However, this is what we believe: If Chinese laws are to go onto the world stage, laws related to the digital economy. We are making it is most likely to be the efforts now in this regard, and although it is difficult, we are full of confidence that the data rights law will thrive.

Key Laboratory of Big Data Strategy
January 16, 2020

Index